Ephemeral Coast

Visualizing Coastal Climate Change

Edited by

Celina Jeffery

University of Ottawa

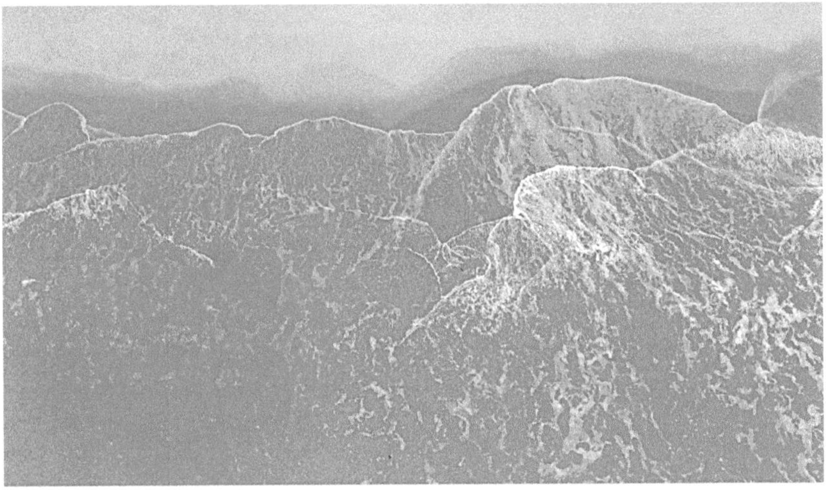

Series on the History of Art

VERNON PRESS

www.vernonpress.com

In the Americas:
Vernon Press
1000 N West Street, Suite 1200,
Wilmington, Delaware 19801
United States

In the rest of the world:
Vernon Press
C/Sancti Espiritu 17,
Malaga, 29006
Spain

Series on the History of Art

Library of Congress Control Number: 2022933660

ISBN: 978-1-64889-424-4

Also available: 978-1-64889-409-1 [Hardback, B&W]

Cover designed by Vernon Press.

Cover image: Julia Davis, *Undercurrent*, 2017, 4K Video, stereo sound, 11:00 minutes endless loop (still). Image courtesy of the artist. This installation premiered in the 'Ephemeral Coast' exhibition, *These Waters Have Stories to Tell*, at the Glynn Vivian Art Gallery, Wales, UK. 2018.

Table of Contents

List of Figures

Acknowledgements

I would like to thank the artists, writers, and scientists for generously participating in the curatorial research project *Ephemeral Coast,* 2014-2019. *Ephemeral Coast,* as a curatorial research project, was generously supported by the Faculty of Arts at the University of Ottawa, Canada and by the Social Sciences and Humanities Research Council, Canada. In turn, I would like to thank Amanda Roderick and Mission Gallery for her support in organising *Ephemeral Coast* in the Swansea, UK region.

I am especially grateful to the authors and artists of this edited anthology who have battled covid-restrictions, child-care, teaching online, artistic careers, all the while working on their individual contributions to this volume.

I would also like to pay respect to and gratitude to the Algonquin people, who are the traditional guardians of the land upon which I live in Ottawa, Ontario, Canada. I acknowledge their longstanding relationship with this territory, which remains unceded.

Foreword by David Rothenberg

This morning I took a walk down to the coast. Ten minutes down the street, I came to the edge of what some call a river that flows both ways, and others claim is a fjord. There stood a man with a telescope watching for migrating birds. "Some days I see nothing, other days a few thousand fly by. I write down what I see."

Every day at the coast is different. And the water's edge never stays the same. "What I like about it is that you're right here in the moment. No past, no future, no to-do list, achievements. Nature just happens. It's always good to live like that… sometimes."

I agree with him. In fact it was just what I was thinking on the walk down in the incipient Spring sunlight. When in doubt… go outside. With all our devastation and destruction, intentional or otherwise, nature endures now and will still endure in the moment long after humanity's run is done.

That's why I always return to learn from nature, to try to respond to its immediacy even though I know whatever I make will pale beside the original model.

Aristotle was wrong. Humanity does *not* exist to finish what nature started. Nature never needed us but, unfortunately, we are here. So then he is also right—if we are to survive, and to live on this planet gracefully, then we must learn to imitate nature in its manner of operation, to work more like nature works and less like our artificially intelligent minds.

I leave the bird watcher and walk North along the coast. The town park is all fenced off, the site of a massive remediation scheme. You see, its coastline is collapsing due to the unexpectedly rapid water rise. The ramparts are crumbling, after two '500-year' floods in one decade. No one was ready for this but of course we knew it was going to happen. To keep the coast from being ephemeral, it is being solidly rebuilt. It's the least we can do.

Celina Jeffery's expansive *Ephemeral Coast* project has brought her clear curatorial vision to exhibitions, events, and travels all over the planet, creatively exploring the fragility and resilience of our changing coastlines. She has a knack for picking the most interesting artists, the most interesting projects, and the most provocative ways of presenting them to a global public.

This book is a parallel presentation of all the work she has done in the curatorial field, and I hope it will inspire all of you to combine the wisdom of immediacy with an inspiration to act, to improve, and to celebrate the world around us so humanity may live up to the great changes we need to face in the decades to come. It's up to no one else but us.

David Rothenberg
Cold Spring, New York
March 2022

Introduction

Celina Jeffery

University of Ottawa

Ephemeral Coast: Visualizing Coastal Climate Change considers the ways that art can offer a means through which to discover, analyze, re-imagine and re-frame emotive discourses about the ecological and cultural transformations of the coastline. This edited anthology takes ephemerality as its central conceptual framework and presents a series of essays to create interconnections between environmental and social considerations of the coast, a succession of embodied creative practices, and shifting regional geographic identities. As a conceptual rubric, 'ephemeral coast' acts as a kind of framing device, which recognizes the turbulence of the ocean's edge in the contemporary, or what Philip E. Steinberg calls the ocean's 'radical indeterminacy'.[1]

Comparative in scope, the essays engender creative strategies for understanding new and uncertain coastal ecologies and the loss, expulsion or destruction of their associated cultures, habitats, species, and ecosystems. The ephemeral is negotiated by the authors as a possible theoretical, methodological, and experiential proposition. The book presents a series of specific case studies of artistic practices and creative strategies that seek to capture the rewriting of cartographic maps that are being reshaped by rising seas, coastal flooding, erosion, and catastrophic weather induced by climate change. These complementary visual studies consider the fracturing of the map's edge as both uneven and uncertain, affecting already vulnerable populations differently, and how being at the water's edge may become associated with concepts of 'inundation'[2] and of disposability, lived and felt locally and in the everyday. The anthology also looks at the historical, mnemonic, and contemporary transitional conditions of 'conflicted' coasts spaces in which empire, modernity and globalization press on coastal erosion and incursions, proliferate it with trivial plastics, pollution and disposable attitudes and bring vulnerable communities into uncertain futures. Here, the ephemeral coast is a place of hauntings but also of potential disruption and resistance, situating vibrance and turbulence as an aesthetic and ontological space, where visual stories and artistic practice are possible ways to think through and experience the incomprehensibility of disappearance and inundation. Tiffany Lethabo King's concept of the shoal as an ecotone, a liminal space of difficult passage, an interruption, and an interpretive frame is important here.[3]

The shore as "an edge, a boundary, a transitional zone," argues American nature writer, John A. Murray, lends itself eloquently to the aesthetic realm of the imaginary.[4] Tidal seas at the water's edge, framed by the temporal horizon, has given rise to a plethora of aesthetic attitudes often underscored by the potential feelings of fear through immersion; and it is arguably this sense of unending permeability and rupture between land and sea that makes the coast so rich for artistic engagement. This 'edge of the sea' is famously described by marine biologist, nature writer and activist, Rachel Carson, as a 'magical zone', a dual, fertile and productive space, which has given rise to resilient and enriching exchanges between territory and unbounded aqueous ecosystems, community and biological life of the ocean.[5] Muscongus Bay, on the coast of Maine, became a particular point of inspiration for her investigation of the littoral zone in *The Edge of the Sea* (1955); it was also a source of inspiration for her burgeoning engagement with conservation.[6] For Carson, the shore is a place of deep time, "where the drama of life played its first scene on earth and perhaps even its prelude"[7] and is constantly morphing, merging, blending, and as she states, there is no finality or permanency, but is a place in which "man is an uneasy trespasser."[8]

Rebecca Solnit and Rebecca Snedeker's *Unfathomable City: A New Orleans Atlas* (2013), is a compendium of essays, prose and maps about New Orleans' shifting and disappearing coastal culture and geography, 'the colossal erosion of recent times', in which land and water permeate with such veracity that former cartographic demarcations are fruitless.[9] The myriad of gas and oil incursions in the critical ecological habitat of the bayous and wetlands of southeast Louisiana, which is home to Indigenous delta clans[10], is partly responsible for the disappearance of the 'buffer' wetlands that break hurricanes.[11] The catastrophe of Hurricane Katrina in 2005, combined with the Exxon Mobil oil spill of 2010, the largest oil spill in US history, which covered 2000 km of the Gulf of Mexico, became shocking signifiers of the violence of 'anthropogenic drivers' upon underprivileged and marginalized communities in particular. Solnit also cautions against the lack of focus on the long-term consequences of such environmental catastrophes,[12] which continue to erode and inundate the Gulf Coast and create instability for its communities. Monique Verdin, an Indigenous Houma (Ouma) storyteller and artist, writes that her home is 'disappearing' into the Gulf at an aggressive speed: "an acre of land is lost from our shores, with 50 to 60 percent of all loss occurring within the Barataria-Terre-bonne estuary" in which many of her ancestral peoples live.[13] Similarly in 2016, the Biloxi-Chitimacha-Choctaw tribe of Isle de Jean Charles, a community near New Orleans, was given 'climate refugee' status, the first of its kind in the USA, due to the disappearance of the bayous. [14] The *bayou*, a Choctaw word meaning 'slow moving stream', is being subsumed by the salt waters of the ocean, as described by Elizabeth Rush, author of *Rising Dispatches from the New American Shore*

(2018).[15] Successions of hurricanes, land loss and flooding have re-written this portion of Louisiana's atlas, forcing communities out of their ancestral homes of two hundred years: "Once the salt started to get into the water table", writes Charles Brunet, a member of the community, "that was when everything started to die."[16]

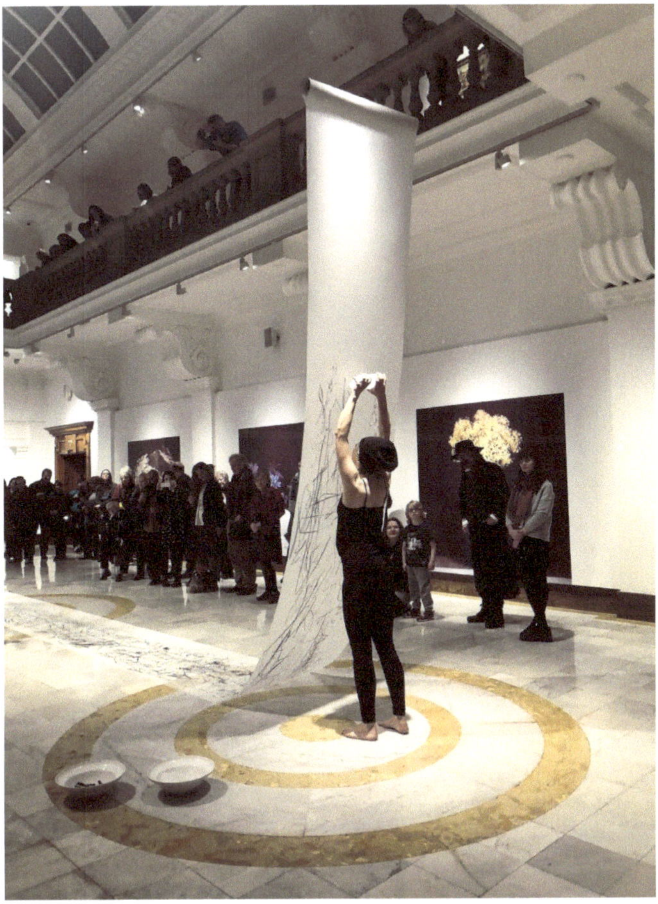

Figure i.1: Jaanika Peerna, *Glacier Elegy (Swansea)* - participatory performance with drawing, sound and ice. Featured in the *Ephemeral Coast* exhibition *These Waters Have Stories To Tell*, 2018, Glynn Vivian Art Gallery, Swansea, UK. Image courtesy of the artist and Ephemeral Coast.

Rob Nixon's pivotal book, *Slow Violence and the Environmentalism of the Poor* (2011), discusses the gradual, often anonymous and invisible consequences of climate change, oil spills, resource extraction, pollution and war – whose consequences manifest through generations and on scales of violence that are hard to grasp, imagine and narrate by those living outside of the community itself.[17] Nixon's discussion of environmental refugees in the 'hydrological-zones' of mega dam construction, for instance, involves an understanding of the loss of both place and time in which historical connection to ancestral lands are involuntary displacements.[18] In such instances of slow, inter-generational violence, blame is hard to attribute, violence may not appear to be violence, yet it has clear impacts on communities like that of Isle de Jean Charles – water slowly seeps into houses, soil is eroded, land disappears, and the Industrial canals and pipelines have allowed salt water to compromise the wetlands and brackish waters, while levee systems have never been built Nixon's writing asks us to acknowledge environmental threats as recast not only in the future but also to consider such threats for the world's most vulnerable and particularly, for the Global south. Thom Davis also speaks of the "the potential of bearing witness to the shifting temporalities of violence", in which "toxic pollution, species loss and climate change" are the silent yet brutal killers of those directly experiencing them – communities whose stories are often considered inconsequential and whose political agency and resiliency is so often denied.[19]

Ephemeral Coast (2014–2020) was a curatorial research project situated in coastal regions internationally including South Wales, Mauritius, Baja California Sur and Mexico with artistic connections to Ontario, Canada, many parts of the United States, Eastern Europe, Australia, the Arctic, among others.[20] Artists located in these regions, climate change experts and writers from the arts and humanities, worked together to foster creative engagement with coastal climate change and oceanic degradation, which manifested in the form of a series of international collaborations, exhibitions, symposia and publications. The curatorial premise sought to embrace the literal ebb and flow of oceanic movement in dialogue with the notion of the ephemeral as a condition of the contemporary coast and its myriad of anthropogenically driven ecological and social issues. The idea of the 'ephemeral' involved mining both material and metaphorical understandings of the ocean's edge, reinscribing very specific stories of encounters of the edge of the sea, and thinking through the creative possibilities of working through borders and thresholds.[21]

This iteration of *Ephemeral Coast* – as an edited anthology, presents a series of creative propositions about the nature of material transactions within coastal waters; of the agentive properties of those waters; as well as the possible mnemonic histories concealed within its waves. The themes of conflict, flux, inundation and saturation are a central inquiry for many of the contributors. Such characterizations are frequently contextualized within the colonial legacies and concomitant capitalist framings of the ocean as container, sewer and resource of extraction. The essays present reflections on the ongoing impacts of oceanic degradation and habitat loss as acts of environmental injustice and seek to offer an opportunity to rethink our relationship with the coast as a place that is at once tumultuous, porous, and transformative, but also a generative space of possibility. Therein, the themes of oceanic turbulence, of relational materiality, of blue futures, of care and the entanglements of thinking through the shape of things to come, feature prominently. Written by artists, art historians, designers, curators, theorists and philosophers, the essays in this book discuss the reshaping of climate-changed[22] coastal cartographies, with case studies of infringements, disappearance, and forecasts of the future, negotiated through the lens of artistic theory and practice. The coast here is most often considered a space of transformation – an ephemeral, shifting and conflicted space that manifests in both particular but also planetary ways.

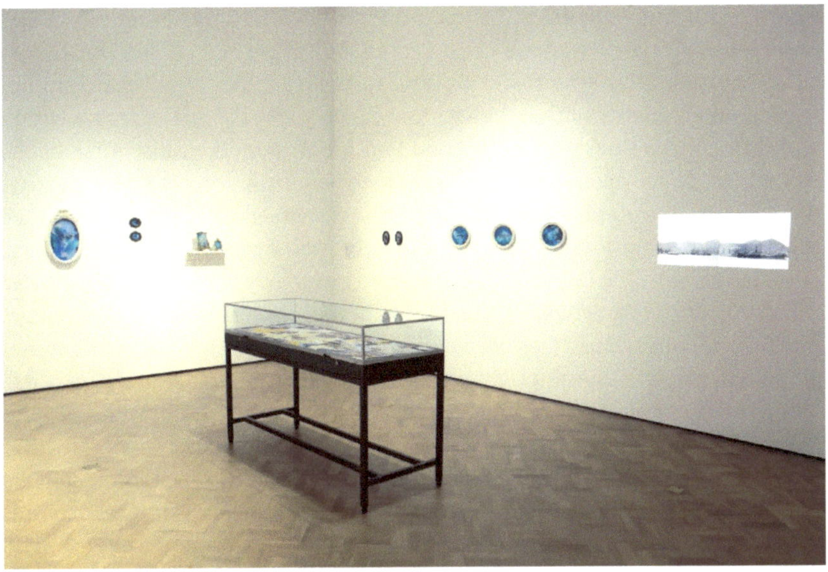

Figure i.2: Shiraz Bayjoo, Installation View, *These Waters Have Stories to Tell*, 2018. Glynn Vivian Art Gallery, Swansea, UK. Image courtesy of Ephemeral Coast.

Anthropocene Oceans

In the 2019 'Special Report on the Ocean and Cryosphere in a Changing Climate', the Intergovernmental Panel on Climate Change (IPCC) cites oceanic acidification and deoxygenation, ocean warming, sea-rise level, cryosphere changes, and extreme weather events as key outcomes of anthropogenic activity.[23] Attributable factors include population growth and coastal development, socioeconomic inequality, pollution, sedimentation extraction, industrial fishing, and seabed mining, among other anthropogenic drivers.[24] These significant changes in the ocean and cryosphere are having impacts of varying scales on coastal cities of different geographies, small islands and developing islands, deltas and Arctic coasts, with an array of ecological, economic and human impacts, swinging in pendulum between the extremes of drowning and drying out. At its most abject, the ocean's edge is quite literally suffocating by increasing global temperatures, with coastal regions experiencing temporal but pervasive systems of dead zones. These clusters of factors, combined with industrial fishing, have led some ocean activists, like artist Mark Dion and environmental journalist Claire Nouvian, to use the term 'oceanocide' to register how acts of anthropocentric activities are literally destroying the ocean.[25]

It is one of the tasks of the nascent fields of the Blue Humanities and Critical Ocean Studies to query how these anthropogenic activities within the world's oceans register within and through the arts and humanities.[26] Rather than rehearse the universalizing disposition of the scientific discourse of the Anthropocene and ideas of the 'Great Acceleration'[27] the task of Blue Humanities seeks to elevate eco-systemic contamination, to explore more-than-human agency, and to highlight that the extreme effects on social justice issues within and through the unevenly distributed and highly gendered discourse of the 'Anthropocene' are paramount.[28] Whereas the scientific 'Anthropocene' focuses on the epochal, the 'oceanic turn' engages with embodied experience of weather, species relations, history, and temporality.[29] A number of overlapping theoretical positions are possible thereafter, summarized by Melody Jue in *Wild Blue Media: Thinking Through Seawater* (2020) as including: global climate change; Indigenous cultural histories of seafaring and navigation; shipping routes and global capitalism; the alterity of marine organisms; the Middle Passage; technologies of ocean mapping; marine extraction and more.[30] Rather than compounding the universalisms (which risks the production of further racialization) of the scientific concepts informing the Anthropocene ocean, Jue argues that idea of 'milieu specific analysis' assists in the breaking down of this meta-narrative, proposing how we can consider an ocean as a space of thought, as well as a conceptual space of displacement.[31] This ontological turn gives rise to new oceanic imaginaries on which the future of humanity is very much reliant.[32] In *Vast Expanses, A History of The Oceans* (2018), oceans historian Helen M. Rozwadowski similarly writes of the necessity to reframe the ocean not as a singular, mono-force, but as a human ocean with multiple histories of seas and coastal waters.[33] Here, accounts of the historically informed sense of the ocean as timeless, separate and inert give way to the idea of oceans as locations of dynamic change with entangled histories to be read through an acknowledgement of both 'deep time and profound connectedness'.[34] As a result, Rozwadowski calls for human histories of the oceans that acknowledge the shifting lenses through which the oceans have been used.

The desire to create new allegorical narratives of the ocean as particular, material and ontological – as opposed to the colonial rendering of the ocean as universal 'pure nature' – is central to Elizabeth M. DeLoughrey's essay, 'Oceanic

Futures: Interspecies Worldings' (2019).[35] Oceans feature as a central argument of DeLoughrey's book, *Allegories of the Anthropocene* (2019), which weaves together histories of the past and narratives of the present into a kind of simultaneity, as a means of breaking down the universalizing tendencies of the Anthropocene.[36] As a founder of 'critical ocean studies', DeLoughrey uses the idea of a 'tidalectic' methodology to recast the ocean as agentic, embodied and ontological, focusing on the materiality of the ocean and its more-than-human inhabitants.[37] DeLoughrey describes oceans as the new space of empire that is viewed by the West as a space of propriety and as a frontier of capitalism, citing bioprospecting, among other harmful practices. The future of the ocean, she argues, is reliant on Indigenous ontologies; through a discussion of Māori culture, she makes a case that the ocean can be reframed beyond materialist space, as a living force with its own sense of mutable time and agency.[38]

It follows then that all our respective fields of study (art history, post-colonial studies, and eco-criticism, among others) could engage with this sense of oceanic estrangement, push its own limits, and expand the range of how theory can work. How can such a reading of shore as inundated, tidalectic, and agential be reintroduced to our respective forms of study, to challenge epistemological models, networks, and objects structures? Or to present different narratives? In what ways can 'ephemeral coast' be considered a metaphor, a theory, or even a method? This edited anthology curates a series of coastal imaginaries positioned at the ocean's edge, written by artists, curators, art historians, art theorists and philosophers, that are sensitive to complexities of the unstructured and migratory material and immaterial quality of water.

The book considers how artists are observing the effects of anthropogenic drivers upon coastal geographies (coastal cities and mega cities, small islands, deltas, Arctic coasts). Contributors discuss how artists and designers face the ocean's edge in the era of the Anthropocene, charting the effects of new cartographies of flooding and drought, and in turn, they consider the effects of industrial fishing and habitat degradation within the world's oceans to develop new perspectives. The anthology therein explores the concept of ethical witnessing and Rob Nixon's idea of 'slow violence' at the water's edge. The authors consider incursions upon borders and plastic pollution, as well as decolonial processes and possibilities, as imagined by artists. The capitalist excess of single-use plastics, microplastics from the cosmetic industry, as well as plastic fibers from the fashion industry, have become so pervasive that they have embedded themselves into the ocean floor, penetrated the ocean's food chain, and imbricated themselves within every shoreline on the planet. The statistics are overwhelming: humanity has produced an estimated 8.1 billion tons of plastic since the 1950s,[xliii] while the absorption of microplastics and its associated toxins into plankton – the foundation of the marine food web – is thought to be considerable.[xliv]

Complex interactions between local communities and coastal resource extraction are discussed by artist, filmmaker and educator, Diana Heise, who frames local and global instances of artisanal fishing as a series of ethical, societal and cultural issues. In her essay, 'The Sea We Make', Heise reflects upon her film, *The Sea We Make* (Lamer Nou Fer, 2016) - which featured in two *Ephemeral Coast* exhibition, she explores the methods of artisanal fishermen in Mauritius and Vermont struggling to address the catastrophic effects of the Anthropocene-ocean. The cumulative effects of by-catch, habitat loss and degradation caused by over-fishing, pollution, ocean warming and acidification are causing cascading rates of extinction: the 2015 Living Blue Planet Report describes a decline of 49% of marine life between 1970-2012.[xlii] The essay discusses the use of creative practice to comprehend the effects of the Anthropocene on the coastal ecologies of Mauritius and the Lake Champlain Islands, with a particular focus on film-making as a means to explore lagoon ecologies as an indication of ocean acidification, declining fish populations and the prospect of mass extinction.

Celina Jeffery's essay, 'Mapping Arctic Shores: Visual Stories of Entangled Histories' brings attention to the idea of how ephemerality interfaces with artists engaging with the circumpolar areas of the USA and Canada, in which regional ice-sheets, glaciers and sea-ice are experiencing the most unparalleled climate incursions, primarily due to global warming. The focus here is on the work of Indian American photographer, writer and activist Subhankar Banerjee, the Inuvialuk artist Maureen Gruben, and the photographer Robert Kautuk who is based in Kangiqtugaapik (Clyde River). The essay queries how such artists, who seek to give voice to both the visible and invisible imaginaries of the pan-Arctic shore as a transitive cultural and geographical border are witness and subject to profound anthropogenic drivers such as global warming, displacement, food security, water quality, and certain species extinction.

In 'From Sea to Source: A Pilgrimage Along the Water's Edges', Andrea Hurst and Belinda Du Plooy reflect upon their academic engagement initiative at Nelson Mandela University, a coastal university in Port Elizabeth, South Africa. *The Tributaries Project* (2019) was an experimental research project that comprised a series of walks or 'journeys' along the coast to explore the potential of water as a lens to think through social cohesion in South Africa's extremely diverse, postcolonial communities. Here, the writers explore the concept of the pilgrimage as a means of tracing a kind of transhistorical line of inquiry along the edges of various bodies of water 'from sea to source' – a concept that also became the platform for a curated exhibition.

Anna Paluch's 'The Baltic Waterways: Mapping Cross-Cultural and Ecological Awareness of the Baltic Sea', considers how several artists and projects in the region 'perform' the sea. Situating her discussion in the context of how artists engage with the forbidden and traumatic historical encounters with the Baltic coast, with its geopolitical and militarized histories, she considers how this transacts with possible futures. Paluch traces how artists such as Antti Laitinen, artist collective SIMKA, and Marta Krześlak reclaim a sense of violation to address the scientific and ethical concerns of anthropogenic impacts in the Baltic Basin. Subsequently, Paluch argues that meta-narratives of the Baltic Sea can be disrupted, personalized and transformed to address and shape public imagination and activism.

Catherine Bonier's essay 'Woven Imaginations: Stories of fluidity and fixity in coastal Louisiana', links stories and material practices found in the Mississippi Delta – ephemeral, she argues, long before the climate crisis, but now exasperated beyond comprehension. Bonier considers design decisions and dilemmas of environmental scientists, engineers, artists, architects and urban planners working in this region. The essay considers how aesthetic imagination can contend with the environmental impact of climate 'changed' on local communities, transforming a study of 'seascapes' into an examination of industrial incursions into the shoreline, with far-reaching implications for biological and cultural life within these vulnerable communities.

Sherena Razek's 'From Ongoing Nakba to a Palestinian Hydro-commons: Reading the Jordan River and the Dead Sea as Ecopolitical Refusal', considers how Palestine's 'bodies of water' may be read through the lens of environmental 'Nakba' – a kind of disappearance. Razek subsequently discusses documentary photography and the 'lack' of traditionally conceived contemporary art forms, to interpret the highly conflicted coast. Thereafter, she considers how Palestinians are reimagining and renegotiating relationships to a partly arid but immensely cultivable homeland while forcibly displaced from Palestine and within the diaspora. She proposes a potential path back/towards a worldly and repaired sovereignty that reimagines water as an indivisible source of life rather than a resource for extraction.

Global warming has resulted in the rise in ocean temperatures and an increase in sea levels of 10-20 cm in the twentieth century and is expected to rise between 25-100 cm by the year 2100, resulting in the inevitable disappearance of small islands and a great many coastal regions.[39] Such a massive shift in atmospheric heat and sea-level rise is the context of the essay, *Three Lines in Space: The Aesthetics of Data Visualization of Sea-level Rise in the Research-based Artworks of Andrea Polli, Timo Aho and Pekka Niittyvirta, and Paul Maher*, Jakub Zdebik. Here, the flooded shoreline becomes a marker of how the Anthropocene-ocean intersects with the twenty-first-century reality of a warming world, with new shifting planetary seasons, and the still relatively unknown prospect of the rapidly melting Arctic.[xl] Zdebik considers how artists such as the Norwegian duo Timo Aho and Pekka Niittyvirta, as well as the American sound artist Andrea Polli, are responding to this new ocean-climate nexus by mapping coastal rising sea levels. Zdebik uses Gilles Deleuze and Félix Guattari's concept of the smooth and striated space, and Peter Sloterdijk's notion of atmospheric islands, to consider ways that geography-oriented theory can be mobilized to shed light on data-driven art.

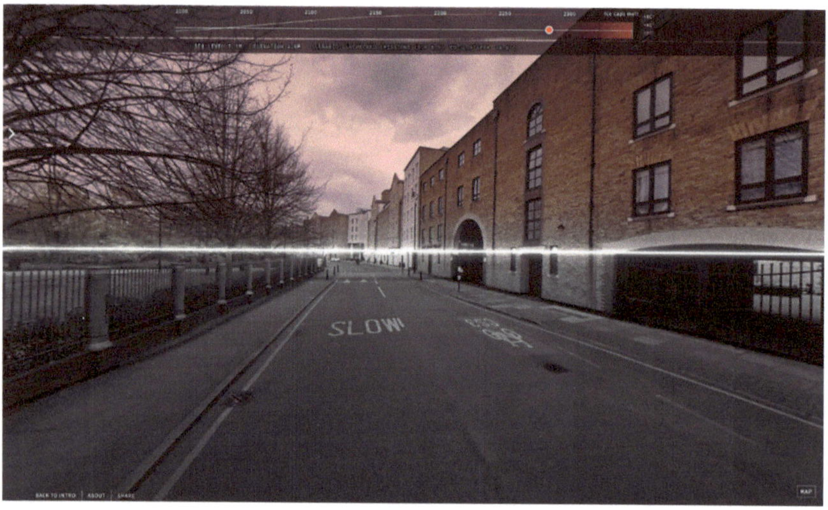

Figure i.3: 'London', from the *Coastline Paradox* 2020 project, an experimental artwork by Timo Aho and Pekka Niittyvirta in collaboration with Google Arts & Culture using data from Climate Central and the IPCC. https://experiments.withgoogle.com/coastline-paradox. Image courtesy of the artists.

In 'The Ocean Behind Glass', Ian Buchanan considers the culture of aquariums – from their physical iterations in the home to public conservation initiatives – as spaces in which humans 'manage' fish. Buchanan details how aquariums create a sense of the one-to-one relationship between humans and aquatic life as if they are 'vast assemblages' of pets. Through a discussion of the role and consumption of aquatic life in cinema, television and aquariums, Buchanan asks us how these large-scale, pristine environments create a spectacle of consumption rather than of care.

Practice-led research is a methodological basis for many of the authors presented here, each of whom are artists, curators, and designers. Other essays engage with topographies of knowledge that 'think with water'[40] to use Astrida Neimanis's term: they offer alternative narratives of flooding or erosion which reframe the practice of managing water as a purely scientific or as economic resource, and in its place mine both the ecological changes of particular coast lines through memory, colonialism, and imaginings of the future. [41] All essays attempt to present the 'complex entanglements with water'[42] that Neimanis speaks of, the complex assemblages of creative knowledge and experience which comes with an understanding of coastal waters as particular, but also at times, the basis of collective memory and action.

Notes

1 Philip Steinberg in "Turbulent Waters in Three Parts" by Jessica Lehman, Philip Steinberg, and Elizabeth R. Johnson, *Theory & Event*, Vol. 24. No 1, 192-219 (John Hopkins University Press, 2021): 194.

2 See Jaimey Hamilton Faris's discussion of inundation in "Sisters of Ocean and Ice: On the Hydro-Feminism of Kathy Jetñil-Kijiner and Aka Niviâna's Rise: From One Island to Another," *Shima (Sydney, N.S.W.)* 13, no. 2, (2019), https://doi.org/10.21463/shima.13.2.08.

3 Tiffany Lethabo King, *The Black Shoals: Offshore Formations of Black and Native Studies.* (Duke University Press, 2019), https://doi.org/10.1215/9781478005681.

4 John A. Murray, "Introduction", *The Seacoast Reader*, Ed. John A. Murray (New York: The Lyons Press, 1999), xvii.

5 Rachel Carson, "The Marginal World", *The Edge of the Sea* (Boston and New York: Mariner Books, 1998), 3.

6 'Walking in Rachel Carson's Footsteps', *The Nature Conservancy*, accessed March 24th, 2021, https://www.nature.org/en-us/about-us/where-we-work/united-states/maine/stories-in-maine/the-nature-conservancy-in-maine-rachel-carson-walking-in-her-footsteps/.

7 Carson, *The Edge of the Sea*, 7.

8 Ibid., 249.

9 Rebecca Solnit and Rebecca Snedeker, *Unfathomable City; A New Orleans Atlas* (Berkeley, Los Angeles, London: University of California Press, 2013), 3.

10 Monique Verdin, "Southward into the Vanishing Lands," Ed. Rebecca Solnit and Rebecca Snedeker, *Unfathomable City; A New Orleans Atlas* (Berkeley, Los Angeles, London: University of California Press, 2013), 19.

11 See John Tibbetts, "Louisiana's Wetlands: A Lesson in Nature Appreciation," *Environ Health Perspective* (January 2016), 114. Also, 'Louisiana Coastal Wetlands: A Resource At Risk', *USGS: Science for a Changing World*, accessed November 20th, 2020, www.pubs.usgs.gov/fs/la-wetlands/.

12 Rebecca Solnit, "Are We Missing the Big Picture on Climate Change," *The New York Times*, December 2, 2014, https://www.nytimes.com/2014/12/07/magazine/are-we-missing-the-big-picture-on-climate-change.html.

13 Monique Verdin, "Southward into the Vanishing Lands," *Unfathomable City; A New Orleans Atlas* (Berkeley, Los Angeles, London: University of California Press, 2013), 19.

14 Coral Davenport and Campbell Robertson, "Resettling the first American 'Climate Refugees'", *The New York Times*, May 3rd, 2016, https://www.nytimes.com/2016/05/03/us/resettling-the-first-american-climate-refugees.html?_r=0.

15 Elizabeth Rush, *Rising: Dispatches from the New American Shore* (Minn.: Milkweed Editions, 2018), 20.

16 Chris Brunet, "On Opportunity" in Elizabeth Rush, *Rising*, 165.

17 Rob Nixon, *Slow Violence and the Environmentalism of the Poor* (Cambridge, Mass. And London: Harvard University Press, 2011).

18 Nixon, *Slow Violence*, 162.

[19] Thom Davies, "Slow Violence and Toxic Geographies: 'Out of Sight' to Whom?'", *Environment and Planning C: Politics and Space* (April, 2019), https://doi.org/10.1177/2399654419841063.
[20] Much of the project is highlighted on the website: http://www.ephemeralcoast.com.
[21] A fuller discussion of *Ephemeral Coast* was published in my essay, "From the Shore to the Coast: Curating the Front Line of Climate Change," in the issue *Curating the Sea* edited by Pandora Syperek and Sarah Wade, *The Journal of Curatorial Studies*, Vol. 9. Number 2, (October 2020).
[22] Margaret Atwood, "It's Not Climate Change — It's Everything Change", *Medium Magazine*, 2015, https://medium.com/matter/it-s-not-climate-change-it-s-everything-change-8fd9aa671804.
[23] IPCC, 2019: *IPCC Special Report on the Ocean and Cryosphere in a Changing Climate*, [H.-O. Pörtner, D.C. Roberts, V. Masson-Delmotte, P. Zhai, M. Tignor, E. Poloczanska, K. Mintenbeck, A. Alegría, M. Nicolai, A. Okem, J. Petzold, B. Rama, N.M. Weyer (eds.)]. https://www.ipcc.ch/srocc/ . Accessed February 23rd, 2021.
[24] *IPCC Special Report on the Ocean and Cryosphere in a Changing Climate*, 667.
[25] See Claire Nouvian's, "Deep Sea Fishing is 'Oceanocide'," *CNN*, September 13th, 2010, http://www.cnn.com/2010/OPINION/09/10/eco.nouvian.fishing/.
[26] There have been many important contributions to the concept of Blue Humanities of which the following is an abbreviated list: John R. Gillis, 'The Blue Humanities.' *Humanities* 34, no. 3 (May 2013): 10-13. Steven Mentz. "Toward a Blue Cultural Studies: The Sea, Maritime Culture, and Early Modern English Literature." *Literature Compass* 6, no. 5 (2009): 997-1013. Serpil Oppermann. 2019. Alaimo, Stacy. "Introduction: Science Studies and the Blue Humanities." *Configurations (Baltimore, Md.)* 27, no. 4 (2019): 429–32. https://doi.org/10.1353/con.2019.0028.
Serpil Oppermann. "Storied Seas and Living Metaphors in the Blue Humanities." *Configurations* 27, no. 4 (Fall, 2019): 443-61, https://login.proxy.bib.uottawa.ca/login?url=https://www.proquest.com/scholarly-journals/storied-seas-living-metaphors-blue-humanities/docview/2313764847/se-2?accountid=14701. Elizabeth M. DeLoughrey, 'Toward a Critical Ocean Studies for the Anthropocene.' *English Language Notes* 57, no. 1 (2019): 21–36. https://doi.org/10.1215/00138282-7309655
[27] Will Steffen, Wendy Broadgate, Lisa Deutsch, Owen Gaffney, and Cornelia Ludwig, "The Trajectory of the Anthropocene: The Great Acceleration", *The Anthropocene Review* 2, no. 1. (2015): 81–98, https://doi.org/10.1177/2053019614564785.
[28] See for example Richard Grusin, *Anthropocene Feminism* (Minneapolis: University of Minnesota Press), 2017; and Kathryn Yusoff, *A Billion Black Anthropocenes or None* (Minneapolis: University of Minnesota Press), 2019.
[29] Elizabeth M. DeLoughrey "The Sea Is Rising: Visualising Climate Change in the Pacific Islands," *Pacific Dynamics* 2, no. 2, (2018): 187.
[30] Melody Jue, *Wild Blue Media; Thinking Through Seawater* (Durham and London: Duke University Press, 2020), 16.
[31] Jue, *Wild Blue Media*, 16-17.
[32] Elizabeth M. DeLoughrey, *Allegories of the Anthropocene* (Durham: Duke University Press, 2019), 136.
[33] Helen M. Rozwadowski, *Vast Expanses: A History of the Oceans*, (London: Reaktion Press, Ltd., 2018).
[34] Rozwadowski, *Vast Expanses*, 12.

[35] DeLoughrey, *Allegories of the Anthropocene.*
[36] Ibid., 134.
[37] Ibid., 133.
[38] Ibid., 141-2.
[39] Dorrik Stow, *Oceans, A Very Short Introduction* (Oxford: Oxford University Press, 2017), 76.
[40] Astrida Neimanis, Cecilia Chen, and Janine MacLeod, Eds. *Thinking with Water* (McGill-Queen's University Press, 2013).
[41] Ibid.
[42] Astrida Neimanis, "Alongside the Right to Water, a Posthumanist Feminist Imaginary," *Journal of Human Rights and the Environment*, Vol. 5 No. 1 (March 2014): 17.

I.

The Sea We Make

Diana Heise

Kansas City Art Institute

Abstract

This essay addresses the use of creative practice to comprehend the effects of the Anthropocene on the coastal ecologies of Mauritius and the Lake Champlain Islands. Here, I consider the regional context of these two locations, illuminating the particularities of their post-colonial and ecological existence. I outline my research methodology and accounts of scenes from the film, rooted in meditating on breaking with conventional ethnography and repositioning cinematic form as well as the camera's ability to turn action into performance, to make correlations between the human and the more-than-human. This writing addresses filmic representation's unique ability, due to its ephemeral nature, to grasp conceptually the forces of the real that are enacted on these ecologies. Through the lens of swiftly shifting ephemerality, the film and this writing ask for a break with patriarchal and colonial concepts that envision the environment as a resource to pilfer, abuse and deplete. Instead, this work is making an argument for modes of attunement within the shifting uncertainty of the Sixth Extinction, to position human bodies as intrinsically tied to oceanic bodies.

Keywords: Anthropocene, Mauritius, Lake Champlain Islands, Documentary film, artisanal fishing, Sixth Extinction

***

From 2012 to 2016, I produced a film entitled *The Sea We Make* (*Lamer Nou Fer* in Mauritian Kreol), witnessing the methods of artisanal fishermen in Mauritius and Vermont struggling to thrive in the Anthropocene. I made this work as I was grappling with the effects of the results of climate change, including the loss, the anxiety, and the apparent differences in the watery vista from my familial home in the Champlain Islands. These shifts change not only my present and future but transform the past and my childhood into a memorial, an environment that my grandchildren will not inherit. This work was made with grief and saddened resistance.

Keeping with the thematic vision of this volume, this essay addresses the use of creative practice to comprehend the effects of the Anthropocene on the coastal ecologies of Mauritius and the Lake Champlain Islands. Here, I consider the regional context of these two locations, illuminating the particularities of their post-colonial and ecological existence. I outline my research methodology and accounts of scenes from the film, rooted in meditating on breaking with conventional ethnography and repositioning cinematic form as well as the camera's ability to turn action into performance, to make correlations between the human and the more-than-human. This writing addresses filmic representation's unique ability, due to its ephemeral nature, to grasp conceptually the forces of the real that are enacted on these ecologies. Through the lens of swiftly shifting ephemerality, the film and this writing ask for a break with patriarchal and colonial concepts that envision the environment as a resource to pilfer, abuse and deplete. Instead, this work is making an argument for modes of attunement within the shifting uncertainty of the Sixth Extinction[1], to position human bodies as intrinsically tied to oceanic bodies.

Regional contexts

Mauritius is in the southwestern Indian Ocean, some 800 kilometers east of Madagascar in a chain of islands known as the Mascarene archipelago. This volcanic remnant has no close physical neighbor, and its stark isolation makes it vulnerable to cyclones and ripe for seclusion. Although it was not inhabited by a consistent civilization, it was known and used by many, including the Arabs, the Swahili,[2] and later the Portuguese. Privateers, who acted at times as rogue pirates and in other instances were funded by rival powers, used the location to their advantage, may it be stocking up on supplies or marooning unwanted adversaries.[3] Biologically separate before the age of globalization, the Mauritian landscape was heavily affected by the influx of visitors who may not have always stayed long but would deposit other species such as monkeys, goats and rats.[4] Accounts of the large tortoises and the fearless Dodos generated an image in the Dutch imagination of Mauritius as a site of plenty after the first Dutch encounter in 1599. Coupled with anxiety over potential French or British occupation,[5] the psychological need to ensure territory in the European colonial race to claim space and the desire for ebony to build their crafts en route to the Dutch East Indies[6] resulted in the sporadic attempts by the nascent Dutch government to establish a viable colony, beginning in 1638. Powered by the capitalist machine of the Dutch East India Company (VOC) and despite their typical attention to land management, ebony was quickly harvested under threat of foreign invasion. Instability plagued the colony, whether it be unruly soldiers, famine, the perceived and actual threat of escaped slave encampments, the rival encounters with others inhabiting the island, or mysterious diseases. There were attempts by more environmentally minded leaders to maintain the ecology, including considerations of soil erosion and deforestation,[7] but the administration of the island was so difficult that such methods were not readily employed. Attempts to stabilize the colony centered on the importation of slaves[8] from the complex social network of the Malagasy, which in turn resulted in escapees, or maroons, to form independent thriving settlements, while others found return passage with French ships.[9] The Dutch settlement failed, and they vacated the island in 1710.

The French came late to the race for colonial territory, claiming Mauritius despite its difficulties to colonize, beginning their efforts in 1721.[10] Their 'successful' establishment of a colony was laid on enslaved bodies, with the drastic increase of the slave population, sourcing individuals from across the Indian and Atlantic Oceanic Worlds, including Madagascar, Mozambique, Bengal, Goa and Gorée on the West coast of Africa. While there are some records outlining the need to improve the working conditions for enslaved people[11] and follow the Code Noir, there is a great silence in the historical record on the experience of these humans, which opens one to think of the indescribable horrors that most likely ensued.

Agricultural enterprise did not reshape the landscape of Mauritius until after the transfer of power from the French to the British in 1810. Despite abolition, the colonial government maintained a plantation society "that engendered continued dependence on a cheap, coercible and abundant labour supply."[12] Slavery was replaced with a system of indenture, primarily sourcing workers from the Indian subcontinent. The British government regulated this system of supplying cheap labor to its colonies, setting up offices in Indian cities such as Chennai and Kolkata. Mauritius was used as the testing ground "because of its previous experience with Indian workers, its large expanse of virgin land and its proximity to the source of supply,"[13] becoming the model for the other British sugar colonies. Differing from slavery yet still full of abuses, indentured laborers were able to keep contact with their family abroad and the possibility of reconnection alive. Those who did stay began purchasing pieces of land, as the plantations were cut into portions called morcellements, cementing the influence of these immigrants.[14] In 1910, this formal system of emigration from India ended, whose descendants now make up two-thirds of the population,[15] while sugar cane cultivation still dominates the landscape.[16]

Accounts throughout Mauritian history during the time of slavery speak to the practice of maroonage, where slaves escape from the plantation.[17] The storytelling around maroon heritage rings loud in contemporary Mauritius, centering around a mountain in the Southwest of the island called Le Morne.

With the rise of heritage dialogues, research into maroon legacies and ecotourist development, Le Morne has been cast as a traditional fishing village. After abolition, many newly freed slaves moved to the coastal regions, making fishing their livelihood.[18] Many indentured laborers also followed the same trajectory after completing their contracts. With the establishment of the Le Morne as a UNESCO World Heritage Site, the government also funds the Le Morne Heritage Trust, which generates research and events to highlight and engage the cultural landscape, including the forms of fishing found in this area. According to anthropologist Rosabelle Boswell, there is a need to resist essentializing this activity and the identity of Le Morne's inhabitants, particularly as livelihoods change, while respecting the historical and contemporary role of cultural heritage, such as fishing.[19]

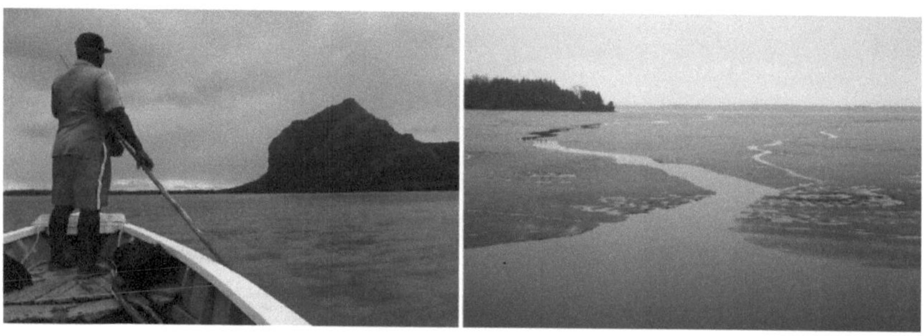

Figure 1.1: Le Morne Mountain, Mauritius and City Bay, North Hero USA, Stills from *The Sea We Make* © Diana Heise.

In contrast to the tropical environment of Mauritius, the Champlain islands are in the deciduous forest region of North America, located on the body of water bearing the same name. This lake acts as a border between Vermont and New York, stretching into Canada. Also, in comparison to Mauritius, humans have inhabited this region since Paleoindian hunter-gatherers moved into the area nearly 11,300 years ago. Before contact with Europeans, the last group of indigenous peoples to inhabit the area were the Iroquois and Algonquin nations, more specifically the Mohawk and Abenaki peoples.[20] The Abenaki named the lake, Petawa-bouque,[21] although various translations have been found including "'alternate land and water,' 'the Water that Lies Between' or 'double lake,'" referring to the island chain as dividing the lake into two.[22] The two largest islands, now referred to as North Hero and South Hero, were called 'gitsimenahan' or 'big island.'[23]

The first Western colonialist to set eyes on this body of water was the French sea captain and empire builder, Samuel Champlain in 1609,[24] some 10 years after the Dutch landing in Mauritius. Upon entering the lake that now bears his name with his Algonquin allies, according to his journals, he passed a series of islands. His guides informed him that these islands had formally been inhabited by local people but 'had been abandoned for a long time because of the war between the Algonquins and the Iroquois."[25] According to this journal, at this time, the lake acted as a border between these two peoples and the islands appear to have been a type of DMZ between them. There is also more recent evidence to suggest that these islands and much of the Champlain valley were cooperatively shared and managed hunting areas between these two peoples and a transportation thoroughfare.[26]

Champlain would not return to this lake, but the French would establish their first settlement in Vermont, a fortified building called Sainte Anne on Isle La Monte, an island west of North Hero in 1666,[27] as the wars between the Iroquois and the French mounted. This area would be contested for the next century and a half, leading to the decimation of the First Nations peoples, the American Revolution, the independent Vermont republic and Vermont's eventual entrance into the United States.

Vermont historian Allen Stratton's research into the founding of the towns located on the Champlain Islands speaks to the original land grants proposed in the wake of the American Revolution. Two of the most prominent revolutionary figures in Vermont were the brothers Ira and Ethan Allen, leaders of a group known as the Green Mountain Boys. These men played significant roles in securing the Champlain region. Upon British surrender, the Allen brothers petitioned the newly formed republic of Vermont for state ownership of this land in 1779, disregarding an earlier claim in 1769 by a New York state resident.[28] These disputes continued as Vermont vied to join the union as the 14th state, but needed to settle ownership discrepancies, particularly the islands of Lake Champlain. Ira Allen redrew the map and asked the representative from Connecticut to present it as his own. This measure passed the newly formed American Congress unopposed, and Vermont joined the United States with jurisdiction of the Champlain Island region.[29] Ethan Allen included his own naming of this area as the Two Heroes, later known as North and South Hero, brashly titled after himself and his brother Ira.[30]

Despite not owning property themselves, the Allen brothers systematically worked to dispossess the indigenous Abenaki who lived in the area.[31] The wars between the English and French and their Indian allies displaced many First Nations peoples, resulting in various subgroups of the Western Abenaki moving into the island region, primarily in Missisquoi Bay and North and South Hero.[32] The Allen brothers fanned fears of the Indians as raiders and trespassers. They cultivated this racism to cement the Abenaki as a threat to white settlers, turning to the newly formed government for bureaucratic interventions that undermined indigenous land rights.[33] A few Abenaki were able to hold onto their land at Missisquoi Bay, but most, which it appears includes peoples living on the Champlain islands, moved because of the ecological damage inflicted by white settlerism. With the loss of moose and deer populations decimated by the colonists and the lack of land on which to grow food, the Abenaki were left in starvation conditions.[34] Researchers cite the linguistic and cultural influence of the Abenaki on communities in present-day Canada, most likely resulting from the forced migration of these First Nations people north of the Vermont border.[35]

By 1790, the lack of affordable farmland in southern New England drove families north.[36] The Champlain Valley's alluvial plain was known for some of the richest and most fertile soil in the region, resulting in the population increasing over 150% by 1810.[37] The period between the 1780s to the 1820s would result in the drastic reorganization of this region, as infrastructure typical of white settlerism was constructed. On the Champlain Islands, the first settlers were anxious to ready the land for agriculture in the warmer months, clear-cutting and burning the virgin forest. Much of the oak and pine were logged and floated into Canada to build ships for the French monarchy as well as to mills established by the Allen's in Swanton and others around Burlington.[38] To survive the long winters, residents would use various means, including ice fishing. The practices of ice fishing are believed to harken back to the First Nations peoples who first inhabited the area.[39] This practice is still popular today, as recreation, a food source or to supplement income, selling fish to local markets and neighbors. Ice shanties dot the winter lake, warmed by heaters, creating social environments outside homes, an antecedent for cabin fever over the long winters.

The ecological health of each location is under threat today. Mauritius is surrounded by a coral reef that protects its shores from beach erosion. There are varieties of coral also found in the lagoon that are the basis of the ecosystem. According to Mauritian oceanographer Vassen Kauppaymuthoo (and most climate scientists today), the global burning of mass quantities of fossil fuels has acidified the oceans. Corals are particularly sensitive to this acidic shift, which breaks down their calcium-based skeletons.[40] According to the non-government organization the Reef Collective, the temperatures in the lagoon reached above 30 degrees Celsius in 2009, bleaching the corals and making them more sensitive to environmental change.[41] These shifts are also noticeable by local fishermen, including Judex Rampaul, the president of a fisherman's union outside the capital, Port Louis, and Fabien Auguste in Le Morne. Each of them also confirmed that pollution from development runs into the lagoon and is damaging the aquatic ecology. Both have witnessed profound effects on the environment's health. According to Rampaul, multiple species of fish that he saw all his life are now gone. The current catch is also smaller, not given the time to grow to full capacity before being plucked from the sea by commercial fishing enterprises. Certain European countries and Japan have fishing rights that are not closely regulated, over-harvesting the waters and making it hard for local fishermen to earn their livings.[42] To procure the amounts of fish needed, local fishermen in Rampaul's union must go farther outside the lagoon, putting themselves at risk from rough seas in their small boats. In Le Morne, fish are precured inside the lagoon, and this catch is also being affected negatively by the weakened and dying coral.

The ecological future of the Champlain Valley is similarly bleak. According to a 2014 study, the temperatures are expected to increase by 0.468C by 2100, twice as fast as the historic modeling indicated.[43] In the same timeframe, both annual snowfall and the number of days below 0 degrees Celsius are expected to decrease by 50% or 45 days, respectively.[44] This shift explains the resulting thinner ice that inhabitants have witnessed, significantly affecting the ice fishing community. These temperature increases also affect the types of fish that live in the lake, producing shifts in natural predators and changes in food sources.

Lake Champlain also suffers from problems with environmental run-off. After the clear cutting enacted by the early European settlers, the Champlain Valley now is dominated by dairy agriculture. Due to field management practices such as manure/fertilizer use, tillage types and timing, crop selection and harvest methods,[45] eutrophication is occurring from high phosphorus levels in runoff, resulting in noxious algal blooms and other disruptions in the lake's ecology.[46] As environmental restrictions to maintain ecological health are primarily voluntary, 90% of the lake segments are not meeting water quality targets. These materials entering the lake have also been proven to affect fish health as cancer-causing chemicals found in these aquatic animals now exceed levels healthy for humans to consume.[47]

Each location continues to engage in artisanal methods of procuring fish. In Rampaul's union, there are no large trolling nets, and the lines are cast by hand. In Le Morne, small boats are taken out into the lagoon and fisherman swim, walk and have a snorkel, using a large metal spear to pierce their catch. In North Hero, holes in the ice are drilled with a hand crank and the line is dropped. This expertise is passed down generationally and can be equated as a form of folk knowledge, learned through experimentation and ancestral understanding of their respective environments. These fishing methods also do not over-consume their ecologies; the methods themselves are too labor-intensive to overtake the balance within the environment. Rampaul explained that industrial fishing will take the largest fish, who should be left to lay eggs and the smallest before they have had a chance to grow and leave their offspring. Hands can be more precise than the machine.

To contextualize these fundamentally different engagements with ecology, we need to consider colonialism's legacy on these environments. Colonialism refers to the geo-political and economic system where imperial powers established settlements in locations outside of their traditional borders to generate power and profit. Neel Ahuja frames the rise of the idea of "'matter' – physical objects making up the universe and its constitutive systems and elements – has developed in tandem with the spread of colonial forms of knowledge and settlement."[48] This inquiry, powered by the modern sciences, reshaped their understanding of the more-than-human world and separated "inanimate matter, the living biological body, human culture and the spiritual domain into distinct spheres."[49] This philosophical shift easily allows matter, as well as, human bodies to be viewed as resources for capitalist gain, justified with the notion that the colonialist methods are more profitable and efficient than indigenous ones. Also, by separating culture and spirituality, justifications for barbarism were connected to religious edicts, weaponizing the missionary process against First Nations and enslaved peoples. Colonial myths of underdevelopment veil the widespread violence, hunger, social inequality, and environmental degradation generated by colonial warfare and settlement.[50]

Despite apparent differences, each location is marked by imperial colonialization and its methods of shifting landscapes. Both the French and English colonial systems were struggling to take hold of these areas. Both were known locations by indigenous people, yet not developed under the definitions of settlerism, justifying colonial claims and land speculation. Mauritius and North Hero are islands, making them isolated and thus vulnerable, particularly to ecological shifts and weather. According to Eve Tuck and Wayne Yang, the system of settlerism requires a notion of civilization in which excess is produced for profit,[51] which requires increased labor due to the geographical isolation of these locales. In Mauritius, this need translates to slavery and indenture. In North Hero, this demand led to aggressive modes of clear cutting, taxes were always paid in labor,[52] and the reorganization of land for unsustainable agricultural production. Both were reshaped by the worldview imposed by colonialism, matter turned to profit, where western modern notions of ownership are still used to justify the continued abuse of the environment and its inhabitants.[53] Today, the ecological damage found in each location reveals the deep trauma that colonialism has impressed upon these landscapes.

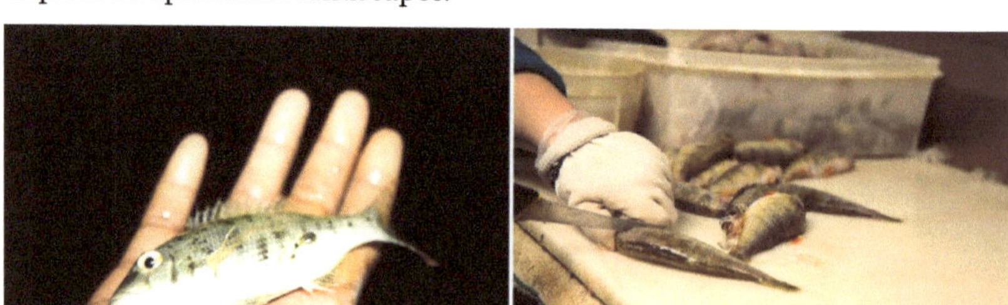

Figure 1.2: Baiting Fishing, Mauritius and Ray's Seafood, Burlington VT, USA, Stills from *The Sea We Make* © Diana Heise.

My method to engage with each community resulted from a deep immersion into both locations. In Mauritius, I became entrenched in the heritage movements, working with activists and artists to produce films to protect endangered cultural practices. I learned Mauritian Kreol and was sensitized to the post-colonial social structures of the country. I asked my activist friend Stefan Gua if he could introduce me to members of the local fishing union, resulting in my interviews and visual engagements with Judex Rampaul and his community. Stefan was also able to put me in touch with ecologically engaged NGOs and climate change researchers to interview for this work. I had also conducted research and attended gatherings at the Le Morne Heritage Trust and their staff put me in touch with Fabien Auguste. I would stay in Fabien's guest apartment and go fishing in the mornings. In Vermont, I am familiar as I had grown up there. I met with Mickey Dattilio, a neighbor and a longtime friend of my uncle and contacted the local fish shop for permission to film.

From this position of community awareness, the methodology behind *The Sea We Make* draws from dialogues to produce ethnographically engaged work without perpetuating a colonialist worldview, to, in Trinh Minh-ha's words, 'speak near-by.'[54] Ethnographic and anthropological methods have long been tied to mapping societies into Western notions of historical world consciousness,[55] locking non-Western peoples and their cultures as static objects of study with fixed identities.[56] This type of work purports itself as a scientific endeavor to "'collect data' for the knowledge of mankind,"[57] made valid by the interpretative forces of the anthropological academy. Meaning is solidified, not because other interpretations are necessarily wrong, but because it escapes anthropological control.[58] In this pursuit of collecting data to support their own worldview, anthropologists looked to photography and film for a stable document, "a vitrine filled with illustrative evidence, seemingly inert."[59] Just as they would learn that their subjects are not objects for museum cases, lens-based media would reveal that "the camera delivered an exorbitant excess which frequently had its own story to tell."[60] Images make their own arguments, at times in opposition to the anthropologist or ethnographer's intentions.

Deviating from this colonialist approach, *The Sea We Make* works self-reflexively, embracing the camera's "inherent inability to recognize, discriminate and filter."[61] Voices are heard, and humans are seen, but the film resists conventional uses of cinema on multiple levels. The narration is destabilized from a singular point of view moving between poetic musings and interpretations of research, creating a difficulty of naming the distinction between 'subjects' and 'objects.' The work is built on an episodic structure, breaking with modes of monological storytelling in order the highlight polyvocality. The film also breaks with contemporary uses of moving images to generate news, entertainment or perpetuate expectations of spectacle. Spectacle, according to E. Ann Kaplan and Ban Wang in *Trauma and Cinema,* is "the tendency of the global mass media to turn history into simulacra."[62] The film does not negate its referenced environment, but works to creatively resist "cinematic capitalism" and the entangled matrix between visuality and modernity.[63] The film instead is creating an ecology, as defined by Matthew Fuller as "the massive and dynamic interrelation of processes and objects, beings and things, patterns and matter."[64] Within this ecological thinking, the film is more in line with notions of the 'ecological sublime" in which Adrian J. Ivakhiv describes as a method which "does not romanticize the violence but simply presents it as a given, like an inexorable fatal tide."[65]

From this standpoint, this film is not intended as a biography of those pictured. I was given permission and invited to film, but the goal was not to engage or construct character. Instead, these images describe human bodies existing in their environment, wishing to thrive, just as the fish navigate their own ecology to find food and reproduce. This equating of human and fish bodies embraces current dialogues from Anthropocene feminist perspectives on renaturalization[66] as a method of garnering a more holistic relationship between the human and more-than-human. The film posits a reconceptualization of "human agency as part of nature or matter rather than in opposition to it."[67] This viewpoint is not a return to justifications of gender inequality, patriarchal marginalization, colonial conquest or white privilege, but a reversal from the modernist project of separating nature from culture. This turn, as Stacy Alaimo describes in *Bodily Natures,* is "not circumscribed by the human but is instead accountable to a material world that is never merely an external place but always the very substance of ourselves and others."[68] This notion of 'other' is embodied within human bodies or can be described as "trans-corporeality: the contact zone between human corporeality and more-than-human nature."[69] After attuning ourselves to these coastal environs, the film asks us to consider the bodies of humans and the bodies of fish as components of one another, tied together in a dance of survival.

The immersive experience of film is also key to engaging questions around ecology in the Anthropocene, from which I will borrow Jacques Rancière's notions of meaning-making to unpack. Despite art's relationship to mimicry and imitation throughout its history, Rancière claims that its current potency lies in its potential dissemblance. Works of art simultaneously provide and undo a viewer's relationship to perception and our meaning-making process. Instead of reinforcing our prescribed ideas, it offers an alternation between resemblance and a discrepancy. Rancière states, "the commonest regime of the image is one that presents a relationship between the sayable and the visible, a relationship which plays on both the analogy and the dissemblance between them."[70] By embracing this dialectic, there is the potential to be released from the maze of simulacra, simulation and spectacle, to be returned to the concrete. Lens-based methods, such as filmmaking, become an ideal method to navigate this process as they can closely mimic the mechanics of the human eye while providing disembodied representations. Through immersion, these images can make a viewer feel like you are right there, although you are not. We can use these simulations to hold onto the ephemeral. As the coastlines shift and disappear, as the corals die and the fish deplete, the image, burned into digital memory drives, persists, remains and reminds, although their mimicked physical mirrors do not.

Just as human activity is shifting global ecologies, this film is creating a sea, a current and a coast to first allow us to grieve and experience loss. Borrowing from Ban Wang and E. Ann Kaplan discussion of trauma, the film gives the audience a viewpoint to act as a witness, opening "a space for transformation ... through empathic identification without vicarious traumatization — an identification which allows the spectator to enter into the victim's experience through a work's narration."[71] Secondly, the film creates a viewpoint to consider our changing future condition. To understand multispecies livability, 'it is not enough to watch lively bodies.' We must also see 'where the "assemblages of the dead gather together with the living. In their juxtaposition, we see livability anew.'"[72] Film and its methods of montage mimics what Deborah Bird Rose refers to as the "Double Death --, that is, extinction, which extinguishes time yet to come."[73] From this extinction, we are creating something new, with violence and toxicity. Through these virtual and ephemeral means, we can understand, perhaps, our own concrete actions and potentially enact a new ethic that addresses the "relentless force of the real."[74]

In this time that has been dubbed the "Great Acceleration,"[75] the ethic posited in *The Sea We Make* makes space to reflect upon the embedded trauma of climate change while offering an immersive space of attunement. The film looks closely at the progress of global development and its resulting climate change as a collective of local experiences instead of an insurmountable global totality. Echoed by Anna Lowenhaupt Tsing, Heather Swanson, Elaine Gan and Nils Bubandt in *The Art of Living on a Damaged Planet*, one way to understand this Acceleration is "through immersion in many small and situated rhythms. Big stories take their form from seemingly minor contingencies, asymmetrical encounters and moments of indeterminacy. Landscapes show us."[76] The stance of this film is to attune to these rhythms and see what these simultaneous landscapes can reveal. Its methodology is a form of deep listening, a noticing that "attunes us to worlds otherwise."[77] By shifting to a perspective of regionalism, the film posits a correlation between artisanal approaches to landscape to valorize a more balanced engagement with local ecologies.

Images from the film

The Sea We Make is organized into eight sections: *Danger, Underwater, Death, Three Visual Notes on the Process of Fishing, Judex's Images, Fish Shop, Fish Culture,* and *Our Development.* At the beginning of each section is an introductory voiceover that moves between giving research-based information to offering poetically styled questions and musings. After this introduction, the video images proceed without narration, taking a position as a keen observer.

As we are not watching this film together, let me create a series of images via story. We see tropical white beach water with shaggy pine trees on shore. There is a mountain in the distance and just beneath the surface a mound of murky green. This green is darker than the trees on shore and rounded in shape, echoing the shape of the mountain behind it. The camera turns sideways, defiant of horizons and land-defined gravity to enter the turquoise water, while placing its focus on the mound of green. Made clear from lack of reflection and refractions, this green is sea foliage growing over a hard structure. Currents move the anchored plant. As the camera shifts upward, the space beyond the bound of the water's surface is revealed: clouds, sky and the contorted pine trees growing on shore. At this stage, we hear a voice ask, "As people, how do we connect with a space that does not support our existence? A space without breath?" This section continues, including underwater images from other locations around Mauritius, including a boat in the lagoon.

A minute later, the camera is once again out of the water, now revealing winter trees and a diagonal plane of ice over a large bay. Grey, overcast, the ice matching the color of the sky. Submerging into a hole through inches of ice, the camera reveals a green murky interior. This green is lighter than the green of the previous image, not a leafy green from photosynthesis. The camera twists and the film cuts to a light blue and glassy white image of cold enclosed ripple-less water from under the ice.

Taken from the section entitled *Underwater,* these filmic representations acquaint the viewer to the bounded space of underwater existence: buoyancy, currents, the upper limit of life above, the density of water and ice. As the voice insinuates, this space is inhospitable to humankind. We choke and drown here. Our bodies are in danger. But the camera lets us linger longer than our lungs allow and attune ourselves.

Once acquainted with underwater space, the third episode, *Death,* invites us to look at the corals growing inside the lagoon of Mauritius. While looking from above the water of these animals, the voiceover informs about the human-produced environmental factors that are depleting the ecosystem. After this information is conveyed, there is a close-up image of a sandy beach. We can hear the surf, but the camera does not reveal the water. There are imprints of sandals and footprints marking the sand.

With a few strands of seaweed intertwined, we see rock-like structures, worn down and smooth. The camera moves in a roaming fashion, inspecting this bony material. Irregular with holes and nobs, these are the bones of deceased coral. Their intricate structures have been tumbled by the sand and sea movements, smoothing their shapes to seem closer to stone. As in the underwater section, the orientation of the horizon line is ignored and now the camera angle remains parallel to the ground. The film cuts to a larger pile of these remains. As the images continue, the piles become larger and the viewpoint closer. We can see more clearly that it is indeed a mass boneyard of coral bodies. Cushioned by larger tufts of seaweed, these skeletons retain a ghostly trace of their past anatomy.

The movement of the camera ceases to simply roam; it now follows a rhythmic pace of stopping to reveal, turning circularly and tracking again. The performativity of these movements reminds that there is a human body behind this camera, interacting with this scene, subtly breaking the filmic immersion in an endless maze of this cemetery. Relief from this motion and viewpoint comes when we see a singular coral skeleton surrounded by a bed of wet sand. The sound of the waves is finally connected with its image, as the water laps gently over the bone and retreats. We see another three filmic images of waves lapping over the coral as if to gently return these bodies to their watery environment, for what I would infer as, a more proper burial.

After establishing this presence of death, human and fish bodies are introduced in the section entitled *Three Visual Notes on the Process of Fishing*. In the first 'note', we hear the rumble of a motor engine with dark night images of an industrial plant in the distance. There is a murky dark void in the bottom half of the screen with slight glimmers of refraction. Water. The film cuts to an image of two male bodies at the front end of a boat, leaning over the bow. The camera follows a long-woven line while we hear a stomping sound, revealing a foot pounding on the hull. The line is connected to a net that is submerged in the water, taunt. We hear murmurs of conversation between the men, as the net is dragged back into the bottom of the boat. No fish, some seaweed. We see the weights around the edges of the net and the fine white mesh material being held in the hand of one person. The motor engine sound returns over an image of black, white and red ripples. New location. More hunting.

Concentrating in close-up, the image focuses on the bow of the boat, a man's lower body and feet, the dark void of black water and the weighted bottom of the net. Green seaweed is littered about, contrasted by the red edges around the craft and the white of its bottom. Two feet shuffle and twist, the lower body adjusts and balances, finding a tension from which to cast the net into the void.

A small piece of seaweed clings to the human's leg. With a point of the right foot and weight transferred to his back leg, the net is released, and we can hear the resulting sound. The image cuts, as we wait, watching the dangling mint green line. The right foot is now positioned on the red edging of the boat, toes gripping, hand-over-hand to retrieve the mesh web, water droplets shimmering. A large white sheet of plastic sits in the bottom of the boat, made bright and more extreme by the portable LED light on the camera. The net is placed on the plastic and shook, the weights making a muted rhythmic sound against the hard fiberglass. There is a singular small silver fish in the net. One fish. That's it. Now, this process is to catch bait. It is not expected to see large fish that would be found outside the lagoon. But the laborious nature of this work is apparent, when only one fish is returned to the boat after much effort. A hand reaches down to retrieve the flailing gilled animal and it is placed in a blue plastic bucket, the size of a rain barrel, filled with sea water.

The images in this section continue outlining the process. More locations, increasing sunlight, more fish, more labor. We continue to be immersed in how hard this artisanal method looks. Industrial modes would not require such physical work. Yet, as mentioned earlier, the increase of scale found in industrial systems would result in a less targeted catch, taking all the fish from the lagoon. In this instance, ancestral knowledge does not equate to antiquated methods of the past but instead a recognition that taking all the babies and the elders will not maintain the wisdom and longevity of a community. By its scale, the artisanal method bounds the abilities of humans to take, which results in safeguarding the health of the waters and their inhabitants. In the next two notes, we watch similar processes in North Hero and Le Morne.

The approach of the camera does not ask the people pictured to describe this labor and its potential difficulty in words. Instead, immersed in this scene, the detail capturing abilities of the camera allow the viewer to relate in closer proximity than our actual human bodies would allow. Due to this sense-saturating approach without explanation, there is a non-hierarchical correlation produced between the human bodies and the fish bodies. These entanglements between people and the more-than-human world, which move from consumption into symbiosis, identity and culture, are undetachable. These humans' bodies appear as belonging to this environment instead of being opposed to it. If we can reposition our viewpoint of all human bodies as belonging to the ecologies that we inhabit, if we can break the colonial mentality of environment as 'other' material resource to be extracted, perhaps a new ethic of engagement can be embodied.

The bait fishing shoot was organized by Judex Rampaul and in the process of making this film, he transferred to me an archive of his videos and photographs, which I edited into the next section. These images reinforce the cultural and biological entanglement that Rampaul's community has with the coastal ecology of his home. There are images of large, 10-foot-long or more fish with multiple men posed around them, donned with fatigue and smiles. The porch of his house stores the equipment for fishing, which he documents visually. We see videos of younger men preparing the nets and hooks, while Judex asks them in a persistent manner to explain what they are doing. He follows his daughter around the store attached to their home, as she describes how to remove the scales of a pinkish red fish with a small brush and where the catch is eventually stored in the freezer. Family, mentorship, and a way of life are revealed, forms of connectivity and care that are made more vulnerable as the ecology changes.

The next three sections reiterate this correlation between human bodies and fish bodies, in which we see fish brought out of their context, flailing, dead, cut, frozen, cut again, roasted and at times hung on a wall. During a celebration for the annual Abolition of Slavery public holiday in Le Morne, we see a fish roasting on a long stick that has been driven through its mouth into its body cavity. The branch is then propped up by the sand around a wood-burning fire to cook it. This process is a cultural remnant, not a daily occurrence but an important staging to valorize the community and their historical ways. In the image, a man on a boat stands directly behind the fish at an equal scale. As the subtle ripples of the sea sway the craft, the man's body moves behind the outline of the aquatic body, revealing and collapsing of two forms into one.

Intercut with this scene are images of fish mounted to a cabin wall. The voiceover tells that the fishing culture in Vermont does not manifest as historical reenactment as it does in Mauritius. Instead, the remnants of this activity result more in physical objects of sport, such as the preservation of fish through taxidermy. The reverence for these animal's manifest as the need to keep and possess them. Teeth gnashed, color preserved, and mounted on wood, these bodies are not allowed to decompose. Instead, their forms act as reminders of the human sensation produced when engaging an activity of mental focus, physical strength and curiosity. When screened in an installation context, these preserved animals are ten times their own size. This scale shift places the viewers' bodies, not just the participants' imaged, into play.

The Sea We Make concludes with the last voiceover asking the viewer to consider the effects of 'advances' in global development, both physically and psychologically. The last images of the film depict hunting for octopus with Fabien August in the lagoon off Le Morne. He stands in waist-deep water, and we see a tentacled animal dragged out of its hiding place of branching coral with a metal rod. After being disemboweled, the creature is placed in the bottom of the boat and the camera lingers on the anguished movement of this body and its slow death. This imagery moves from the physical to the symbolic, as after inclusion of the previous equations between the human and more than human bodies, this gutting implies that human bodies are just as vulnerable. This reality is even more present now after the oil spill of 2020 gushed over 1000 metric tons of oil fuel after crashing into a coral reef in the South-Western region of the island. This event makes devastatingly clear that all bodies are at risk.

As seasoned professionals consider the response to the oil spill in Mauritius troublingly mismanaged[78] and high levels of phosphorus runoff continue spew without oversight into Lake Champlain, what have we humans gained by scaling up our activities to meet global demands and privileging a conception of our environments as a resource for commodity-driven extraction, propelled since the colonization of each location? This statement is not intended to place blame as people attempt to support their families in the context of contemporary capitalism but aims to ask us to examine the system of exploitative practices that actively undermines ecological health. By a consideration of these two local situations, the film is asking its audience how we may move through ephemeral representations to address what Elizabeth Grosz refers to as "the relentless force of the real."[79] The images of the film stay locked in their non-corporeal state, functioning as ghosts of another time. Yet, because of experiencing the work and as discourse around new materialism and feminist renaturalization grows, symbolic and ontological considerations invite us to build a potential new ethic. adrienne maree brown writes in her activist-oriented text, *Emergent Strategy*, that in following the science of emergence as a method to grow social justice movements, we can consider biomimicry, adaptation, non-linearity and resilience as paths for generating and turning toward greater equity.[80] As we watch birds, bugs and trees murmurate and adapt, the hope is that humans can learn to do the same, without causing harm.

While writing this essay, our contemporary dialogue has been shifted by the events of George Floyd's death and calls to dismantle systemic racism. Land recognitions are announced at lectures and symposiums, like eulogies, pronouncing which nations once lived on lands before settlerism. Mauritians are protesting the botched government and international response to the MV Wakashio spill, while donating their hair which helps soak up the oil, attempting to protect the fragile ecosystem from further damage. Meanwhile, the heated denial of climate change and calls to defund the fossil fuel industry has led to a stalemate of political action in the United States. The implications of colonialism and neo-liberal policy lay bare the trauma that has been inflicted on all the bodies in our intertwined ecologies. Some of the most vulnerable are the ones on the edges, the ones of the islands, those with little room to spare, those who have been pushed to the societal margins by racism and neo-imperialism, those humans and more-than-humans that dwell in and by physical and social coasts. The entangled branches of history, cultural practice, and ecological impact need to be held within the same viewpoint, understood as inter-related kin, as not to underestimate the damage inflicted and the healing that is required. With the aid of artistic practice, we need to stay close to the pain, to not forget, to attune, to root into our collective bodies, so that we are ready for action to occur collectively and intersectionally.

Notes

[1] Elizabeth Kolbert, *The Sixth Extinction: An Unnatural History* (London: Bloomsbury, 2014), 3.
[2] Richard Allen, *Slaves, Freedmen and Indentured Laborers in Colonial Mauritius* (Cambridge: Cambridge University Press, 1999), 9.
[3] Megan Vaughan, *Creating the Creole Island: Slavery in Eighteenth-Century Mauritius* (Durham: Duke University Press, 2005), 5.
[4] Vaughan, *Creating the Creole Island*, 4.
[5] Ibid., 6.
[6] Ibid., 8.
[7] Ibid., 71.
[8] Major studies of slavery in Mauritius include: Teelock, *Bitter Sugar*; R. Allen, *Slaves, Freedmen, and Indentured Laborers*; and Vaughan, *Creating the Creole Island*.
[9] Vaughan, *Creating the Creole Island*, 9.
[10] Allen, *Slaves, Freedmen and Indentured Laborers*, 11.
[11] Vaughan, *Creating the Creole Island*, 64.
[12] Vijayalakshmi Teelock, "The Mauritius Truth and Justice Commission: 'Eyewash', 'Storm in a Teacup' or Promise of a New Future for Mauritians?" in *Emancipation and the Remaking of the British Imperial World*, ed. Catherine Hall, Nicholas Draper, and Keith McClelland (Manchester: Manchester Univ. Press, 2014), 207-222, 217.
[13] Marina Carter, *Voices from Indenture: Experiences of Indian Migrants in the British Empire* (Leuven: Leuven University Press, 1997), 19.
[14] Allen, *Slaves, Freedmen and Indentured Laborers*, 142.
[15] Ibid., 17.
[16] Despite much of the landscape is still growing cane, post-independence economic stability came mostly from investment in offshore banking, the textile industry and the growth of the Informational Technology market. According to the World Bank, Mauritius had the second highest GDP per capital in Africa in 2019.
"GDP per Capita (Current US$) - Sub-Saharan Africa," accessed November 13, 2020, https://data.worldbank.org/indicator/NY.GDP.PCAP.CD?locations=ZG.
[17] See Vaughan, Allen, Teelock.
[18] Krish Seetah, et al, "The Mauritian Archaeology and Cultural Heritage Project: Exploring the Impact of Colonialism and Colonisation in the Indian Ocean," *Antiquity* 85, no. 330 (2011): 1-6.
[19] Rosabelle Boswell, "Heritage Tourism and Identity in the Mauritian Villages of Chamarel and Le Morne," *Journal of Southern African Studies* 31, no. 2 (2005): 283-295, https://doi.org/10.1080/03057070500109466, 290.
[20] Philip G. Terrie, *Contested Terrain: a New History of Nature and People in the Adirondacks* (Blue Mountain Lake, NY: Adirondack Museum, 2008), xx.
[21] Gordon M. Day, "Abenaki Place-Names in the Champlain Valley," *International Journal of American Linguistics* 47, no. 2 (1981): 143-171, https://doi.org/10.1086/465683, 151.
[22] Day, Abenaki Place-Names, 152.
[23] Ibid., 153.

[24] Ralph Nading Hill, *Lake Champlain: Key to Liberty* (Woodstock, VT: The Countryman Press, 1995), 18.
[25] Ibid., 18.
[26] Day, *In Search of New England's Native Past*, 43.
[27] Ralph Nading Hill, *Lake Champlain: Key to Liberty*, 29.
[28] Allen L. Stratton, *History, Town of North Hero, Vermont: an Account of the Discovery, Settlement, and Interesting and Remarkable Events* (North Hero, VT: Stratton, 1976), 13.
[29] Stratton, *History, Town of North Hero*, 14.
[30] Ibid., 14.
[31] Colin G. (Colin Gordon) Calloway, *The Western Abenakis of Vermont, 1600-1800: War, Migration and the Survival of an Indian People* (Norman, OK: University of Oklahoma Press, 1994), 225.
[32] Calloway, *The Western Abenakis*, 86.
[33] Ibid., 227.
[34] Ibid., 231.
[35] Day, *In Search of New England's Native Past*, 146.
[36] Jacqueline Carr, "Local History and the Vermont Borderlands, 1790-1820," *Vermont History* 84, no. 1 (Winter/Spring 2016): 70–92, 72.
[37] Carr, *Local History*, 72.
[38] Stratton, *History, Town of North Hero*, 74.
[39] I. Sheldon. Posen, *You Hear the Ice Talking: The Ways of People and Ice on Lake Champlain* (Plattsburgh, NY: Clinton-Essex-Franklin Library System, 1986), 27. According to I. Sheldon Posen, there has not been extensive archeological research in the Lake Champlain area to confirm Native peoples use of ice fishing, but as other nearby northern nations used these methods, it is more than likely that the practice was used here too.
[40] Interview with Vassen Kauppaymuthoo, 2014.
[41] Interview with Reef Collective, 2014.
[42] Interview with Judex Rampaul, 2013.
[43] Justin Guilbert et al., "Impacts of Projected Climate Change over the Lake Champlain Basin in Vermont," *Journal of Applied Meteorology and Climatology* 53, no. 8 (January 2014): 1861-1875, https://doi.org/10.1175/jamc-d-13-0338.1, 1870-1.
[44] Guilbert, "Impacts of Projected Climate Change over the Lake Champlain Basin in Vermont," 1872.
[45] L. T. Ghebremichael, T. L. Veith, and M. C. Watzin, "Determination of Critical Source Areas for Phosphorus Loss: Lake Champlain Basin, Vermont," *Transactions of the ASABE* 53, no. 5 (2010): 1595-1604, https://doi.org/10.13031/2013.34898, 1601.
[46] Ghebremichael, Veith, and Watzin, "Determination of Critical Source Areas for Phosphorus Loss: Lake Champlain Basin, Vermont," 1595.
[47] James J. Pagano and Andrew J. Garner, "Concentrations, Toxic Equivalence, and Age-Corrected Trends of Legacy Organic Contaminants in Lake Champlain Lake Trout: 2012–2018," *Environmental Research* 184 (2020): 10, https://doi.org/10.1016/j.envres.2020.109329.
[48] Neel Ahuja, "Colonialism," in *Gender: Matter*, ed. Stacy Alaimo (Farmington Hills, MI: Macmillan Reference USA, 2017), 237-251, 237.
[49] Ahuja, *Colonialism*, 237.
[50] Ibid.
[51] Eve Tuck and K. Wayne Yang, "Decolonization Is Not a Metaphor - Center for Latin ..." *Decolonization: Indigeneity, Education Society*, Vol. 1, No. 1, (2012): 6.

[52] Stratton, *History, Town of North Hero, Vermont*, 48.
[53] Adrian J. Ivakhiv, *Ecologies of the Moving Image: Cinema, Affect, Nature* (Waterloo, Ontario: Wilfrid Laurier University Press, 2013), 257.
[54] Nancy Chen, '"Speaking Nearby": A Conversation with Trinh T. Minh–ha', *Visual Anthropology Review*, (1992) 82–91. doi: 10.1525/var.1992.8.1.82, 82.
[55] James Clifford and George E. Marcus, *Writing Culture: the Poetics and Politics of Ethnography* (Berkeley, CA: University of California Press, 2011), 165.
[56] Faye Ginsburg, "The Parallax Effect: The Impact of Aboriginal Media on Ethnographic Film," *Visual Anthropology Review* 11, no. 2 (1995): 69, https://doi.org/10.1525/var.1995.11.2.64.
[57] Trinh T. Minh-Ha, "Documentary Is/Not a Name," *October* 52 (1990): 92, https://doi. org/10. 2307/778886.
[58] Minh-Ha, "Documentary Is/Not a Name," 93.
[59] Christopher Pinney, "Bruises and Blushes: Photography 'Beyond' Anthropology," in *Documentary across Disciplines*, ed. Erika Balsom and Hila Peleg (Berlin: Haus der Kulturen der Welt, 2016), 20-38, 22.
[60] Pinney, *Bruises and Blushes*, 22.
[61] Ibid., 24.
[62] Ban Wang and E. Ann. Kaplan, "Trauma and Cinema: Cross-Cultural Explorations," in *Trauma and Cinema: Cross-Cultural Explorations*, ed. E. Ann. Kaplan and Ban Wang (Hong Kong: Hong Kong University Press, 2008), 1-22, 3.
[63] Ivakhiv, *Ecologies of the Moving Image*, 37.
[64] Matthew Fuller, Media Ecologies: Materialist Energies in Art and Technoculture (Cambridge, MA: MIT Press, 2007) quoted in Adrian J. Ivakhiv, *Ecologies of the Moving Image: Cinema, Affect, Nature* (Waterloo, Ontario: Wilfrid Laurier University Press, 2013), 348.
[65] Ivakhiv, *Ecologies of the Moving Image*, 109.
[66] Lynne Huffer, "Foucault's Fossils: Life Itself and the Return to Nature in Feminist Philosophy," in *Anthropocene Feminism*, ed. Richard A. Grusin (Minneapolis, MN: University of Minnesota Press, 2017), 65-88, 65.
[67] Ibid., 68.
[68] Stacy Alaimo, *Bodily Natures* (Bloomington: Indiana University Press, 2010), 158, quoted in Lynne Huffer, "Foucault's Fossils: Life Itself and the Return to Nature in Feminist Philosophy," in *Anthropocene Feminism*, ed. Richard A. Grusin (Minneapolis, MN: University of Minnesota Press, 2017), 65-88, 69.
[69] Lynne Huffer, *Anthropocene Feminism*, 68.
[70] Jacques Rancière, *The Future of the Image* (London: Verso, 2009), 7.
[71] Ban Wang and E. Ann. Kaplan, "Trauma and Cinema: Cross-Cultural Explorations," in Trauma and Cinema: Cross-Cultural Explorations, ed. E. Ann. Kaplan and Ban Wang (Hong Kong: Hong Kong University Press, 2008), 1-22, 16.
[72] Anna Tsing et al., "Haunted Landscapes in the Anthropocene," in *Arts of Living on a Damaged Planet*, ed. Anna Lowenhaupt Tsing et al. (Minneapolis, MI: University of Minnesota Press, 2017), 1-15, G5.
[73] Tsing et al., *Haunted Landscapes*, G7.
[74] Lynne Huffer, *Anthropocene Feminism*, 70.
[75] Will Steffen, Wendy Broadgate, Lisa Deutsch, Owen Gaffney and Cornelia Ludwig, "The Trajectory of the Anthropocene: The Great Acceleration," *Anthropocene Review 2*, no. 1 (2015 81-98, quoted in Anna Lowenhaupt Tsing et al., *Arts Of Living On A Damaged Planet*, (Minneapolis: University of Minnesota Press, 2017), G5.

[76] Tsing et al., *Arts Of Living On A Damaged Planet,* G5.
[77] Ibid., G11.
[78] Nishan Degnarain, "Five Glaring Issues With The Oil Spill Response In Mauritius Today," September 18, 2020, https://www.forbes.com/sites/nishandegnarain/2020/09/18/five-glaring-issues-with-the-oil-spill-response-in-mauritius-today/?sh=52ce0b755d7b.
[79] Elizabeth A. Grosz, *Becoming Undone: Darwinian Reflections on Life, Politics, and Art* (Durham, NC: Duke University Press, 2011), 85 quoted in Lynne Huffer, *Anthropocene Feminism,* 70.
[80] adrienne maree brown, *Emergent Strategy* (Chico, CA: AK Press, 2017), 50.

II.

Mapping Arctic Shores: Visual Stories of Entangled Histories

Celina Jeffery

University of Ottawa

Abstract

In this essay, I consider how artists in the Arctic regions of the USA and Canada (Turtle Island) use visual imagery – mainly photographic and performative video, to convey histories and produce creative interventions that complicate the climate discourse imagery of a so-called 'empty,' melting Arctic. Here, I examine the work of Subhankar Banerjee, an Indian born, American activist and photographer, who presents images of caribou migrations and hunts in Alaska that reject the prevalent narrative of the 'white' north, by drawing attention to the connection between the evisceration of certain forms of vulnerable social life and trends in Arctic climate biodiversity loss, toxicity and intrusion by the oil and gas industries. I also acknowledge the work of Inuit photographer Robert Kautuk, based in Clyde River, Nunavut who creates evocative photography situated as a form of Inuit self-determination. Finally, I think through the work of Inuvialuk artist Maureen Gruben who highlights the impacts of melting ice on Indigenous hunting livelihoods, particularly in areas of the Canadian Arctic coast most vulnerable to climate change. All three artists use their work to act as a literal and metaphorical investigation of ice as an ecosystem, a home, a signifier of global climate change, and perhaps, a form of resistance to the oil, gas and mining interests of the South.

Keywords: Arctic, Inuit art, climate change, colonialism, Indigenous

***

> "Suddenly something huge and white loomed out of the darkness and grew in size and whiteness, a marvelous whiteness in contrast to the inky sea, on the dark waves of which it rocked and swayed. This was the 'rst oe' gliding by us. Soon more came, gleaned far ahead, rustling by us with a strange rippling sound, and disappearing again far behind...I felt instinctively that I stood on the threshold of a new world."[1]
>
> Description of an "Ice Blink" from F. Nansen and H.M. Gepp's *The First Crossing of Greenland*, 1890

> "The ice is melting. A way of life that has existed for thousands of years is changing so rapidly that there is no precedent in either geological or human time scales. Arctic life has always been about the need to respect and adapt to the vagaries of cold, wind, ice, snow, land, and sea. But it is not just Inuit who have to contend with these changes. What happens in the Arctic will change the world for all of us."[2]
>
> Shelley Wright in her book *Our Ice Is Vanishing = Sikuvut Nunguliqtuq*, 2014

Fridtjof Nansen's description of Arctic glaciers by the Norwegian polar explorer and adventurer is evocative of the geophysical discourse that has dominated readings of the Arctic as an oceanic imaginary: life threateningly cold, intrepid, vast and wild, with limited biophysical diversity, and an ultimate playground for colonial, 'masculinist fantasy'.[3] It followed a long lineage of colonial exploration and exploitation in the Arctic, often in search of the Northwest Passage, in which 'discovery' was infused by the myth of disappearance and hence doubled as denial or erasure of Indigenous presence.[4] Thus Queen Elizabeth I famously named Baffin Island, an Inuit homeland for thousands of years, as *Meta Incognita* or 'the unknown limits' after privateer Martin Frobisher (1535–94) claimed the region for the Queen and named it Frobisher Bay, now modern day Iqaluit. Frobisher falsely stated that the shore was 'empty' when in fact he was known to have murdered Inuit inhabitants during his three voyages to the region. Implicit within this colonial framing of the circumpolar regions is the concept of *terra nullius*, designating a vast 'wilderness' whose fragile and sparse terrain is devoid of human and more-than-human populations (a term that signifies entanglements across species) and their respective ecosystems, and which continued to guide Arctic colonialism and discourse throughout the twentieth century. *Terra nullius* was a key principle in informing the colonial conception of Arctic glaciers as inert, unoccupied and never changing – a 'nobody's land' with resources that would eventually be seen as there for the taking. Photographic images (often unattributable) taken of the Canadian north in the 1880s by explorers, whalers, artists, ethnologists and geologists, many of whom were sent by the Canadian government or through the Hudson Bay Company to see if there were possible shipping routes for goods such as the Northwest Passage, reiterated this version of Nordicity as an aesthetic sublime of pristine wilderness and rugged terrain at the coastal edges that was nevertheless occupied by so-called 'ethnographic' subjects that by the early twentieth century had been 'discovered'.[5] Photographic images by the likes of Captain Joseph-Elzéar Bernier (1852-1934) or Canadian photographer Geraldine Moodie (1854-1945), for instance, present staged portraits of Inuit families that 'perform' their ethnographic culture and are otherwise decontextualized from their culture and land. In such examples, the identities of the sitters were most often omitted, and names were rarely acknowledged or, in other cases, intentionally misspelled to make Inuit names to be more pronounceable to people living in the South.[6] Both series of photographs played a role in the Canadian colonization of the north in which *Terra nullius* was followed by the so-called discovery of Indigenous peoples and then by occupation, resource extraction, exploitation and acquisition.[7]

According to Indigenous Studies professor Maura Hanrahan, there is a direct line of inquiry from the early wave of Arctic colonialism through to the current climate crises, a "through-line" she argues, "from the early polar explorers to Canada's expeditions from the 1880s onward to the establishment of Canadian law and other institutions on Inuit land to present-day scientific and social science research in the Arctic." [8] Contemporary imagery of the climate crises in the Arctic often continues this reiteration of the discourse of *terra nullius*, focusing heavily on the far north as somehow beyond the social; from depictions of the sublime, to images of the catastrophic melting of glaciers, ice fractures and pools of meltwater on ice shelfs, or the resulting shifts in seasons and opening up of new pathways or 'frontiers' for the fossil fuel industry. The continued framing of the Arctic as an 'abstract space (and thus security commodity)' as opposed to an actual homeland, Jason Dittimer argues, refashions the Arctic as an 'exclusionary' and 'contested' space open to multiple and competing definitions.[9] Thus, while the effects of global warming are drastically redrawing the map of the Arctic Ocean and broader Arctic regions by opening up routes, the 'abstract' colonial framing of the Arctic by the global south as indeterminable and 'fragile' and thus, open to forces of geopolitical interests in security and resource extraction is ultimately enabling a resurgence of intervention.[10] Andrew Stuhl suggests that while the Arctic is now conflated with global warming as a kind of 'far-off land' that pays the price for the world's carbon emissions, it is more important to understand histories and trajectories of Indigenous peoples[11] and transitive and entangled cartographies. Although the Arctic Ocean and its coasts have been dominated by scientific discourse, particularly regarding physical geography and social sciences, how are such entangled narratives thought of by visual artists – particularly Inuit artists – and how do they invite thinking through the Arctic's ephemeral coast differently?

In this essay, I consider how artists in the Arctic regions of the USA and Canada (Turtle Island) use visual imagery – mainly photographic and performative video, to convey histories and produce creative interventions that complicate the climate discourse imagery of an empty Arctic. The work of Subhankar Banerjee, an Indian born, American activist and photographer, presents images of caribou migrations and indigenous hunts in Alaska that reject the prevalent narrative of the 'white' north, by drawing attention to the connection between the evisceration of certain forms of vulnerable social life and trends in Arctic climate biodiversity loss, toxicity and intrusion by the oil and gas industries. Inuit photographer Robert Kautuk, based in Clyde River, Nunavut whose evocative drone photography and digital atlas project (the *Clyde River Knowledge Atlas*) is situated as a form of 'Inuit self-determination in research'[12] and includes an important mapping exercise that reinscribes Inuit place names and provides details of their significance, including an archive of photos, videos and stories that convey historical dimensions of hunting and food insecurity. Finally, I reference the work of Inuvialuk artist Maureen Gruben[13], whose installation, performance and video works highlight the impacts of melting ice on Indigenous hunting livelihoods, particularly in areas of the Canadian Arctic coast most vulnerable to climate change, while also acting as a means of literal and metaphorical investigation of ice as an ecosystem, a home, a signifier of global climate change, and perhaps, a form of resistance to the oil, gas and mining interests of the South.

Entangled histories of the Arctic Ocean

Sverker Sörlin and Dolly Jørgensen have addressed the lack of *historiography* of the circumpolar regions, noting that its historically ascribed 'emptiness' was linked to the colonial denial that there could be a human and even more-than-human history.[14] Sörlin, an historian and Arctic Humanities researcher, also describes the turn in 'issue-based' knowledge such as planetary climate change being produced over the past ten years, as needing to replace discipline-specific routes. He argues that an Arctic Humanities must be imbricated in pluralistic knowledge with Indigenous presence that ultimately addresses the ethical conditions of our contemporary world through integrated methodologies.[15] A humanities perspective can give rise to new contexts, alternative paths of thought, and allow for new imaginations of histories and futures.[16] In this essay, I am interested in an art historical reading of the Arctic's ephemeral coast within a humanities context that acknowledges its entangled history.

The Arctic Ocean was not formally recognized as an *ocean* – in the 'meta-geographical' sense – until 1921, when the International Hydrographic Organization declared it the world's smallest ocean, (the fifth ocean having recently been identified as the Antarctic ocean).[17] Having been continuously remapped throughout the twentieth century, the Arctic Ocean space was rearticulated in 1986 to include smaller northern seas.[18] Currently, five coastal states – Canada, the USA, Russia, Norway, and Denmark – are contesting land claims via the United Nations Convention of the Laws of the Seas, each motivated by claims to "natural resources, security and indigenous status and rights."[19] The rhetoric of the ocean's edge as a frontier has been pervasive in the Arctic context and has informed substantial trajectories of colonial expansion and occupation, guided by the increased desire for marine trade routes. In the era of mid-twentieth century capitalism, resource extraction dominated concepts of the ocean frontier as a space of opportunity – a 'margin' according to Philip E. Steinberg – whose physical dynamism could at once prevent surveillance and control, and yet inversely, be closed by sovereign states, was codified in the United Nations Convention on the Law of the Sea (UNC-LOS). [xli] Global warming is having a significant impact on the Arctic Ocean and its surrounding coastal zones in Alaska, Canada, Greenland, Norway and Russia. The Sixth Assessment Report of the Intergovernmental Panel on Climate Change, published in August 2021, describes climate change as effecting every inhabited area of the planet, with the Arctic "*likely* to be practically sea ice free in September at least once before 2050 under the five illustrative scenarios considered in this report, with more frequent occurrences for higher warming levels." [20] The damning report states that the process of global warming will continue exponentially in the world's oceans, Antarctica, and the Arctic, over and above any other region in the world. [21] Further, the report found that Arctic sea ice 'was smaller than at any time in at least the past 1000 years',[22] and is likely to be ice-free by the end of the century, the result of human activity, yet it fails to fully articulate a dominant fact: that climate change is largely the product of a select few countries contributing to an uneven Anthropocene.

As the Arctic warms and sea ice melts, the Northwest passage – which became ice-free for the first time in 2007, is opening to commercial shipping and oil drilling, creating an opportunity for a kind of colonial expansionism.[23] The 'New North' as it has recently been dubbed, denotes a conflation of global warming, melting ice and literally new pathways for investment, rehearsing the colonizing principles of the past while staking a claim to its future ownership.[24] Andrew Stuhl argues that this New North is dependent on the erasure of the 'old North' as an 'isolated and inhospitable' place designated to fuel exploration and colonial land claims at the expense of Indigenous and more-than-human presence.[25] As the 'marvellous white' ice disappears, so the opportunities for drilling for oil, coal, gas, and minerals emerge; and as some estimate, 25 per cent of the world's remaining fossil fuels are buried in the Arctic Ocean.[26] The Arctic has become symbolic of where future loss and the constantly morphing and melting present intertwine, with a constant impact on the lives of Indigenous peoples; yet the discourse of climate change often depicts the imagery of the far 'north' as beyond the social lives of Indigenous communities.

Shelf or land fast ice is a type of salt water ice that forms on the perimeter of the shallow coastal waters, as in the islands of the Canadian Arctic Archipelago, and which if the temperatures remain cold, provide solid stretch of thick ice from land to sea.[27] In the Spring, as temperatures warm, floe edges are formed to create a new edge – sometimes extending great distances, where the coastal sea-ice meets the open ocean and provides a 'frozen shoreline' from which Indigenous peoples have traditionally relied upon the extraordinary marine ecosystems. As the Arctic Spring sun warms the waters, the algae emerge from ocean floor to the surface and attracts a plethora of prey and wildlife to the floe.[28] Warming temperatures have made the Spring floe treacherous and hazardous to fish, meanwhile, pack and multi-year ice are disappearing and has been replaced by annual ice. [29] The traditionally nomadic Inuit of the circumpolar regions and the entire system of migration and seasonal transformation of Arctic biodiversity has been irrevocably interrupted.

Since the emergence of climate change discourse in the 1980s, the Arctic has been at the center of global warming discussions, and the retreat or disappearance of 'marvellous white' tidewater glaciers has become iconic imagery in media, popular culture and in the work of art activist groups. The turn of the twenty-first century witnessed renowned glaciers, such as the Muir Glacier in the US state of Alaska, notably retreat. Named after the Scottish naturalist and explorer John Muir, who travelled there in 1879 and 1880 by ship, the Muir Glacier, like all the glaciers inhabiting Glacier Bay National Park, began to retreat simultaneously while thinning dramatically, signalling that warming air and water temperatures were transforming the Arctic's coastal regions.[30] NASA's *Images of Change,*[31] which chronicle 'before and after' satellite photographs of prominent sites of environmental degradation and global heating, features the Muir Glacier in 1941 and again in 2004, documenting its process of disappearing.

The organization, *Chasing Ice*, founded in 2007 by James Balog, similarly grappled with visualizing the fleeting passing of these great glaciers by using a technology he developed called Extreme Ice Survey (EIS).[32] EIS[33] was created to capture consecutive images of depleting and vanishing glaciers internationally. The resultant documentary film of the same name features imagery reminiscent of late Romanticism, with magnificent and sublime glaciers in the landscape tradition, but packaged in the kind of data-oriented, technologically classified visual proof of climate change discourse. Rather than acknowledging local narratives and the effects of shifting weather patterns on Indigenous communities, then, the film primarily visualizes 'calving events', the breaking of ice from the edge of a glacier that signifies the rapid and intense effects of the global warming upon the Arctic. In this regard, visualising climate change through EIS is limiting, in part because it lacks historicity in favour of images of immediate and staggering loss, but also because it ignores the relationships between these locations and their more-than-human as well as Indigenous peoples who consider the glaciers to be sentient and responsive to the behaviour of humans.[34] The social and cultural impacts of Arctic heating encompass less reliable ice coverage for hunting, thawing permafrost, damaged infrastructure, erosion of shoreline through storm surges, unpredictable weather patterns and of course, rising sea levels.

Julie Cruikshank, whose research involves Indigenous oral histories, recounts that the first peoples of the Yukon and Alaska consider glaciers as agential, as 'shapeshifting', and "as occurring within a deeply moral universe where natural-cultural histories are always entangled."[35] The work of Subhankar Banerjee provides an early example of an artist seeking to create specific representations of Indigenous lives as at once intertwined through historical and contemporary relationships with the land and sea, while also in the process of disentangled, fragmented and challenged by the ever increasing pressures exerted by the neo-colonial south, including global climate change and its concomitant engagement with resource extraction. Banerjee is an artist, writer and activist who has been engaged with Arctic climate change awareness and social justice issues in the Arctic since the early 2000s. As an artist-researcher in the Alaskan Arctic National Wildlife Refuge (known as the 'Refuge') in 2001-2002[36], Banerjee engaged with the Indigenous communities of the Gwich'in people and the Iñupiat people – who reside in coastal regions, to discuss the impacts of climate change and oil development in the area adjacent to the Beaufort Sea,[37] where sea ice is depleting, and permafrost is now known to have thawed at great speed. The Arctic National Wildlife Refuge was established by the Eisenhower administration in 1960 as the 'Last Great Wilderness' with eight million acres are designated 'wilderness area', but with a few Indigenous populations living therein.[38] The Refuge covers some 80,000 km2 from the Beaufort Sea coast and coastal tundra of the Brooks Range to the boreal forest and is the largest conservation area in the United States. Its history as a conservation site has been undermined and very publicly violated by the oil and gas industries that view it as a last standing frontier; while the First Nations people of the land were urged to move from the regions around its three major rivers to the 'Arctic Village', thus separating them from their traditional land claims and hunting lifestyles.

During Banerjee's research at the Refuge, the artist dialogued with Gwich'in Nation people and chronicled the effects of drying lakes, wildfires, disruption to caribou migration, and what is perhaps a more unusual effect of permafrost thawing – a phenomena knowns as 'drunken forest' in which larch trees lose their grounding and start to tip over and fall. At the time of Banerjee's research and photographic series were produced, the oil and gas industries had been pushing for onshore oil drilling, as well as offshore oil and gas drilling in the Beaufort and the Chukchi Seas. A US Geological Survey estimated that there are 90 billion barrels of oil, 1669 trillion cubic feet of gas, and 44 billion barrels of natural gas liquids in this region.[39] Banerjee's subsequent images of coastal Arctic Alaska, which were censored in an exhibition at the Smithsonian Institute by the Bush administration in 2003,[40] depict intensifying environmental changes – from the retreat and thinning of the ice to the thawing of the permafrost, to rising sea levels and intense storms – that all have a significant impact on coastal erosion and force local, Indigenous populations and more-than-human species and ecosystems in Alaska to adapt, retreat or decline.[41] His photographic series, *Oil and the Caribou* (2002), bring these collisions of Indigenous communities and the fossil industry into dialogue, while also suggesting a different narrative than the data-driven and catastrophizing imagery of films like *Chasing Ice.*

Banerjee's work includes aerial photography such as *Caribou Migration I* (2002), which depicts the Porcupine River caribou herd crossing the Coleen River. This area of coastal plain is the major calving region for the caribou, and it is also one of the most contested regions in the US, due to the lobbying of oil and gas industries. The Gwich'in Nation, who call themselves the caribou people, live with and rely upon this species for hunting. Banerjee's image both comments upon and literally visualizes this entangled tradition, while also contextualizing the disruption of migration in caribou (*Rangifer tarandus*), whose access to important habitats have been affected by both global warming and industrial incursions in the landscape. The use of aerial imagery helps to literalize this relationship that is deeply significant for Indigenous communities in the region (of which there are approximately 9000 Gwich'in in the Northwest Territories).[42] These communities and the caribou are both affected by freeze-thaw cycles, diminished access to foraging and oil drilling.

Most dramatic changes are happening to the sea ice in the region, which is retreating rapidly and what remains is thinning; such freeze-thaw cycles of the tundra are causing caribou to migrate farther to search for food, only to be met by starvation. These 'icing events', in which rain during the fall and winter months is followed by dramatic freezing patterns, prevent animals like caribou, reindeer and muskoxen from moving around and breaking through the ice to find food; at times, the animals ingest ice to satiate hunger and die of hypothermia.[43] Extinction patterns have existed in the Arctic for at least one hundred years; one example is the extinction in 1990 of the Arctic reindeer in East Greenland that travelled to West Greenland to search for food, likely as the result of climate change.[44] By 1977, the Western Arctic Caribou population declined by 80 per cent and by 1980, scientists began to register and monitor the warming trends in the sea ice.[45] Then, in the early 2000s, sea ice was melting in the Arctic at such a staggering rate that images of polar bears drowning were widely circulated in the media; and far less noted, but no less impactful, was the severe effect on the habitat for seals, particularly Ribbon Seals, which live on the edges of sea ice.[46]

When Banerjee returned to Arctic Village in the Refuge in 2007, he produced a series of photographs entitled, *Gwich'in and the Caribou,* one of which titled

Caribou Hunt – Jimmy John focuses on the challenges that global warming presents to Indigenous life.[47] The image depicts a caribou hunt at close range, with Jimmy John skinning a Caribou, while blood trails across the snow. It is indicative of the mutual relationship between *Gwich'in* and the caribou, whose past and future are ultimately reliant upon each other. In contrast to the dominant image of the pristine/melting white Northern landscape, Banerjee sought to demonstrate the sustainable, transitional, and interconnected multispecies lives of the First Nations peoples. Banerjee's book, *Arctic Voices: resistance at the tipping point* (2012), is testimony to his positioning of the local inhabitants as witnesses.[48] For the Indigenous authors of this testimonial, the Arctic is home, a vast ecosystem that is neither wilderness nor terra nullius, as *Gwich'in* elder and cultural activist Sarah James writes: "Caribou are not just what we eat; they are who we are. They are in our stories and songs and the whole way we see the world. Caribou are our life. Without caribou we wouldn't exist."[49] The visibility of Indigenous voices has been much enhanced by recent documentaries such as *Qapirangajuq* (2010) that give light to the expertise and opinions of Northern communities.

Qapirangajuq: Inuit Knowledge and Climate Change (2010), is the first Inuktitut-language film concerning climate change and wildlife conservation in the North from the perspective of the Inuit.[50] Interviewing elders and hunters, the film draws attention to the impact on social factors of climate change, the constant adaptation to unsettled and extreme weather patterns, and the daily lives of Inuit people and the local communities. Directed by Nunavut based film maker Zacharias Kunuk and researcher and filmmaker Dr. Ian Mauro, it features interviews with Inuit residents, mainly elders and hunters, who discuss their lived experience of the climate crisis, their sustainable relationship to the land and sea, and makes a case that their future must be guided by Indigenous knowledge. The film also posits a kind of counter-narrative to the climate discourse presented by climate science, including detailed, local, and personal accounts of the changing behaviour of seals and fur thickness, the increase in raven populations and polar bears, and how the warming weather is making navigation over thinning ice difficult and treacherous. 'Inuit Qaujimajatuqangit', which means doing things in an Inuit way[51], brings to light the voices of elders who counter the standard discourse of climate science and wildlife welfare by questioning the acquisition of climate knowledge itself and offering a worldview of relationality, adaptation, and cultural revitalization.[52]

Climate scalability

Robert Kautuk is an artist – primarily a photographer, cultural worker and educator, who lives in the Clyde River or Kangiqtugaapik (which means 'a nice little inlet') – who similarly engages with the social, embodied and cultural context of coastal regions in Nunavut.[53] Clyde River is a hamlet located on the east coast of Baffin Island's Patricia Bay; nearby is the Barnes Ice Cap, known as one of the oldest and most 'spectacular' ice caps in Canada. Clyde River / Kangiqtugaapik is characterized as a low coastal plain, extending some 400 kilometers long, with the distinctive black cliffs of Black Buff acting as a local landmark. Whalers (late nineteenth century) and the Hudson Bay Company traded there (from 1923); government programs fostered a local art market in soapstone carvings and silkscreens comparable to the Kinngait Studios, while Nunavut's new cultural college, Piqqusilirivvik, is in Clyde. Seal hunting and fishing remain important for the community, who historically also moved inland for caribou hunting, while polar bear, walrus, beluga, and narwhals were hunted in the fall seasons in the shallow fjords and inlets.[54] Where the intertidal zone was once known, trusted and capable of withholding the seasonal hunting habits of the Inuit community, the thinning and waning of the ice surrounding the Qikiqtaaluk Region present many challenges.

In 2015, Kautuk and Mike Jaypoody founded and created the *Clyde River Knowledge Atlas,* in dialogue with the Ittaq Heritage and Research Centre, as a means of collating research on climate change from an Inuit knowledge system and perspective within and for the community.[55] For Kautuk and Jaypoody, the digital atlas – which is made available to Inuit and is a form of 'Inuit self-determination in research'[56] – includes an important mapping exercise that reinscribes Inuit place names and details of their significance. The project also assembles an archive of photos, videos, and stories. Low broadband and limited infrastructure, however, inhibit both production and access to digital photographic practice.[57] Place names are written in Roman alphabet as well as Inuktitut syllabics, while recordings of pronunciations accompany some of these names (many recorded by Kautuk), and aspects of the website allow you to overlay conservation interests, such as detailing calving regions that are of critical wildlife concern.[58] Another facet of the atlas is an account of historical weather patterns that is organized by the community-driven Silalirijiit Project meaning "those who work with or think about weather" in Inuktitut.[59] The sea ice map, which is based on Indigenous Elders' knowledge in dialogue with that of scientists, shows shifting ice patterns from 1978-2016 and significant diminishing of the ice. The cyber atlas, in this way, is characteristic of the pivot away from climate change cartography that focuses solely on conventional approaches to capturing data, toward a mixed method approach that also draws on Indigenous knowledge that seeks to promote and protect northern languages, culture, ecologies and people. This generation of modern elders as Shelley Wright argues, "remember what it was like to grow up on the land while learning the old skills as they had been passed on for generations, although as time goes by this treasury of knowledge is disappearing."[60]

Kautuk is known for his video, photography and aerial surveys using drones, some of which are taken in collaboration with researchers involved with the Arctic Institute of North America (AINA)[61] and the Ilisaqsivik Society.[62] Kautuk's drone photograph *After Cutting Up Two Walruses, Igulik* (2016) presents an aerial image of an ice floe in which two walruses have been hunted and skinned by three people.[63] A boat is attached to the floating ice, which is shaped like an island that sits on a deep, blue jade green sea. Blood runs across the ice from the skinned meat and carcass of the walrus; the physicality of the photograph is palpable and tells the story of co-existence. Drone imagery, which may be considered a continuation of attempts to colonize the resources of the sea and its inhabitants, as well as document climate change, is in a way, inverted by Kautuk's aerial images. As curator Wanda Nanibush writes, "In this context, a photograph of a walrus hunt is an act of resistance."[64] In this regard, Kautuk's image is also a creative response that contributes to the narrative about connectivity and the convergence of human and more-than-human entanglement in the broad and intersecting relationships between climate change, sovereignty and the survival of traditional Inuit relationships with the sea as a habitat, tradition, and interdependency, or what Donna Haraway described as 'symbiotic makings'.[65] Kautuk's images of Inuit living within and off the coast detail an ecosystem within and through which the lives of Inuit interact with non-human others. The photographs are neither metaphors of the 'magnificent white' Arctic, nor are they catastrophizing its imminent doom, as is suggested in *Chasing Ice*. Kautuk's *After Cutting Up Two Walruses, Igulik* also resists the detached stance of southern culture from their food sources and asks the viewers to immerse themselves in the textures, voices, and agencies that the image presents. This is not an Arctic Ocean melting at the edges, bustling for routes to create further capitalist overflow. It is an image that presents a living ecology albeit a precarious one and a literal fragment of a community, of a way of life, which can push against the anthropogenic systems of aestheticized and sanitized food industries.

Anna Lowenhaupt Tsing ascribes the theory of *nonscalability* to note the need for attention to diversity of life on earth and draws "attention to the mounting pile of ruins that scalability leaves behind."[66] Tsing argues that digital technology belongs to this process of scalability or the 'expansion-oriented world' and in this regard, helps us recognize the complexity of ecological non-scalability by eliciting sensitivity to the 'conjuncture' and 'friction' inherent in this theory; a kind of entanglement that notices the relationship between ice, blood, and hunt, histories and contexts that are unfamiliar to the south, and which is unread by data-driven science.[67] The non-scalability of localised voices, visual representations of those who live a community in their own terms that convey the temporal anxiety of weather upon entangled lives, is significant also as an assertion of cultural identity and sovereignty. The political cannot, as Inuit curator and art historian Heather Igloliorte explains, be separated from the land, "For Indigenous peoples, language and culture are rooted in the land. Knowledge is place-based, embodied, and inter-relational. This worldview, and the artistic practices based in it, has become politicized by settler colonialism, which is characterized by a historical and ongoing dispossession of Indigenous peoples from their lands."[68]

Artist Maureen Gruben is from the Tuktoyaktuk region of Inuvialuit, a hamlet located in the Inuvik Region of the Northwest Territories. Gruben works in performance, sculpture, installation art, and video to address the relationship between Indigenous land rights, climate, and Inuit culture. Much of her work is zero waste, made in dialogue with or co-produced with the community, and combines reclaimed materials from the land, her home and industry like the use of beluga intestine alongside digital technology like USB charging cords.[69] In *Stitching my Landscape* (2017), Gruben placed red broadcloth over the ice in the Pingo National Landmark site near Tuktoyaktuk in a performative act that took place between April 19-25, 2017, as part of the 2017 *Landmarks* initiative, in which ten artists were invited to produce site-specific works in national parks across the country to engage with Canada's sesquicentennial as a country. Eventually the work formed an installation and then video, exhibited at the National Gallery of Canada's *Àbadakone/Continous Fire/Feu Continuel* (November 2019) exhibition among others.[70]

The installation took place in the canal surrounding the Ibyuq Pingo in the Pingo National Landmark, on the shore of the Beaufort Sea and Arctic Ocean, near Gruben's home and in a region experiencing severe climate-related impacts. The Park preserves eight geological ice-cored canonical hills, known as pingos, which are formed by permafrost,[71] and Gruben's installation took place on the second-largest pingo in the world, the Ibyuk Pingo. These ice-cored hills have historically acted as cartographical markers for hunting and navigational aids for the Inuit of the Northwest Territories.[72] Gruben's installation involved the laying of the red cloth but also the collaboration of the community and permission to drill one hundred and eleven ice fishing holes along the shoreline in a zig-zag formation one thousand feet in length, which the artist then threaded with red cord.[73] The video and subsequent photographic stills are aerial, and highlight a light-drenched bright white snow, contrasting with the red ribbon interweaving through the landscape.

The artist's threading of the ice was a performative act of "endurance and of careful devotion" deeply rooted in the traditions of tattooing and the embroidery of parkas. [74] In *Stitching my Landscape,* the artist also makes several commentaries on her personal experience of her family's relationship to the land. The red weave was intended to recall the seal hunt, once undergone by her brother, in which red blood and guts would spill across the ice after the harvest.[75] In addition, the video uses the sound of Gruben's father's chiseling snow but slowed down to resemble a heartbeat. The stitching of the ice is also a reference to Gruben's mother, a seamstress, who recycled materials like cotton flour sacks to repurpose for use in the household.[76] Here the stitching is inevitably a metaphor for the desire to literally hold the sea ice together: "every year during these storms' Gruben states, 'we can witness our land drop into the ocean."[77] The use of the Inuvialuit Delta motif[78] the red zigzagging to literally keep the ice together "was like we were closing up the ice road," stated Gruben.[79]

The marine ecosystem and shores of the Beaufort Sea have presented Indigenous communities and wider ecosystems alike with some of the most intense impacts of climate change including: severe land erosion; rapid thinning of ice cover and thickness; more storms and stronger winds; marine mammals migrating farther from communities; earlier breakup and later freeze-up of sea ice; less reliable shore-fast ice; and, more rain and warmer weather.[80] Gruben considers ice an 'intimate materiality'[81] and her enduring engagement in *Stitching my Landscape* is not just a sculptural signifier for the urgent effects of global warming and for the land as a material that continues to be contaminated and colonized; it also signals hope in a communal action and a position of solidarity among and with Indigenous communities. Here, Gruben dislodges 'ice' from notions of exceptionalism, saviorism and the neoliberal systems that have informed climate imagery and disrupts the idea of the Arctic as an 'abstract' space of contestation and uncertainty by literally interweaving perspectives of Indigenous and more-than-human others. Such webs of connections can lead, as Maria Puig de la Bellacasa suggests, to further ideas about care and specifically, to the kind of ethical thinking that renders care within environmental contexts as an ethical-political issue. In this way, the idea of care becomes a proposition that can generate 'more caring relationalities' and detailed assemblages to generate responsive notions of care.[82]

Gruben's reworking of the ice in *Stitching my Landscape* maybe considered a form of 'geographical inscription', which Denis Cosgrove argues is counter to the typical geographical representation of cartography, a kind of mapping exercise that dominates climate discourse.[83] In this regard, Gruben counters both the kinds of totalizing ecological discourse which frames both google earth[84] and even arguably, NASA's *Images of Change* and which maybe said to echo the kind of universalizing and omnipresent vision which guided European colonial 'discovery', occupation and then cartography. [85] In this regard, Gruben's aerial imagery in the video version of *Stitching My Landscape* implies a counter narrative of the visual discourse of climate change in which verticality and aerial viewing can act as a means of identifying territorial and environmental degradation, but fails to acknowledge entangled perspectives – of people and more-than-humans which Gruben's work addresses.

These artworks by Maureen Gruben and Robert Kautuk thus situate Inuit land, in dialogue with community, history and culture to foster possibilities of decolonial vision and material creative expression. In both bodies of work, these artists disrupt the neo-colonial narrative of calving glaciers and inert melting ice to speak of the daily lives, struggles and acts of resistance to the effects of heating and pollution brought to their communities. In this regard, as J. Martineau and E. Ritskes argue, the work may be thought of as acts of 'decolonial aesthetics' that challenge the individualization of Eurocentric art production and instead speak of community, land and the desire for material decolonization to "remain rooted in a politics of land and place, as well as to embrace a fugitive aesthetic of liminal exploration."[86] In this regard, Banerjee, Kautuk, and Gruben all highlight the environmental and economic estrangement from traditional sources of food and subsistence that have constituted their deep connected to the shorelines of the Arctic Ocean, and which has become major cultural and political issues for Indigenous people in the North.

Our responses to addressing climate change and biodiversity loss must be planetary in scale. The artists discussed here offer a means of thinking through the relationship between planetary scale and 'nonscalability' as described by Tsing. They invite the viewer to simultaneously witness the entangled ecosystem of the pan-Arctic coast as social, political, ecological and ontological, and to recognize the specific disentangled and violent unpacking of this relationship through resource extraction, global heating, and resultant phases of extinction and ecocide. Each of these artists – Banerjee, Kautuk and Gruben rescale the macro imagery of climate change, both literally in their sense of focus on the fragmentation, thinning and thawing of ice, and in their dialogue with the social lives of Indigenous communities and kin. These bodies of artwork thus rescale the ecological fragmentation of ice as incomplete; as a phase which is closely bound to the need to reframe the future of the Arctic.

Notes

1 Description of an "Ice Blink" from Nansen, Fridtjof, and Hubert Majendie Ge, *The First Crossing of Greenland* (London and New York, Longmans, Green, and Company. 1890), 149-150.

2 Shelley Wright, *Our Ice Is Vanishing = Sikuvut Nunguliqtuq: A History of Inuit, Newcomers, and Climate Change* (McGill-Queen's University Press, 2014), 22.

3 Jason Dittmer, Sami Moisio, Alan Ingram, and Klaus Dodds, "Have You Heard the One About the Disappearing Ice? Recasting Arctic Geopolitics," *Political Geography* 30, no. 4 (2011): 202–14, https://doi.org/10.1016/j.polgeo.2011.04.002.

4 Wright, *Our Ice Is Vanishing*, 100.

5 See exhibition *Arctic Images from the Turn of the Twentieth Century*, National Gallery of Canada, 2014.

[6] Natan Obed, 'How to overcome the reassure of Inuit identity in archival photos: Reclaiming our names', *Inuit Art Quarterly,* June 9th, 2021. https://www.inuitartfoundation.org/iaq-online/how-to-overcome-the-erasure-of-inuit-identity-in-archival-photos . 'Project Naming' was founded by the Government of Nunavut and the Library and Archives of Canada to identify the individuals depicted in historical photographs held in the collection.
[7] Maura Hanrahan, "Discovering' Inuit Women: Photographer Geraldine Moodie and the Advancement of Canadian Sovereignty in the Arctic", *Western Geography,* Volume 24, accessed October 8th, 2020, http://www.geog.uvic.ca/wcag/WesternGeographyV24_InuitWomen_Hanrahan.pdf.
[8] Hanrahan, *"Discovering" Inuit Women,* 3.
[9] Jason Dittmer, Sami Moisio, Alan Ingram, and Klaus Dodds, "Have You Heard the One About the Disappearing Ice? Recasting Arctic Geopolitics," *Political Geography* 30, no. 4 (2011): 202–14, https://doi.org/10.1016/j.polgeo.2011.04.002.
[10] Dittmer et al, *Have You Heard,* 2.
[11] Andrew Stuhl, *Unfreezing the Arctic: Science, Colonialism, and the Transformation of Inuit Lands* (Chicago: The University of Chicago Press, 2017), 4.
[12] *Clyde River Knowledge Atlas,* accessed September 1st, 2021, https://clyderiveratlas.ca/index.html?module=module.clyderiver.aboutatlas.
[13] Maureen Gruben website, accessed September 10th, 2021, https://www.maureengruben.com/about.
[14] Sverker Sörlin and Dolly Jørgensen, *Northscapes: History, Technology, and the Making of Northern Environments* (Vancouver, UBC Press, 2013), 1-2, https://books.scholarsportal.info/uri/ebooks/ebooks3/upress/2014-01-21/1/9780774825733.
[15] Sverker Sörlin, "Why We Should Develop Arctic Humanities", Lecture: September 29, 2020, *The Arctic Environmental Humanities Workshop Series,* https://www.bu.edu/pardee/research/the-arctic-environmental-humanities-workshop-series/
[16] Ibid.
[17] Sverker Sörlin, "The Arctic Ocean", *Oceanic Histories,* Ed. David Armitage, Alison Bashford and Sujit Sivasundaram (Cambridge: Cambridge University Press, 2017), 270.
[18] Ibid., 271.
[19] Ibid., 273-4.
[20] IPCC, 2021: *Climate Change 2021: The Physical Science Basis. Contribution of Working Group I to the Sixth Assessment Report of the Intergovernmental Panel on Climate Change* [Masson-Delmotte, V., P. Zhai, A. Pirani, S. L. Connors, C. Péan, S. Berger, N. Caud, Y. Chen, L. Goldfarb, M. I. Gomis, M. Huang, K. Leitzell, E. Lonnoy, J. B. R. Matthews, T. K. Maycock, T. Waterfield, O. Yelekçi, R. Yu and B. Zhou (eds.)]. (Cambridge University Press). In Press, https://www.ipcc.ch/report/ar6/wg1/downloads/report/IPCC_AR6_WGI_Citation.pdf. 10.
[21] IPCC, *Climate Change 2021,* 21
[22] Ibid., 22.
[23] Helen M. Rozwadowki, *Vast Expanses: A History of the Oceans* (London: Reaktion Books, 2019), 221.
[24] Andrew Stuhl, "The Politics of the 'New North': Putting History and Geography at stake in Arctic futures", *The Polar Journal,* 3:1, (2013): 94-119, DOI: 10.1080/2154896X.2013.783280.
[25] Andrew Stuhl, *Unfreezing the Arctic: Science, Colonialism, and the Transformation of Inuit Lands* (Chicago: The University of Chicago Press, 2017), 3.
[26] Alex Shoumatoff, "Dispatch: The Arctic Oil Rush", *Vanity Fair,* April 14th, 2008. http://www.vanityfair.com/news/2008/05/arctic_oil200805.

[27] Wright, *Our Ice Is Vanishing*, 5.
[28] Susan Nerberg, *Life at the Arctic Floe Edge*, March 27th, 2019, https://www.canadiangeographic.ca/article/life-arctic-floe-edge.
[29] Wright, *Our Ice Is Vanishing*, 5.
[30] Jonathan Watts, "As glaciers disappear in Alaska, the rest of the world's ice follows," *The Guardian Newspaper*, May, 1st, 2021, https://www.theguardian.com/environment/2021/may/01/as-glaciers-disappear-in-alaska-the-rest-of-the-worlds-ice-follows.
[31] NASA, *Images of Change*, accessed: August 18th, 2021, https://climate.nasa.gov/images-of-change/?id=376#376-muir-glacier-melt-alaska
[32] *Chasing Ice*, accessed August 20th, 2021, https://chasingice.com.
[33] *Extreme Ice Survey*, accessed August 20th, 2021, http://extremeicesurvey.org/about-eis/.
[34] Julie Cruikshank, *Are Glaciers 'Good to Think With'? Recognising Indigenous Environmental Knowledge, Anthropological Forum*, 22:3, (2012): 239-250. DOI: 10.1080/00664677.2012. 707972.
[35] Julie Cruikshank, *Do Glaciers Listen? Local Knowledge, Colonial Encounters, and Social Imagination* (Vancouver: UBC Press, 2005), 243.
[36] Banerjee returned to Alaska and travelled to the Yukon between 2005-7.
[37] Subhankar Banerjee, "In the Warming Arctic Seas," *World Policy Journal*, 32, no. 2, (2015): 18–27, https://doi.org/10.1177/0740277515591539.
[38] *Protect the Arctic*, accessed September 20th 2021, https://www.protectthearctic.org/history-of-the-arctic-national-wildlife-refuge.
[39] Banerjee, *In the Warming Arctic Seas*, 24.
[40] Lisa E. Bloom, "Disappearing Ice and Missing Date: Climate Change In the Visual Culture of the Polar Regions," *Journal of the New Media Caucus*, (Summer, 2010) v. 06 n. 01.
[41] See Banerjee *In the Warming Arctic Seas* and the artists' website: http://www.subhankarbanerjee.org
[42] Gwich'in International Council, accessed June 2nd, 2021, https://gwichincouncil.com.
[43] Banerjee, *In the Warming Arctic Seas*, 21.
[44] "Caribou." *Caribou - New World Encyclopedia. N.p.*, n.d. Web. Dec. 10th, 2016. *Assessment, Arctic Climate Impact. Arctic Climate Impact Assessment - Scientific Report*, (Cambridge: Cambridge University Press, 2005).
[45] Maya Lin, *What is Missing*, accessed May 20th 2020, https://www.whatismissing.net/timeline/arctic_timeline
[46] Ibid.
[47] http://www.subhankarbanerjee.org/photohtml/arctic-photo-white-04.html
[48] Subhankar Banerjee, *Arctic Voices: Resistance at the Tipping Point* (New York: Seven Stories Press, 2012).
[49] http://www.subhankarbanerjee.org/photohtml/arctic-photo-white-04.html
[50] *Isuma*, accessed June 19th 2021, http://www.isuma.tv/inuit-knowledge-and-climate-change/movie-no-subtitles
[51] https://www.suzannemethot.ca/wp-content/uploads/2019/03/Inuit_Knowledge_and_Climate_Change.pdf
[52] Keavy Martin, "Introduction," *Stories in a New Skin Approaches to Inuit Literature* (Winnipeg: University of Manitoba Press, 2012).
[53] Qikiqtani Inuit Association, *Qikiqtani Truth Commission, Community Histories 1950–1975*, (Inhabit Media Inc. 2014), https://www.qtcommission.ca/sites/default/files/community/community_histories_clyde_river.pdf
[54] *Qikiqtani Truth Commission*, 14.

[55] *Clyde River Knowledge Atlas*, accessed June 9th, 2021, https://clyderiveratlas.ca/index.html?module=module.clyderiver.aboutatlas.
[56] Ibid.
[57] See "Looking Down from Up," *Collapsing Lines*, September 2019, Gallery44 and Inuit Art Quarterly, http://collapsinglines.ca/en/september-2019/.
[58] An example of the Longstaff Calving Area: https://clyderiveratlas.ca/index.html? module=module.clyderiver.conservation#eyJ0IjoieCIsImkiOiI4NWJjNjgwMzE3YjgzMjJhYTNkYTU4ZDg4NjI3ZjkwNSIsInMiOjE2MjM2OTUwNzE2OTV9
[59] https://clyderiveratlas.ca/index.html?module=module.clyderiver.weatherstation datavisualizer
[60] Wright, *Vanishing Ice*, 33.
[61] Aina News, "Update: The Return to Nova Zembla", *Infonorth* 72, Iss. 4, (December 2019): 478-480.
[62] John Geohegan, "Robert Kautuk: Looking Down from Up," *Inuit Art Quarterly*, November 7, 2019, https://www.inuitartfoundation.org/iaq-online/gallery-44-emerging-arctic-photographer-spotlight-robert-kautuk.
[63] The walrus hunt occurred outside of Iglulik and was part of a Piqqusilirivvik Inuit Cultural School program that gives young Inuit an opportunity to learn how to hunt using both traditional and modern techniques. https://www.uphere.ca/articles/summer-school
[64] Wanda Nanibush, "Notions of Land," *Aperture*, September 27, 2019, https://static1.squarespace.com/static/5b5f44a15cfd790e0236897b/t/5dd131a0d6c0de799e34ef80/1573990842797/aperture+wanda+nanibush+.pdf
[65] As discussed by Anna Lowenhaupt Tsing, "Bodies Tumbled into bodies" in Tsing et al, (Eds.) *Arts of Living on a Damaged Planet: Ghosts and Monsters of the Anthropocene* (Minn.: University of Minnesota Press, 2017), muse.jhu.edu/book/52400. M5
[66] Anna Lowenhaupt Tsing, "On Nonscalability: The Living World Is Not Amenable to Precision-Nested Scales," *Common Knowledge* (18 (3), (1 August 2012): 505–524, doi: https://doi.org/10.1215/0961754X-1630424, 506.
[67] Tsing, *On Nonscalability*, 508.
[68] Heather Igloliorte, Amy Dickson, and Charissa von Harringa, *Among all these tundras* [Exhibition catalogue], (Leonard & Bina Ellen Art Gallery, Toronto, Canada ISBN 978- 1-77252- 012- 5, 2019): 24, http://openresearch.ocadu.ca/id/eprint/2890/.
[69] Tania Willard, "Visceral Materiality and Instinctual Aesthetics," in *Maureen Gruben - Qulliq*, (ECU Press and Libby Leshgold Gallery, 2020).
[70] ÀBADAKONE | CONTINUOUS FIRE | FEU CONTINUEL, National Gallery of Canada, https://www.gallery.ca/whats-on/exhibitions-and-galleries/abadakone-continuous-fire-feu-continuel
[71] Betty Ann Jordan, "Maureen Gruben draws attention to a rapidly changing Arctic with Stitching my Landscape," *Canadian Geographic*, March 15, 2017, https://www.pressreader.com/canada/canadian-geographic/20170315/281552290657334
[72] Pingo National Park, accessed. June 2nd 2020, https://www.pc.gc.ca/en/lhn-nhs/nt/pingo.
[73] Kyra Kodoski, "Stitching my Landscape", *Maureen Gruben website*, accessed June 1st 2021, https://www.maureengruben.com/stitching-my-landscape.
[74] Ibid.
[75] Ibid.
[76] Tara Hogue, "Maureen Gruben. Delta Trim," *Garland Magazine*, November 28, 2019, https://garlandmag.com/article/maureen-gruben/.

[77] Jordan, *Maureen Gruben.*
[78] 'Broder mon paysage', *Repères2017,* 2017, https://reperes2017.ca/info/maureen-gruben/broder-mon-paysage/.
[79] Erin Donnelly, "An Arctic Installation Marks the End of An Era," *Azure Magazine,* August 17, 2017, https://www.azuremagazine.com/article/stitching-my-landscape-arctic-installation/.
[80] Henry P. Huntington, Julie Raymond-Yakoubian, George Noongwook, Noah Naylor, Cyrus Harris, Qaiyaan Harcharek, and Billy Adams, "A Collaborative Analysis of Change and Coastal Community Subsistence Practices in the Northern Bering and Chukchi Seas, Alaska," *Arctic* 74, no. 2, 06, (2021): 113-126, doi:http://dx.doi.org/10.14430/arctic72446.
[81] Eugenia Kisin, "Stitching my Landscape," *Gallatin Today,* Winter 2018, http://gallatin.nyu.edu/about/gallatin-today/climate-change-initiative/climate-initiative/stitching-my-landscape.html
[82] María Puig de la Bellacasa, *Matters of Care: Speculative Ethics in More Than Human Worlds* (Minneapolis: University of Minnesota Press, 2017).
[83] Denis Cosgrove, "Geographic and Cosmological Vision," *Geography and Vision: Seeing, Imagining and Representing the World* (London: I. B. Tauris & Company, Limited, 2008).
[84] Mark Dorrian and Frédéric Pousin, *Seeing From Above: The Aerial View in Visual Culture* (London: I B Tauris, 2013), 290-291.
[85] Denis Cosgrove, *Geographic and Cosmological Vision,* 21.
[86] Jarrett Martineau and Eric Ritskes, "Fugitive indigeneity: Reclaiming the terrain of decolonial struggle through Indigenous art," *Decolonization: Indigeneity, Education & Society* 3.1, (2014): I-XII.

III.

From Sea to Source: A Pilgrimage along the Water's Edges

Andrea Hurst

Nelson Mandela University, South Africa

Belinda Du Plooy

Nelson Mandela University, South Africa

Abstract

The Tributaries Project was an academic engagement project undertaken during 2019 at Nelson Mandela University (a coastal university in Port Elizabeth, South Africa). In this essay, we focus specifically on the pilgrimages, which traced a pathway along the edges of various bodies of water from sea to source. The notion of a "pilgrimage" (a journey, usually for religious reasons, embracing some form of difficulty or suffering, and to a sacred place) might ring strangely in narrowly orthodox academic corridors. However, the notion of a secular "place pilgrimage" has gained contemporary currency and is diversely understood as a journey through/to a particularly evocative site (for example, of "national or ethnic suffering," and one might here add "ecological suffering") in the hope of emotional, ethical, psychological, or social learning or healing. Since, among individual pilgrims, each travelling differently along the "same" pathway, there is a paradoxical combination of diversity and solidarity, a pilgrimage forms a metaphor and pattern for the social cohesion the project aimed to foster.

Keywords: Apartheid, Port Elizabeth, South Africa, pilgrimage, social cohesion

***

The Tributaries Project was an academic engagement project undertaken during 2019 at Nelson Mandela University (a coastal university in Port Elizabeth, South Africa).[1] The primary question behind the project was how to foster social cohesion in South Africa's extremely diverse, postcolonial academic communities, or, that is, how to counteract a sense of individual isolation and group division and emphasize a more prosocial sense of interdependence in a specific university context. The guiding proposition in response to this question was that cohesive communities can be formed when diverse individuals recognize their commonalities because they share pressing species-level concerns. Of these, "water" was selected as the guiding theme for the project aligning it with the thematic of the water's edges in several ways.

The main campus of the university is, in fact, quite literally located right at the water's edge and the entire campus is a coastal/marine nature reserve. Further, Port Elizabeth is an industrial port city, where water in its various forms is a part of the infrastructure and industry of the city, but also the habitat within which large-scale recreation, tourism and conservation activities are situated. The city, lodged in a natural bay, is surrounded by partially protected coastline, consisting of beautiful and expansive beaches, one of the last remaining natural dune fields on earth, and extraordinarily diverse marine life. The city is also close to the large Addo National Elephant Park and the Groendal Wilderness Reserve. Yet, like much of Southern Africa, Port Elizabeth has struggled through a recent, crippling drought on top of complex problems relating to rapid urbanization and expansion, as well as ageing, overburdened infrastructural systems and sprawling informal settlements without infrastructure. It is also the site of toxic industrial activity, associated with the city's two large harbors and industries along the Swartkops River, as well as wastewater contamination, particularly around the estuary where the river meets the Indian Ocean. Adams, Pretorius and Snow detail the effects on water quality of Port Elizabeth's "overloaded and poorly maintained wastewater treatment works (WWTWs), polluted stormwater runoff and solid waste."[2] Port Elizabeth, thus, forms a microcosm that brings humans in constant and intimate contact with water, in ways that play out on the literal multiple edges between water and land. For example, on any given day in Port Elizabeth there will be bathers on the beaches; surfers riding the waves; fishermen on the rocks and river banks; snorkeling or scuba diving around the reefs of the bay; leisure boat cruises; whale and dolphin watching; ships entering the city's two harbors to bunker or dock; night lights of commercial "chokka" (squid) fishing boats; industries and factories using water; and local indigenous cultural groups performing spiritual rituals on beaches and the banks of the river.

It must be reiterated that the project was at its core social rather than ecological, and readers will not find contextualized input on the local impacts of ecological degradation and water pollution. Instead, we discuss an experiment in fostering social cohesion in a local context where identity struggles have produced fractious and violent modes of "othering" amongst extremely fragile subjectivities. The emphasis was on the communality produced by experiencing shared feelings of "eco-awe" (so to speak), "eco-grief," or helpless ecological concern. With the main aim of facilitating social cohesiveness among a diverse academic group, and taking "water" as its unifying theme, *The Tributaries Project* provided an experimental, transdisciplinary, extra-curricular and voluntary engagement experience. It transcended the limitations of conventional academic teaching and learning practices since it took place outside of habitual academic spaces, such as classrooms and laboratories. It was aligned with a strong mandate in the local academy to recognize and elevate subjugated knowledges in a complex postcolonial context. In *Knowledge/Power* Foucault described subjugated knowledges as those "that have been disqualified as inadequate to the task or insufficiently elaborated; naive knowledges, located low down on the hierarchy, beneath the required level of cognition or scientificity."[3] Humanity has a vast heritage of such alternative pieces of knowledge, communicated to us through generations, since prehistoric times, by the storytellers, griots, artists, philosophers, teachers, preachers, and wise ones of diverse cultures, who shaped conceptions of the human condition. The splitting of the arts and sciences and the devaluation of certain kinds of knowledge is a modern phenomenon. Part of the contemporary academic project is to reset the balance, returning to, and paying renewed attention to, art and other subjugated knowledges. These have a value that is different from but equal to the sciences. This, as Foucault recognized, lies in their potential for critique. Underlying *The Tributaries Project* was an added focus on their equally productive potential to foster the emotional and social aspects of ethical learning.

The overall project consisted of three parts. Firstly, the continuity of the project over the year was established through an open weekly seminar series held at one of the university's inner-city campuses, where anyone from the university community could present on a topic related to water. Secondly, in tandem with this, 29 participants took part in one of three experimental pilgrimages along the water's edges from sea to source. In each group, there were nine participants together with the two organizers, who participated in all three pilgrimages.[4] Although all had some form of past or current association with the Nelson Mandela University, most participants had not met before or did not know each other well before their involvement with the project. Participants were diverse across race, nationality, class, age, gender, physical ability, academic disciplines, and seniority, ranging from a first-year student to full professors and every level in between (including a high-school pupil, participating with her academic parent). Thirdly, participants were requested up-front to commit to producing a response to their experience, to be shared and displayed during a culminating week of public events at year-end. The brief was intentionally left wide open, encompassing theoretical work (academic article or presentation), works of creative writing, music, and artwork. The exhibition week was shaped around the responses produced, and it consisted of the public performance of an original four-part music composition, a performance artwork, an art exhibition, a one-day colloquium of academic presentations, and a "narratives" event of poetry reading and stories. Of the 31 contributors to the project's Catalogue, ten had formal artistic training and eight were associated with the university's School of Visual and Performing Arts (lecturers and students). The rest of the project participants had no formal training in art making. Many participants from both groups, however, produced a mix of theoretical, literary, and artistic works.

In this essay, we focus specifically on the pilgrimages, which traced a pathway along the edges of various bodies of water from sea to source.[5] The notion of a "pilgrimage" (a journey, usually for religious reasons, embracing some form of difficulty or suffering, and to a sacred place) might ring strangely in narrowly orthodox academic corridors. However, the notion of a secular "place pilgrimage"[6] has gained contemporary currency and is diversely understood as a journey through/to a particularly evocative site (for example, of "national or ethnic suffering," and one might here add "ecological suffering") in the hope of emotional, ethical, psychological, or social learning or healing. Following this secular understanding of "pilgrimage," the three pilgrimages took pilgrims, at three different seasonal times of the year, along roughly the same route along the water's edges. This offered multiple opportunities for engagement with diverse bodies of water (oceans, wastewater, harbor water, salt flats, river estuary, river, pristine streams, and pure pools). The pilgrimage journey was U-shaped. From joyous heights (literally and metaphorically) in a part of Port Elizabeth's more protected coastline (the sand dunes of Sardinia Bay and the cliff edge of Schoenmakerskop), participants moved from site to site (by foot and in vehicles), heading "downwards" through the industrialized part of the coastline (including the Driftsands Wastewater Treatment Works, the Cape Recife lighthouse, and the Port Elizabeth harbor). Then, at its lowest ebb, the journey took a turn inland, moving into the tragically polluted Swartkops River Estuary.[7] Here one is warned not to dip even a finger in the toxic water. The pilgrimage moved upriver via the Redhouse village, salt flats and notorious Motherwell canal (which regularly spills raw effluent into the river), and finally towards the pristine source of the Swartkops river in the Groendal Wilderness Reserve. Here, participants hiked together towards a high point again, where they could scoop up in their hands the clean, pure water that feeds the river, drinking it in a ceremonious, communal celebration. Since, among individual pilgrims, each travelling differently along the "same" pathway, there is a paradoxical combination of diversity and solidarity, a pilgrimage forms a metaphor and pattern for the social cohesion the project aimed to foster.

In the first part of the essay, we explain the theoretical intent behind the creation of this water pilgrimage experience, with its openness to an artistic response. In the second part, we offer a sense of what the pilgrimages meant for the pilgrims by discussing four of the artworks made in response to the experience. Many exciting original artworks were generated by the project participants.[8] Instead of striving to encompass the 31 responses, we selected only four artworks to discuss here. We discuss these because each explicitly represents a human body in relation to, or "edge to edge" with, a body of water. While we name the individual artists who created the artworks, we do not supply additional biographical details because we discuss artworks that emerged in response to experiences that were, in each case, widely shared by participants on the pilgrimages. Notably, we here subscribe to this de-emphasis on the individual and respect for the communal as it is integral to what is taught through the concept of "ubuntu" in African indigenous knowledge systems (from *umuntu ngumuntu ngabantu* meaning "I am because we are"). This is a prominent aspect of the social cohesion aimed for by the project. The creators of the artworks provided their permission for their work to be discussed and presented here.

The theoretical intent behind the creation of a water pilgrimage as a strategy for fostering social cohesion is complex. Firstly, it draws from the overarching insight that addressing shared and pressing concerns requires an alternative ethic, focused on the interconnections between self-care, social cohesion, and ecological action. In other words, efforts to address such concerns do not only depend on sophisticated information gathering and scientific or technical expertise. They also require social cohesion. They depend on the willingness of vast numbers of ordinary people to make personal attitudinal and behavioral changes, that are both a precondition for, and a result of, fostering and sustaining deeply considered, judiciously respectful relationships with "the other" (in its many senses).

Secondly, the core complex of ideas behind the creation of a water pilgrimage as a strategy for fostering social cohesion was drawn from engagement with Pierre Hadot's account of "aesthetic perception" (another example of subjugated knowledge). Hadot's account is based on his readings of ancient Greek and Roman philosophers in *Philosophy as a Way of Life*[9] and *The Veil of Isis*.[10] It is necessary to lay out this theoretical background in some detail to show how a "place pilgrimage," in this case a passage along the water's edges from sea to source, might be a productive, indirect strategy to foster social cohesion in the South African postcolonial context (where, as mentioned, directly addressing socio-political concerns regularly triggers immediate further divisiveness rather than cohesion).

Hadot notes that "already in antiquity, people were not conscious of living in the world. They had no time to look at the world, and philosophers strongly sensed the paradox and scandal of the human condition: man lives in the word without perceiving the world."[11] In other words, it was commonly noted by ancient Greek and Roman philosophers that ordinary habits of perception are auxiliaries of efficient action that help people manage aspects of the otherwise overwhelming richness of the real by narrowing attention selectively.[12] Still today, as Hadot summarizes it, perception is conditioned by interests and values, according to which people habitually highlight what seems personally useful and downplay the rest. Further, despite what is known intellectually, space remains Newtonian (three-dimensional) for everyday perception, the seconds tick by in regular succession, and the earth is experienced as an immobile, stable ground in relation to which a person moves. Each person feels like the center point of existence, looking out towards a surrounding world. Individuals perceive themselves (mostly) as intact body-subjects (whole beings with definable borders, solidity, and presence), placed in a world of discrete objects that can be manipulated and negotiated. Finally, everyday perception is regulated by habitual ways of thinking that show a general bias towards order, purpose, hierarchies, and boundaries.[13]

It is impossible to deny the pragmatic necessity of habitual everyday perception. Human life itself depends on the capacity to create reflective distance from the overwhelmingly complex "real" or "the world qua world," and fabricate a humanized world consisting of *inter alia* "the objects of our worry, quarrels, social rituals, and conventional values."[14] But the habits of everyday perception have serious drawbacks. Firstly, they narrow our perception to the world of our immediate, utilitarian concerns, and it becomes an effort to look beyond it. Seldom explicitly encouraged, people forget to make an effort, and soon no longer value, or even see, the bigger natural or social worlds.[15] In everyday perception, for example, "nature" becomes merely a problem of the human environment.[16] This problem is often couched as the development of technologies to artificially create objects and environments that are sanitized and modified for human convenience. These are supposedly better than nature itself. Focused on utility and comfort, and blind to the vast and strange natural world, people often now remain removed from, but blankly complicit in large-scale environmental destruction, which in turn contributes to devastating social conflicts. In addition, as Henry Thoreau astutely remarked "society is commonly too cheap. We meet at very short intervals, not having had time to acquire any new value for each other."[17] Even as far back as the mid-1800s he noted that "we live thick and are in each other's way, and stumble over one another, and I think that we thus lose some respect for one another."[18]

Secondly, narrow utilitarian perception also poses multiple threats, stemming from the associated narcissistic self-interest detectable in the egocentric self, chauvinism at the level of the in-group, and anthropocentrism at species level. In the South African context, as an understandable consequence of a traumatic history, everyday perception is strongly characterized by individual and cultural narcissism. This manifests strikingly as an obsessive drive to fix and protect particularizing identity-markers. However, historical struggles for identities in this context have primarily yielded fragile and volatile social relations. Oversensitivities very quickly erupt, ironically creating new forms of violent "othering" and exclusion (the persistent, violent xenophobia directed towards other African nationals is just one example). Regarding *The Tributaries Project* in this context, it is hard to overestimate the value of creating a safe space where project participants could (incompletely and temporarily) let go of a strong insistence on identity-markers (and extremely divisive, violent, and antagonistic local politics) to explore/experience others as *also* "the same." This explains the emphasis (within the temporary space of the project) on the other side of particularizing identity politics; namely, on the sameness we share in being "human" (understood in relation to water as an entity that can, literally and metaphorically, soften barriers and bring us together). Temporarily highlighting the modality of "sameness" in ineradicably complex social relations of sameness and difference should not be mistaken for supporting the erasure of identity struggles. That would be to interpret a complex situation in over-simplified binary terms. The project aimed not for absolute erasure of the particular in the name of a pure universal, but more moderately, temporary reflective dislocations from particularizing identity-markers. It was proposed that achieving this (to be sure, no mean feat) would promote a shift from obsessive narcissistic concern to the "bigger picture" perspective theorized by Hadot. This shift fosters greater capacity for care about "the other" (in diverse forms) required for social cohesion.

Ancient philosophers already made it clear that narcissistic everyday perception traps us in the artificial world of our own making, and the philosophical schools shared a concern to disrupt it in the name of human spiritual development and well-being. In the contemporary academy, both the natural sciences and the hermeneutic arts already entail a de-centering of everyday perception, which creates, in Hadot's words, "a radical rupture with regard to the state of unconsciousness in which man normally lives."[19] Learning in both the sciences and the arts entails the transformation of a self-centered relationship to the world, with the result that students may step back from utilitarian concerns and learn to see how the world works not "in itself" (humans have no access to this) but "for itself" (that is, regardless of whether humans exist).[20] Thus, both the sciences and the arts presuppose in principle that the process, message, product, or expression transcends egotistical self-interest. Further, both fields demand respect for the wisdom of the senses, which is given equal weight to, and must operate in tandem with, intellectual reasoning. Both require and employ creativity and imagination, affirm that understanding may emerge in a flash of inspiration that exceeds systematic orders of reasoning and knowledge accumulation, and either tacitly or explicitly recognize the importance of emotion (feelings of excitement, awe, love, respect, joy) to knowledge acquisition and production.

Recognizing such commonalities affirms the interconnectivity between the sciences and the arts, but aesthetic perception is nevertheless markedly different from scientific perception. As Hadot describes it, aesthetic perception engages perceptual faculties without the underlying motivation to "discover hidden laws, equations, or structures behind phenomena."[21] It therefore does not, like science, entail a "search for the secrets of nature," but an effort to deepen our "familiarity with nature."[22] For example, to grow plants from seeds or walk regularly on the beach is to become familiar with the ways of plants and tides, without necessarily having the scientific knowledge to explain them. This familiarity is not a matter of mastery and objectivization, but what Hadot describes as "a feeling of communion with nature."[23] The feeling of "familiarity" or "communion with nature" is a core concept underpinning *The Tributaries Project*. It is used metaphorically, in the sense that insight into "the way things work" via aesthetic perception in encounters with water, is transferable to encounters with other kinds of others, specifically the human other. This raises some important points.

Firstly, it remains important to recognize that the vast majority of South African cultures and most of the country's inhabitants engage very directly in some form of "mysticism" or ritualized spiritualization of life and nature (including animistic beliefs in the powers of *sangomas*, ancestral spirits, and sacred plants, locations and waters). However, the project's aim to offer opportunities for self-reflective dislocations from narcissistic egotism by engendering the feeling of "familiarity" or "communion with nature" is not intended to imply a strong sense of ego-dissolution (associated with religious rituals, substance use, neurological pathologies, sleep deprivation, trance states, and so on). Nor is a mystical feeling of oneness with nature intended. This is often described as the "oceanic feeling" that Freud, at the request of Romain Rolland, tried to explain in psychoanalytic terms in *Civilization and its Discontents*.[24] Freud himself reported that he had never experienced this feeling, but he found it to be compatible with psychoanalytic theory as a remnant of the primitive infant state that precedes the formation of the more bounded adult ego.[25] There is a connection, however, between this "oceanic feeling" and self-reflective dislocation from egotism. One of the many ways to engage in active, intentional dislocation, is to draw on "imaginative recall" of this more primitive state where ego formation is less settled. This boundary-softening recall aids the active, intentional concentration on the richness of sensations in aesthetic perception. One may use this experience of boundary-softening as a metaphor for any encounter with the other. However, notably, the ego's self-reflective dislocation still requires a working, active, intentional, bounded ego.

Secondly, in drawing from Hadot's account of the wisdom of ancient philosophers, one must pay attention to a significant paradigmatic shift. Most ancient philosophical schools viewed "the natural" in terms of hidden cosmic orderliness, and tied an appreciation of orderliness to beauty and goodness.[26] This set the tone for an intellectual tradition that viewed human well-being one-sidedly in terms of communion with natural orderliness and attunement to beauty.[27] However, contemporary thinking reflects a marked shift towards thinking in terms of the sublime. One must, Hadot notes, "speak of pleasure and wonder in the face of beauty, but also of terror in the face of the sublime."[28] The feeling of the sublime stems from recognition that 'the other' is the site of truth that is always elliptical or partial. Thus, nature is indicated not through attunement to beautiful symmetry, but only elliptically or partially through words/marks/images/signs that cannot properly or fully express it. If aesthetic perception deepens a person's familiarity with nature, such familiarity should yield the insight that in natural phenomena (including humans) order, beauty, and goodness form just one side of the coin. There is also, in equal measure, inexplicability, madness, disconcertedness, horror and abject ugliness. Thus, in aesthetic perception a person is also charged with facing feelings of abjection, vulnerability, and the possibility of being desecrated and of dying. Indeed, a crucial aspect of aesthetic perception is the symbolic encounter with the thought of death – of the self and of the other - which, as Hadot notes, "reveals to us the miraculous character of our relationship to the world: always in peril, always unforeseeable."[29]

Thirdly, familiarity with nature, as mentioned, does not mean knowing all her secrets. Rather, it entails an equal appreciation of a thing's "secretiveness" or transcendence, which is portrayed by some as divinity.[30] To this, one appropriately responds in the spirit of what Heidegger, borrowing from Meister Eckhart, calls *Gelassenheit.* The term denotes a disposition towards the encounter with things that releases the ego's drive towards mastery and keeps it open to the other's mystery.[31] In deep alignment with Heidegger here, Hadot argues that, "wisdom does not merely cause us to know: it makes us 'be' in a different way,"[32] and this means that it ethically changes a person's disposition in a way that is better captured in the figure of the sublime than that of beauty. In short, wisdom should be tied to an ethic of respect and humility, rather than purity and goodness.

Finally, resonating with the figure of the sublime, the idea of the edge also signifies the limiting boundary between the known and the unknown. This inscribes the notion of a precipice, a proverbial place of no return. The pilgrimages brought pilgrims directly and bodily to the water's edges, and beyond, where human bodies merged and engaged with water, sometimes as an experience of unity and cohesion (like the surfer on the wave or the baptismal or sacrificial rituals mentioned above), but also sometimes as conflict (such as those around marine conservation and fish farming, abalone poaching, and bunkering off the Port Elizabeth coast, as well as the municipal crises around the upkeep of water-related infrastructure, interruptions of water supply to large areas of the city and burst pipes leading to massive wastage of water). Pilgrims experienced not only literal edges, but also symbolic, metaphorical, and discursive edges, signifying sites where real and symbolic power plays itself out in relation to water. Entry into unknown spaces is inevitably a humbling experience, for when a limit or boundary (of the known) has been crossed, there is uncertainty, even panic, at not being able to return or to recover again. This resonates with the common expression that one is "on edge." If one is fully open to this experience, it can constitute a productive space of transformation and growth through engagement with the unknown\unknowable other in its many varied forms. For the project's academic pilgrims, this edge signified a space in which to engage with, and open to, knowledge systems and practices outside the conventional academic modes of thinking. The pilgrimages configured spaces in which it was possible to disengage many of the habitual cognitive regulators that underpin everyday perception, such as interest, use value, action, time constraints, means-end thinking, analytical division and simplification.[33] In this sense, it was important for pilgrims to feel a little lost, in the sense suggested by Rebecca Solnitt's *In A Field Guide to Getting Lost* (2010) where she equates the experience of being lost with an inner journey of self-discovery and shows how this has been a recurring theme in artists' and philosophers' consideration of the relationship between humans and nature.[34] This echoes Thoreau's remarks from his mid-nineteenth century vantage point, on the edge of Walden Pond:

> not till we are completely lost, or turned around, - for a man needs only to be turned round once with his eyes shut in this world to be lost, - do we appreciate the vastness and strangeness of Nature. ... Not till we are lost, in other words, not till we have lost the world, do we begin to find ourselves, and realise where we are and the infinite extent of our relations.[35]

The implied ethical task of reflective ego dislocation, thus losing the world of our own making and re-finding our relational, eco-systemic humanity through attunement to nature's "vastness and strangeness" plays itself out at the ephemeral edges of both time and space. The pilgrimages offered a transitory moment of collaboration in historical time, in the sense that pilgrims were all associated in some form or another with the university but were not part of any permanent or formal organized collective, such as a class, department or faculty. Further, the pilgrimage represents awareness of the transitory nature of life (as we know it), against what was previously assumed to be a monolithic and eternal grand plan, the unchanging and inexhaustible backdrop against which humanity set itself. The pilgrimage was, therefore, also necessarily a liminal place, a threshold experience where one experiences the paradox of a simultaneous "both/and" – in the city and in nature; on the land and in the water; human agent and element of an ecosystem; constituted by water (humans are 70% water) and yet external to water, which is also something that can be objectified, manipulated, and consumed.

Simply placing one's body in a liminal space, however, is not enough to experience the vibrant, sensory immediacy, and enveloping intensity of aesthetic perception that dislocates the ego. This is achieved only by an intentional shift and careful attention to perception, which takes time, energy, and concentration. When this perceptual shift is achieved, however, a person's relationship to the world changes; everyday familiarity falls away and, as Hadot notes, people perceive as if seeing again "for the first time."[36] Without such perceptual experiences being explicitly directed, we believe that the pilgrimage experience dislocated participants from the comfort zones of habitual perception and offered opportunities to achieve moments of aesthetic perception that brought them both literally and metaphorically to the edges where imaginative play could happen. Assuming that the resultant changes in relationships to the world are marked and reinforced in a second dislocation whereby one emerges from overwhelming experiences, retreats from the edges, and reflects, pilgrims were requested from the outset, as mentioned, to produce a reflective response to the pilgrimage.

In the rest of this essay, we interpret four of the artworks through which pilgrims tried to relocate themselves and make sense of their experiences. Through the lens of Hadot's account of aesthetic perception, we consider two different experiences of reflective ego dislocation in Lungelo Manona's "Becoming Water" and Thandazani Nofingxana's "*Singqunga Ndawonye*" ("We're running in circles"). We then consider the idea of "monstrosity" in Luke Rudman's "Blue Plastic Monster" and Nonnie Roodt's "Mythopoetics." These interpretations constitute a third act of dislocation and relocation, where we try to "perform" the appropriating hermeneutic process by which experiences of aesthetic perception fostered on the pilgrimages, now insightfully, and sometimes intuitively or unconsciously, rendered into artworks, in turn, help to engender ethical learning in an audience. We should admit that these interpretations are explicitly appropriations. Our tandem wrestling with these interpretations, one another, and the struggle to put insights into words represents part of our own efforts, as fellow pilgrims, towards insightful relocation and ethical learning.

Lungelo Manona's "Becoming Water" (figure 3.1) was inspired by the moment during the pilgrimage when the artist and fellow pilgrims, ritualistically immersed their bodies in the pristine Crystal Pool deep into a ravine at Groendal, where the pilgrimage ended. Other pilgrims shared similar immersive experiences, some also in the ocean at Sardinia Bay. Thus, the reflective dislocation of the ego associated with physical immersion in water represents both the personal and particular of Manona's experience, as well as something widely shared among the three groups of pilgrims. Manona spoke of his work as "a commentary on our broken relationship with water," suggesting to us that the work pulls together both a deep human desire for immersion in life's vital movement and the sorrow of human desecration. This reflects the shared vacillation among most pilgrims between joyful wonder and disheartening eco-grief.

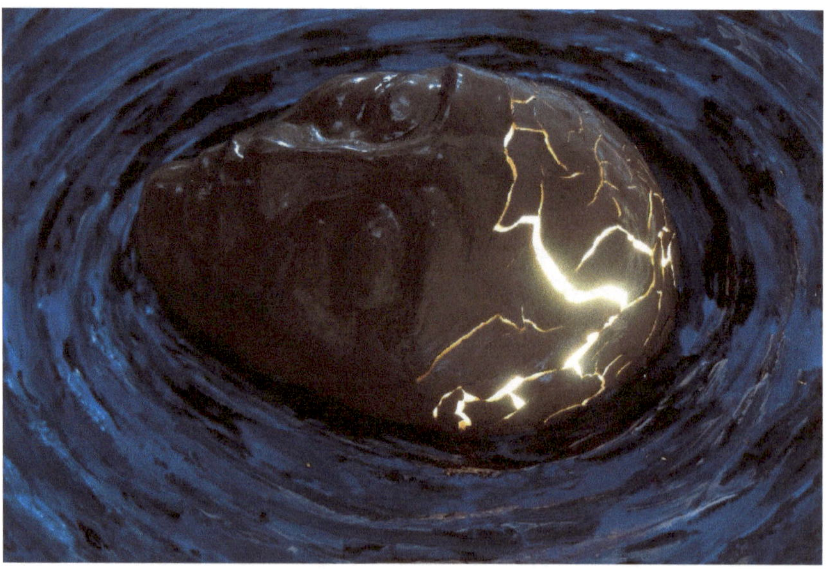

Figure 3.1: Lungelo Manona, *Becoming Water.*
400mm x 250mm. Modelled and glazed clay head, mounted on canvas, painted impasto. A light was placed behind the head. Photo and permissions: Andrea Hurst

The experience of immersion is one of the most prevalent characteristics of aesthetic perception. As Hadot explains this, in an immersive experience, the ego's boundaries blur and there is a feeling of identification with something other. Hadot cites Shitao's description of his shift from a sense of separation to feeling that his Ego was "being-born together … with the Mountains and the Rivers."[37] These sentiments are repeated by later western artists such as Cezanne, who writes: "For my part, I want to lose myself in nature, and grow again with her, like her … In a patch of green, my entire brain will flow with the sap-like tide of the tree."[38] Thoreau expressed the same sentiments when he said, "shall I not have intelligence with the earth? Am I not partly leaves and vegetable mould myself?"[39] Hadot focusses on the power of identification invested in immersive experiences to facilitate well-being in a joyful release.[40] Similarly, Thoreau, immersed in the sights and sounds around his cabin near Walden Pond, described "an infinite and unaccountable friendliness all at once like an atmosphere sustaining me … Every pine needle expanded and swelled with sympathy and befriended me."[41] Aesthetic perception in an immersive experience sensitizes individuals to a vitality that overflows the subject/object relation.[42] But this sensitivity can bring both joy and horror. On the pilgrimages, we encountered not only friendship and peace of mind, but also the much wilder sensations of immensity and smallness, and more disconcerting moments of anxiety, grief, and sorrow.

We found the double edges of aesthetic experience to be particularly striking in "Becoming Water." In this work, a human head, modelled in clay, is mounted on canvas painted with heavy impasto to mimic rippled water. The head is both/either sinking under, or emerging from, the water rippling around it. The work's further complexity emerges by the dint of an electric light shining through the back of the head. While this light is almost invisible in daylight, it becomes increasingly sharp as the day darkens, revealing more starkly and emphasizing the skull's fragility. It is cracked into fissures, like dried mud, but also like the folds of the human brain.

At first glance, particularly if this is during the day, the work evokes the profound sense of dislocating boundary softening associated with immersive experiences. It is easy to recall or imagine floating as the figure does, face to sky, feeling at one with a body of water. In this position, it is no longer possible to look downwards in an objectifying and mastering gaze. Instead, our vision must relax upwards, placing our bodies under sky, clouds, or treetops, giving way, and giving over. The closed eyes of Manona's figure indicate a reflective, meditative, or praying moment of silence, solitude, retreat, reverence, or awe. Yet, closed eyes also recall moments in such an immersive experience when immensity overwhelms and water extends a powerful invitation towards a submerging, sinking, drowning death. Manona explicitly intended the death-mask feel of the figure to suggest the pilgrim's shared sense of the symbolic death of the narcissistic self in "the realization that we are water." Manona writes (on his accompanying label), that "everything we are is made of it," that "our entire lives and existence are dependent on and submerged in it." This, he adds, goes hand in hand with the realization that "we are responsible for so much that degrades and destroys this precious element." In other words, in the mirroring realization that this other is me and vice versa (thus, I am becoming water, as the title implies) there is also the realization that this is no friendly communion from my side, but also the introduction of the ubiquitous poisons of my effluent and waste. This work engenders the profoundly disturbing insight that I risk the death of the other that sustains me.

In an interesting twist, the fact that Manona's figure is made of clay invokes well-known myths of human origin that suppress the fact that we are mostly water, preferring to identify humans with the dry and bounded solidity of earth. This metaphor, generated within the habitual values of everyday perception, is repeated in the familiar words of many burial rituals: "ashes to ashes and dust to dust." However, since we emerge from and through water in the proverbial amniotic fluid of gestation, water seems better suited to signify and ritualize the implied cosmic unity in the substance of all bodies and a dynamic of emergence and return where the self and the other will invariably (re)unite into an originating source. Part of the insight we take from "Becoming Water," as we imagine the softening of hardened clay into life's vital movement and fluidity, is the potential revision of a deep-seated, but misleading, metaphor that identifies humans one-sidedly with solidity and grounds.

Importantly, Manona's figure does not succumb fully to water's implicit invitation to self-annihilation. Instead, particularly as the day darkens, the work emphasizes an eternal, energetic movement between fiery light and rippling water. The cracked skull emphasized by the light communicates a sense of madness, craziness, or insanity, which has multiple, contradictory connotations with negative and affirmative moments. The resemblance to mud-cracks in drought-stricken riverbeds suggest that our selfish everyday interests and desires are burning out of control in ways that threaten to suck dry life's vital resources, destroy its energetic tension, and leave us lethally parched. For us, it evokes the feelings of anxiety, panic, and fear prevalent on the pilgrimages as one's head breaks over the much-discussed, humanly created ecological problems we encountered. But, along with Manona, we also took it to signify the light of hope. Describing the work on the accompanying exhibition label, Manona writes:

> The light that shines through the cracks reflects the hope that I gleaned from my participation in *The Tributaries Project* sea-to-source pilgrimage. It speaks to a journey of becoming more aware of our impact and the necessity of taking responsibility and taking corrective measures in the way we approach our relationship with water, and water itself, especially in our water scarce region of the world.

The cracked skull speaks to this new awareness that is shattering and breaking out of the body (both the personal individual body and the symbolic communal body), because it realizes anew its unity with its surroundings – it is opening up and letting its light out into the world as it shares itself with the other, thereby also simultaneously making itself receptive to and letting the light of the world and the other into itself, opening itself up to change and transformation. The work does not pretend to resolve what Manona describes as "the immense tensions that are evident within humanity's relationship with water." "Becoming Water," instead, exemplifies the idea that aesthetic perception can open a person to responsive dialogical encounters with the other, a skill which becomes transferable to diverse situations and relations.

The traumatic nature of literal and metaphorical reflective dislocation of the ego through aesthetic perception is again evoked by the quite different thematic of Thandazani Nofingxana's "*Singqunga Ndawonye.*" The title is translated from Xhosa as "We're running in circles." Nofingxana put together two mixed media works that combine photography, plastic and tiny sketches made during the pilgrimage. They are small, inviting spectators closer to share intimately a nauseating confrontation with overwhelming human wastage. Reflected by Nofingxana's facial expressions in the photographs of himself in the artwork, the work captures his strong sensory reaction to the encounter with wastewater at the Driftsands Wastewater Treatment Works. The water there is thick with sludge, there is a dizzying smell of chemicals and excrement, and an incessant mechanical churning of wheels that separate solids from fluids. Nofingxana's physical reaction to this intensely sensory experience and the dislocating feeling of abject horror was again both personal and shared. Pilgrims all reported a feeling of severely overwhelming anxiousness. A sense of loss of control and dislocation accompanied the direct confrontation with what usually lies on the other side of the conveniently (out-of-sight-out-of-mind) flushed toilet and opened tap.

In "*Singqunga Ndawonye,*" Nofingxana placed two photographs of himself, at opposite corners, within/against a background depicting churning excremental sludge (Figure 3.2.). The photographic images depict reflections of his own face in the contaminated water as he peers over the rims of large, open-air, concrete sewage tanks. These could just as much have been reflections of any of the pilgrims. Afraid to see, pilgrims nevertheless could not help peering compulsively and with horrified fascination, over the edges of these massive sewerage tanks. We take this to reflect a subliminal sense of our deep connection with the wastewater and the associated anxiety of being discarded or deemed wastage oneself, thus the fear of becoming one with or having one's body fall into, immersed in, contaminated by, or made a part of the wastage. Notably, the encounter at the Driftsands WWTW was cited as one of the most provocative experiences on the pilgrimage, and Nofingxana's work offers multiple further insights that help us understand why this was the case.

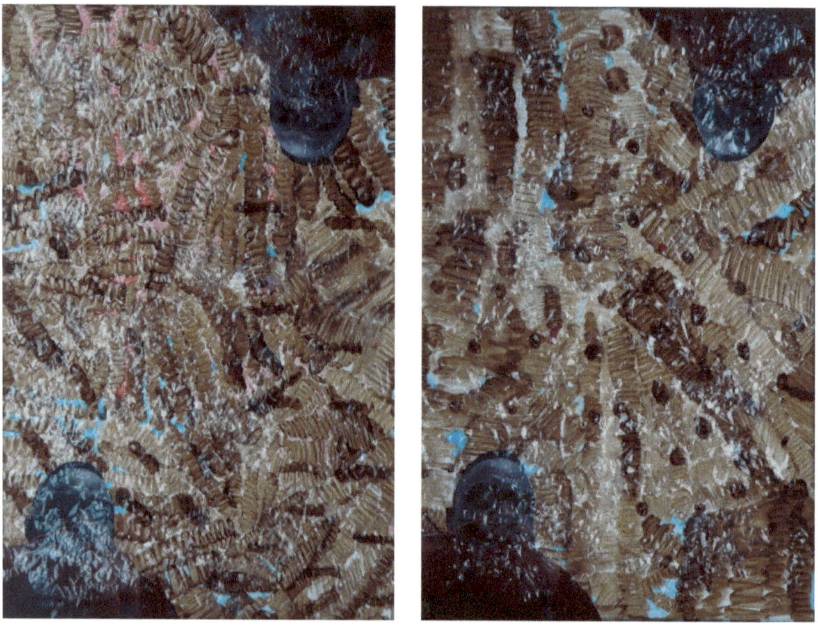

Figure 3.2: Thandazani Nofingxana, *Singqunga Ndawonye.*
2 works, each 195mm x 290mm. Mixed media collage using drawings, photographs and shards of cellophane. Photo and permissions: Andrea Hurst.

Firstly, it is important that Nofingxana renders himself as doubled and/or split. There are two similar photographs, positioned opposite one another in the corners of similar works. This effectively creates an uneasy sense of self-reflective, mirroring dislocation and discomfort, implying an internal vacillation, or the to-and-fro, of a person divided from himself. Notably, the photographs in the work show a figure instinctively covering his mouth with his shirt, not only to keep himself from retching in visceral response to the experience, but also in a self-protective gesture which shuts him off from its assault. The gestures (holding your breath, covering your mouth and nose, looking away, stifling the retching) are symbolic of the self-protective resistance that divides one from what was experienced at the wastewater treatment plant. On the work's accompanying exhibition label, Nofingxana writes: "The title '*Singqunga Ndawonye*,' suggests that even after having learnt so much about the pollution in the city I still buy food packaged with plastic." The contradiction between the work's visceral imagery and its self-critical title reflects the discrepancy between the traumatic, visceral disgust humans tend to feel when immediately confronted with the overwhelming excesses of our own waste (whether this is wastewater, garbage islands or the discarded humans of Mbembe's "Necropolitics")[43] and then the bland, circular return to business as usual, in the name of comforts and conveniences when the moment of visceral disgust passes. This self-critical awareness of internal splitting evokes a feeling of futility associated with being stuck in a repetitive cycle from which there seems to be no escape.

Secondly, the sense of ego-dislocation in the work is compounded by a shift in visual perspective (on the part of the work's spectator) which sees the photographs depicting not reflections, but the artist himself, looking down towards the spectators of the work, from a position above the wastewater. This positions the work's spectators (you and me) within the tanks, submerged in our own toxic effluent. The artist looks out from the artwork at the observer in the tank in a reminder that we are all complicit in the problem of human waste. The work, therefore, serves not only as self-incrimination, but also accusation.

Thirdly, Nofingxana's work offers a double message. "*Singqunga Ndawonye*" expresses an impatient frustration in the absence of solutions to the human wastage that threatens to overwhelm Earth's sustaining ecosystems, which exclaims nihilistically, "we are going nowhere!" And yet, the work itself creates a transformative space, since it demands engagement with that which we cannot bear to see about ourselves. The work's reflection of this dislocating discrepancy between what we initially felt and how we now act offers us a pointed call for self-critique. Many pilgrims shared the worry that the evocative, overwhelming, sensory experiences on the pilgrimage would quickly fade away from consciousness, leaving us, at the end of the journey, right back at the beginning, having, in a sense, gone nowhere. This work highlights a concern reiterated among pilgrims through all the pilgrimages: that to intentionally change behavior on a large scale, drastically and quickly enough to save humans from extinction, seems impossible from where we stand now. The sustained effect of this artwork is to challenge us to find ways beyond the implicit radical nihilism of its title. Taking the work's circular metaphor in a more affirmative direction, one should acknowledge that the change of heart we seek requires constant repetition of, and reflective attention to, the sensory intensity occasioned by aesthetic perception. Only when this reflective repetition becomes a regular part of daily practice can it lead to sustained behavior change.

Taking up the challenge to find a way beyond the moment of radical nihilism most pilgrims experienced at some point on the pilgrimage, Luke Rudman created a large-scale performance art piece, entitled "Plastic Monsters." This artwork was inspired by the shared sense of monstrosity generated by the experience on the pilgrimage of the inescapability of plastic pollution. We found plastic debris washed by the ocean into the rocky cracks and crevices on seemingly pristine beaches and the infiltration spread right into the seemingly untouched heart of the wilderness at Groendal. The intense beauty of the coastline, river estuary and wilderness area exacerbated the travesty of the desecration, as did the knowledge of the contamination of even inaccessible water sources by invisible microplastics.

In his creative response to his pilgrimage experience, Rudman collected discarded plastic trash, from which he created the costumes, body extensions and head-dresses of the twelve performance works he called "plastic monsters." Human bodies (Rudman's own, as well as those of friends, volunteers, and other pilgrims) were the canvasses for his art, bringing to life Walt Whitman's words, "your very flesh shall be a great poem."[44] These human bodies, through body-paint and costuming, were converted into the hybrid forms of mythical monsters, not half human/half creature as in the satyrs, mermaids, and medusas of ancient myths but, in contemporary terms, half human/half plastic. Rudman then orchestrated these twelve figures, each embodying a different facet of plastic pollution, in a peaceful environmental protest on one of the campuses of the university. He also performed, alone, or with other figures, in other venues (local shopping malls) and at public events. These performances were reported in local media and on social media, leading also to national media coverage, television and radio interviews, in which he could raise awareness and spread the message against plastic pollution. This brought him to the attention of Greenpeace, who allowed him to take over their Twitter feed for a time to advocate against plastic pollution; he was invited to perform some of the monsters at the event organized in Cape Town when the Greenpeace ships moored there on their Pole-to-Pole global journey, and he was awarded the Commonwealth Litter Programme (CLIP) Stomp Award for his "Plastic Monsters" artwork.

Our interpretation of Rudman's work takes its cue from his explicit intention to create mythological figures that depict the humanly created monstrosity that is now insinuated into earth's ecosystems, which he names plastic. "Monstrosity" is a much-discussed subject of human fascination. Briefly, a monster is something obscene, unspeakable. It has a shape-shifting power which allows it to re-appear in unrecognizable disguises, and the genuine monster cannot finally be slain, remaining forever beyond our grasp, and posing an eternal, immortal threat of annihilation to mortal beings. This is the source of the terror it evokes.[45] The monster is "the sign that the unknown is in us and around us" and we are advisedly afraid of it since it holds the potential to annihilate us.[46] The most radical form of monstrosity emerges when something I believe I have control over, goes out of control. It emerges when what is trusted as ostensibly familiar and benign is revealed to be alien and lethal, or when what I have created for the good, turns upon me and poses a threat. Most devastatingly, it emerges when the monster I have fled all the way through, is unexpectedly revealed to be on the inside, right inside me, identified as me. What is monstrous, in this case "does not simply mark an alienated or distorted limit-figure of humanity to be overcome, but also designates something like the horror at the core of all human existence and is thus to be defined as a terrifying excess inherent to 'being-human."'[47]

Rudman's creation of "Plastic Monsters" taps into the tendency to create mythical monsters in our literatures to remind ourselves of the truth that we know unconsciously but wish to suppress. Thus, while we might feel terrified by or, as Hadot states, "ill at ease with regard to these creatures that resemble the phantasmagoria of our dreams or the products of our imagination," we should take this feeling seriously as the embodiment of underlying fears and anxieties regarding genuine dangers and threats.[48] In an essay about Hollywood, Joan Didion refers to a line from an old monster movie, in which one character says to the other: "I just can't get that monster out of my mind."[49] In actively creating these monsters, thus getting the monsters out of his head, so to speak, and giving them substance by placing them in the world, Rudman invites engagement with the fears and anxieties that stand in for the silent truth that plastic pollution may pose an ineradicable threat of extinction.

In Rudman's "Plastic Monsters" (Figures 3) a heightened sense of monstrosity is achieved by an intentional dislocation of perspectives. His figures are majestic, larger than life and infused with the grace and beauty of haute couture. As "Blue Plastic Monster" shows, in the costuming and headdresses of many figures, Rudman mimics the familiar conventions of high fashion. He cues the observer to respond affirmatively and admiringly in ways conditioned and coded by the socialized norms and expectations of beauty dictated by fashion magazines, catwalks, and red carpets. In his performances of the work, however, he mingles with the audience, drawing the observers in and inviting a closer look. This evokes the subsequent awful and destabilizing realization that this image of beauty is, in fact, made up of the plastic trash we revile and discard. His figures, therefore, invoke monstrosity in its most devastating senses: humanity's most creative product, familiar and benign, is not only revealed to be something alien (discarded trash) that has turned on us, posing threats of toxic pollution. More radically, this monster, as science keeps unexpectedly revealing, is right on the inside and is now integrated with life itself. This makes it impossible to slay the monster in any direct sense. Herein lies the radical monstrosity implied in Rudman's work.

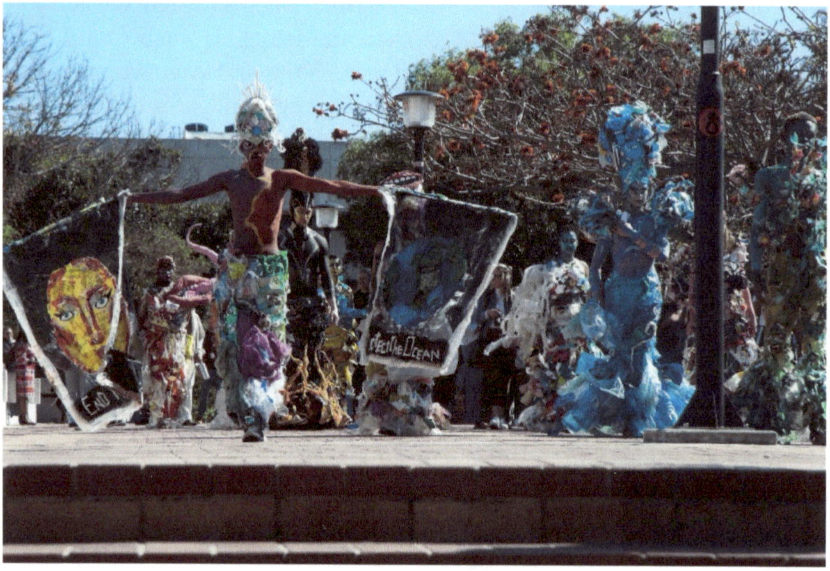

Figure 3.3: Luke Rudman, *Plastic Monsters.*

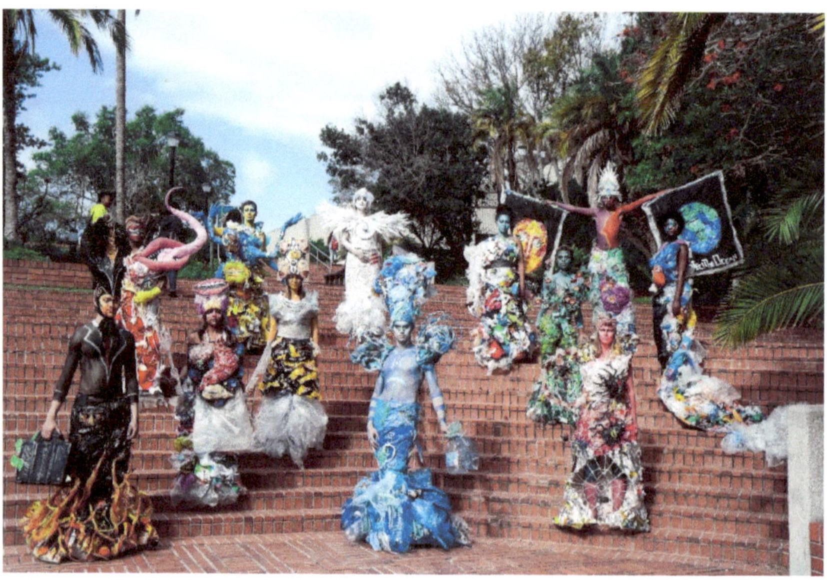

Figure 3.4: Luke Rudman, *Plastic Monsters.*

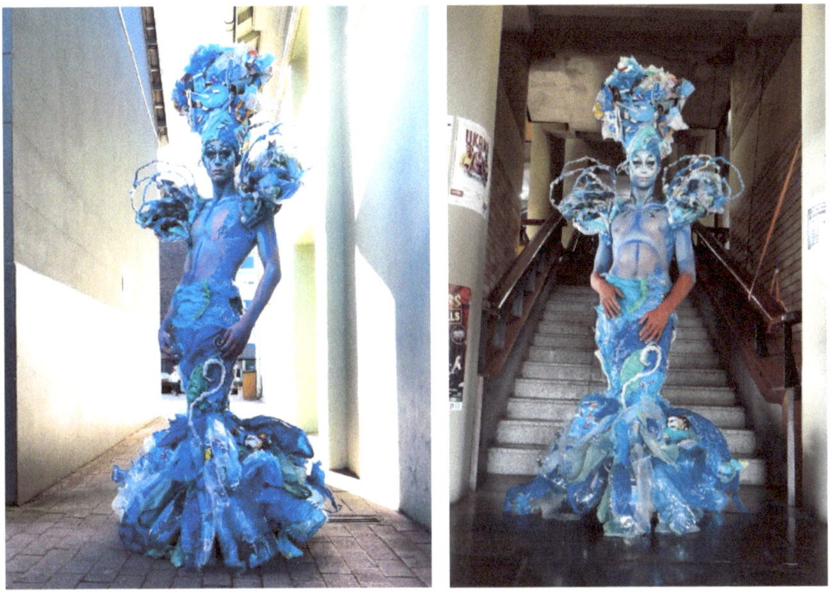

Figure 3.5: Luke Rudman, *Plastic Monsters*.
12 works, using human models of various sizes. Performance artworks using body paint and costuming created from multiple forms of plastic waste collected along and near the Port Elizabeth coastline, undergirded with structures made from upcycled materials such as fabric and wire. Credit for Rudman 1: Stein De Cuyper; Credit for Rudman 2 & 3: Sharon Rudman.

By analogy with the hybridity between the painted human bodies and their plastic-trash extensions, other natural bodies (beaches, estuaries, streams and their multiple life forms, for example), are irrevocably changed by the diverse trappings of human waste that collect in and around them, resulting in what is here presented so vividly – not mere plastic pollution, but the irrevocable integration of trash that is humanly produced and the so-called natural environment. Plastic (and this is just one example) is ubiquitous, having infiltrated every aspect of earthly life to such a degree that, as Kristen Minogue remarks, "it will leave its mark in the fossil record."[50] Some, she adds, have proposed the label "Plasticene" as a way of speaking about "the near-universal spread of plastic around Earth." This has generated a specialized lexicon, including "epiplastic" to denote the state of living on plastic, "plastivore" to describe creatures that have swallowed plastic, "plasticized" for those trapped in plastic debris, "leaching" for chemical contamination from plastics, and "microplastics" as a catch-all for the varied, invisible, major players in plastic pollution.[51] It is difficult to resist the conclusion that earthly bodies, and even earth itself, are already "plastic monsters." This resonates with Anna Tsing's remark that the monster challenges the habitual "modernist figure" of individual organisms with physical integrity, and definite human/non-human edges, since it opens us to the notion of more primary symbiotic entanglements with other species and other individuals.[52]

Such symbiotic entanglement with plastics, would not be cause for concern if plastic lived up to its name. Plasticity as an adjective, meaning 'capable of being shaped or molded', is essential to nature's creative play, and relatedly, plastic is one of humankind's most versatile creations. However, the radical monstrosity of this human creation is captured in a small caveat: not all plastic exhibits plasticity. In the production of unmalleable, unusable waste that cannot be re-formed, or taken up as fuel or nutrients in another form of production, humans have created a ubiquitous substance that has veered away from the perpetual plasticity of natural creativity. In consequence, what we thought we had created for the good, the wonder-substance trusted as inert, safe, and benign, has turned upon us and poses a lethal threat.

Because the observer invariably recognizes and identifies with the human at the center of Rudman's figures, there is a sense of mirroring recognition, both of shared vulnerability (the danger of being engulfed or annihilated by the plastic monster), and worse, tacit knowledge of shared responsibility (of being, in the continued use of plastic products, the monstrous creators of our own possible destruction). Having created his monsters as a form of protest action, Rudman opens hope that human ingenuity will lead us towards finding indirect ways to negotiate (since they cannot be slain) the plastic monsters that threaten to engulf us. By implication hope lies in returning human ingenuity to nature's creative plasticity. Here Rudman's creativity resonates with Tsing's qualified optimism, when she says, "rather than paralyzing our readers with fear, we are hoping, through the wonder of all these arrangements in the world, to mobilize a sense of activity and possibility within this very terrible time that we've created."[53]

Speaking to such hopes, the final artwork we discuss is a piece from Nonnie Roodt's collection called "Trash and Treasure." This collection responded to moments during the pilgrimage when the artist was most struck by the discrepancy between a consumerist throw away attitude and care for the environment around us. These works were made explicitly as resistance pieces that critically speak back into our contemporary behaviors and practices, particularly our tendency to toss unwanted objects heedlessly into the spaces around us, where they become ugly, polluting forms of trash and litter. But Roodt also saw that many of these discarded items, upon careful observation, have an aesthetic value and interest all their own, and may be salvaged and restored. She saw her work as symbolic of the human condition, in which there was a parallel need and potential for restoration and rehabilitation. To enact this dynamic between resistance and rehabilitation she collected objects, during and after the pilgrimage, that had been discarded. Then she converted or re-assembled them into art-objects, in which form they could reclaim value, even beauty and a new significance. Instead of being reduced to junk, they can convey an opposite message – the urgent need for us to take care of our environment, thereby drawing something affirmative out of the negative.

For example, the work we selected to discuss here, "Mythopoetics," assembles items that might have randomly washed ashore in a storm and ended up lodged together in a rock crevice on the beach. It presents a collection of what may, for example, have broken off from the Great Pacific Garbage Patch, an enormous and growing pile of trash that is floating around in the sea, destroying ocean plant and animal life. The bone-colored monochrome of the work suggests a sun-bleached conglomerate that was washed up in or from an era long past. It prompts a sense of death, desiccation, and fossilization – as if it belongs to an imaginary future in which water has vanished from the world, leaving only archaeological traces, or cyphers of its ways, in the heaped remains, the fragments and bare bones, of an organic life that once existed.

Cohesive bodies that might once have been vital organisms, are now reduced to severed and isolated body parts. A partial skull is clearly identifiable, into whose abyssally blank eye sockets we might project an accusation or a plea. What emerges from behind this memento mori death's head, is a combination of desiccated corals, shells, anemones and found objects, all mounted on a solid structure that protrudes from below the piece with what seems like the bony spinal column, spiked tail or sharp teeth of a large leviathan monster, like The Kraken, Moby Dick or Jaws. Thus, the observer glimpses something dangerous and threatening lurking below the surface, suggesting the subliminal and sublimated anxiety and fear that accompanies the ecological and planetary threats in which humanity is sorely implicated.

The most disturbing aspect of this piece is the disembodied protruding human-like hands and arms, salvaged from discarded dolls, that are held up as if in either a posture of submission and defeat ("I give up") or in the sense of signaling for help ("I am drowning"). Read in this context this piece is both an accusation from, and a plea on behalf of, the children of the future. The observer is invited to look at the world and the future and see it, via the skull's empty eye sockets, through the proverbial eyes of a child. It invariably reminds one of the angry words that young climate activist Greta Thunberg furiously levelled at the leaders of the world when she said:

> You have stolen my dreams and my childhood with your empty words. … How dare you! … You are failing us. But the young people are starting to understand your betrayal. The eyes of all future generations are upon you. And if you choose to fail us, I say: We will never forgive you. We will not let you get away with this. Right here, right now is where we draw the line. The world is waking up. And change is coming, whether you like it or not.[54]

This monstrous imaginary phantasmagoria – from a world without water – evokes an imaginary future in which all that is left, if any are left to see it, would be the mysteries of a long past era, when the ocean floor was a vivid, fertile panoply of living forces and wild waters. However, the colorlessness of the piece invites the observer to add color in their own mind, imagining the rich colors of a real living underwater world. Thus, in the heaped remains that make up this artwork one sees the potential for new myths or poetics, which embody a call to restore hope to humanity.

In this essay, we described one aspect (the sea-to-source pilgrimages) of a larger transdisciplinary extra-curricular university project (The Tributaries Project). The pilgrimages (experimental, immersive encounters with the real world outside the conventional classroom context) aimed at fostering aesthetic experience to facilitate critical engagement and social cohesion. We found that the pilgrimages indeed brought about a sense of social cohesion among a vastly diverse and disparate group, focused on the collective interest in, and concern for water. This project validated the necessity for increased and enhanced focus on what Foucault called subjugated knowledges, such as art and other hermeneutic practices, for the important contribution they can make to our understanding of ourselves, others, and our world. This then begs for a reorientation away from the perceived dominance of the sciences as driver of knowledge and for a rebalancing that will entail the acknowledgement of the equal primacy of both science and art and, in fact, of their interdependence and inseparable cohesiveness in the way we experience ourselves, others and the world we share.

We used Hadot's ideas about aesthetic experience here as a lens through means of which we retrospectively conceptualized our experience of *The Tributaries Project* and the sea-to-source pilgrimages. We discussed four of the artworks that were created by participants to illustrate two of the core aspects of aesthetic experience, namely the self-reflective dislocation of the ego and the engagement with monstrosity. The pilgrimages and these artworks pose to us the challenge to consider whether there is a way beyond what seems to have become increasingly stagnating and stultifying encounters with common human problems. This means that we have the potential to imaginatively conceive of alternatives, both for the better and for the worse, for which arts and hermeneutic practices, and the attendant transformative potential of aesthetic perception, is crucially important.

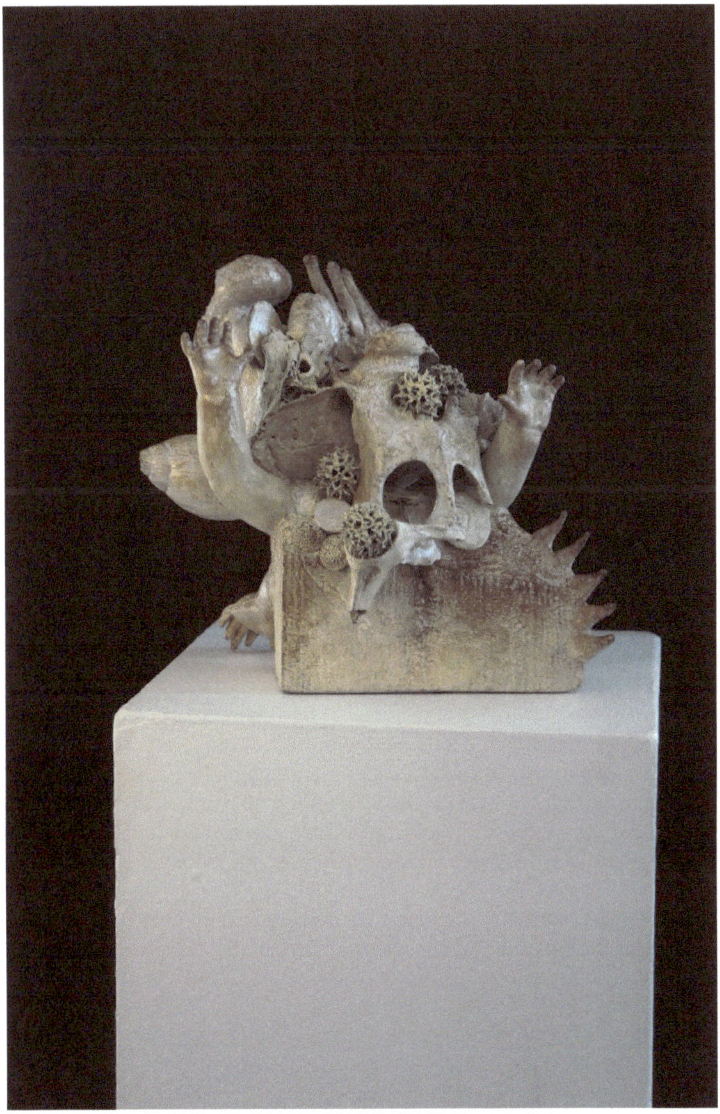

Figure 3.6: Nonnie Roodt, *Mythopoetics*.

The change of heart we seek, that can drive changes in behavior - both individual and collective, local and global - requires a constant return towards, repetition of and reflective attention to the sensory intensity occasioned by aesthetic perception. Ancient philosophical schools all insisted on specifically designed exercises for this purpose and considered these exercises to be a necessary part of regularly repeated daily practice. With *The Tributaries Project* and the sea-to-source water pilgrimages, we borrowed from this ancient wisdom in a small, local initiative that experimentally immersed a group of diverse individuals, who normally would engage with knowledge in the conventional classroom and textbook context and chalk and talk fashion, directly into their local and immediate environment. We learnt that, not only did this create a natural space for critical engagement, but it also organically produced social cohesion among the group. The key to this, we believe, was the introduction of art as a tool to express and communicate the aesthetic perception that occurred during the pilgrimages.

Notes

[1] This work is based on the research supported by the National Research Foundation of South Africa (Grant Number 99188, SARChI Chair in Identities and Social Cohesion in Africa, Nelson Mandela University). Opinions, findings, conclusions and recommendations expressed in this work are those of the author's alone and the NRF accepts no liability whatsoever in this regard.
[2] Janine Adams, L Pretorius and G Snow, "Deterioration in the water quality of an urbanized estuary with recommendations for improvement," *Water SA* Vol. 45 No. 1 (January 2019), 86-96. Published under a Creative Commons Attribution Licence https://doi.org/10.4314/wsa.v45i1.10 Available on website http://www.wrc.org.za ISSN 1816-7950. See also: Janine Adams and Taryn Ridden, *State of Knowledge: Conservation and Management of the Swartkops Estuary*, June 2019. Institute for Coastal and Marine Research, Nelson Mandela University.
[3] Michel Foucault and Colin Gordon, *Power/Knowledge: Selected Interviews and Other Writings, 1972-1977* (New York: Pantheon Books, 1980), 81-2.
[4] Andrea Hurst was the project's leader and main organizer, participating in all three pilgrimages and actively contributing as a participant to the project as a whole. Belinda Du Plooy, via the University's Engagement Office, co-funded the project, participated in the second of the three pilgrimages, and made extensive further contributions as a participant to the project as a whole.
[5] We have elsewhere more fully discussed *The Tributaries Project* as a whole. See Andrea Hurst and Belinda Du Plooy, "Educating for Complexity: 'The Tributaries Project' as a Higher Education Heterotopia," *South African Journal of Higher Education*, (2021).
[6] John Eade and Dionigi Albera, "Pilgrimage Studies in Global Perspective," in *New Pathways in Pilgrimage Studies: Global Perspective*, eds. John Eade & Dionigi Albera (New York: Routledge, 2017), 1-17. ISBN: 978-1-315-63731-0 (ebk).
[7] Adams et al, 'Deterioration in the water quality.'
[8] Full representation and discussion of these may be found in *The Tributaries Project Catalogue* at https://isciachair.mandela.ac.za/Engagement/The-Tributaries-Projects/The-Tributaries-Project-Catalogue

[9] Pierre Hadot, "The Sage and the World," in *Philosophy as a Way of Life: Spiritual Exercises from Socrates to Foucault*, ed. Arnold L. Davidson, trans. Michael Chase (Oxford: Blackwell, 1995), 251-263.
[10] Pierre Hadot, "Aesthetic Perception and the Genesis of Forms," in *The Veil of Isis: An Essay on the History of the Idea of Nature*, trans. Michael Chase (Cambridge, Mass.: Harvard University Press, 2006), 211-229.
[11] Ibid., 258.
[12] Hadot, "The Sage and the World," 253-254; Hadot, "Aesthetic Perception," 211-212.
[13] For more detail see Gilles Deleuze's analysis and critique of the eight postulates of the "dogmatic image of thought" in *Difference and Repetition*, trans. Paul Patton (London & New York: Continuum, 1994), 129-167.
[14] Hadot, "The Sage and the World," 258.
[15] Hadot, "Aesthetic Perception," 212-213.
[16] Hadot, "The Sage and the World," 252.
[17] Henry David Thoreau, *Walden; or Life in the Woods* (New York: Dover Publications, 1995), 89.
[18] Ibid.
[19] Hadot, "The Sage and the World," 254.
[20] Ibid.
[21] Hadot, "Aesthetic Perception," 215.
[22] Ibid., 219.
[23] Ibid.
[24] Sigmund Freud, "Civilization and its Discontents," *SE Vol XXI*, Ed. & Trans. James Strachey, 64-145. (London: The Hogarth Press, 1968), 64.
[25] Ibid.
[26] Hadot, "Aesthetic Perception," 214.
[27] Ibid., 212, 218-219.
[28] Ibid., 214.
[29] Hadot, "The Sage and the World," 260.
[30] Ibid., 228.
[31] Martin Heidegger, "Conversation on a Country Path about Thinking," in Martin Heidegger, *Discourse on Thinking*. Trans. John M Anderson and E. Hans Freund (New York: Harper and Row, 1966).
[32] Hadot, "The Sage and the World", 265.
[33] Hadot, "Aesthetic Perception," 212.
[34] Rebecca Solnitt, *A Field Guide to Getting Lost* (Edinburgh: Canongate Books, 2010).
[35] Thoreau, *Walden*, 111.
[36] Hadot, "Aesthetic Perception," 212-213.
[37] Ibid.
[38] Ibid., 229.
[39] Thoreau, *Walden*, 90.
[40] Hadot, "The Sage and the World," 252.
[41] Thoreau, *Walden*, 86.
[42] Hadot, "The Sage and the World," 251.
[43] Achille Mbembe, "Necropolitics" trans. Libby Meintjes, *Public Culture*, Volume 15, Number 1, (Duke University Press, Winter, 2003), 11-40.

[44] Walt Whitman, Preface in *Leaves of Grass: The Original 1855 Edition* (Value Classic Reprints, 2016).
[45] Gerhard Unterthurner and Erik M. Vogt (eds), *Monstrosity in Literature, Psychoanalysis and Philosophy* (Wien, Berlin: Verlag Turia + Kant, 2012), 9.
[46] Hadot, "Aesthetic Perception," 218.
[47] Unterthurner & Vogt, *Monstrosity*, 9.
[48] Hadot, "Aesthetic Perception," 218.
[49] Joan Didion, *I can't get that monster out of my mind. Slouching Towards Bethlehem: Essays*, (New York: Farrar, Straus and Giroux, 2008), 49.
[50] Kristen Minogue, "Do We Live in the Plasticene? 12 Words to Know for the Age of Plastics," in *Shorelines: Life and science at the Smithsonian Environmental Research Center*. Posted Jan 15, 2020. Accessed July 14th, 2020. (https://sercblog.si.edu/do-we-live-in-the-plasticene-12-words-to-know-for-the-age-of-plastics/).
[51] Ibid.
[52] Charles Carlin, "The Best of End Times: A Conversation with Anna Tsing," https://edgeeffects.net/anna-tsing/ posted September 19, 2017, updated February 12, 2020.
[53] Ibid.
[54] Greta Thunberg, "Transcript: Greta Thunberg's Speech at the U.N. Climate Action Summit," NPR (National Public Radio). *Environment News*, September 23, 2019. https://www.npr.org/2019/09/23/763452863/transcript-greta-thunbergs-speech-at-the-u-nclimate-action-summit.

IV.

The Baltic Waterways: Mapping Cross-Cultural and Ecological Awareness of the Baltic Sea

Anna Paluch

Carleton University

Abstract

This essay looks at diverse artistic activist actions happening over the last twenty years in relation to the Baltic Sea and its inner basin, which attempt to answer Jannok's question of artistic and cultural activism towards the environment. Antti Laitinen (Finnish) looks at personal complex relationships to the Baltic Sea in his works *It's My Island* (2007) and *Bark Boat* (2010). Artist collective SIMKA (Swedish) choreographs relationships between human interventions and the environment in *Baltic Sea – Floating Trunks* (2014). Marta Krześlak (Polish) created a site-specific installation with reference to the forces of nature in dialogue with human activity for the show *Human-Free Earth* (2019), part of the project *Plasticity of the Planet* at U-jazdowski in Warsaw. The artists and projects represented in this essay perform various ways of interacting with and on the sea, sometimes in direct dialogue with the Baltic, and other times, in a broader anthropogenic sense, but their geographies and proximity to the Baltic makes connectivity possible. In these engagements, the artists also tackle the moral concerns of human impact in the Baltic Basin, together with geopolitical histories and futures, and scientific data. Whether deliberately or not, the artists then, are engaging with what historian Dipesh Chakrabarty suggests is the double life of the Anthropocene as both "a scientific life involving measurements and debates among qualified scientists, and a more popular life as a moral-political issue."[1] Antti Laitinen and SIMKA engage with the Anthropocene in the Baltic context on a deeper, more 'moral' level, addressing the direct human impact in and around the sea, but also highlight the human responsibilities of maintaining a mutually respectful relationship with the water's ecosystems. *Plasticity of the Planet* at U-jazdowski follows a similar engagement with the Anthropocene, though the specific work of Marta Krześlak focuses on more of a geopolitical and capitalist history of interactions between humans and the sea.

Keywords: Anthropocene, Baltic Sea, ecosystems, Cold War, art activism

***

Artists from various countries bordering the Baltic Sea express their frustrations with environmental crises, often through culturally specific lenses or politically motivated commentaries. Contemporary musicians, academics and artists from Polish, Latvian, Lithuanian, Estonian, and various Scandinavian communities have turned into climate activists, such as Sámi activist, artist and musician Sofia Jannok. In 2019, Jannok participated in the Baltic Sea Festival with a program that was "a musical protest against the damage being done to the Baltic Sea and to all of the world's oceans"[2] that focused on discussions of sustainability and the environment. Speakers at the conference were encouraged to ask: "Can culture and music help create awareness…Can we actually save the Baltic Sea through the emotional power of music and cross-border collaboration?"[3]

This essay looks at diverse artistic activist actions happening over the last twenty years in relation to the Baltic Sea and its inner basin, which attempt to answer Jannok's question of artistic and cultural activism towards the environment. Antti Laitinen (Finnish) looks at personal complex relationships to the Baltic Sea in his works *It's My Island* (2007) and *Bark Boat* (2010). Artist collective SIMKA (Swedish) choreographs relationships between human interventions and the environment in *Baltic Sea – Floating Trunks* (2014). Marta Krześlak (Polish) created a site-specific installation with reference to the forces of nature in dialogue with human activity for the show *Human-Free Earth* (2019), part of the project *Plasticity of the Planet* at U-jazdowski in Warsaw. The artists and projects represented in this essay perform various ways of interacting with and on the sea, sometimes in direct dialogue with the Baltic, and other times, in a broader anthropogenic sense, but their geographies and proximity to the Baltic makes connectivity possible. In these engagements, the artists also tackle the moral concerns of human impact in the Baltic Basin, together with geopolitical histories and futures, and scientific data. Whether deliberately or not, the artists then, are engaging with what historian Dipesh Chakrabarty suggests is the double life of the Anthropocene as both "a scientific life involving measurements and debates among qualified scientists, and a more popular life as a moral-political issue."[4] Antti Laitinen and SIMKA engage with the Anthropocene in the Baltic context on a deeper, more 'moral' level, addressing the direct human impact in and around the sea, but also highlight the human responsibilities of maintaining a mutually respectful relationship with the water's ecosystems. *Plasticity of the Planet* at U-jazdowski follows a similar engagement with the Anthropocene, though the specific work of Marta

Krześlak focuses on more of a geopolitical and capitalist history of interactions between humans and the sea.

The complexities of the Baltic Basin are tied to the large-scale agricultural developments in Eastern European nations (Poland, Belarus, Northern Ukraine, Eastern Germany, and the Baltic Nations) which occurred within the last 70 years; a direct result of Soviet occupation and push for production, creating a geo-politically motivated environmental issue. Both nitrogenous fertilizer and atmospheric nitrogen (which appeared in greater volumes during the twentieth century) and the increase of phosphorus in surface soils, are responsible for the presence of 'dead zones' in bodies of water according to British-Polish geologist Jan Zalasiewicz.[5] This chemical cocktail enters bodies of water, such as the Baltic Sea, through agricultural runoffs which seep into groundwater, rivers, and casually enter the Sea's borders. Due to the poor circulation of the Baltic Sea (there is only a very narrow exit through Denmark into the North Sea), the nitrogenous and phosphatic fertilizer runoff promote plankton blooms, which sink to the bottom once they die, and then decay, "using up dissolved oxygen and suffocating bottom living faunas."[6] The climate of the area does afford a new stirring of oxygen with the autumn and winter winds, but Zalasiewicz warns that "further atmosphere/ocean warming will cause the seas to become more strongly thermally stratified, and so more prone to oxygen deprivation"[7], and the Baltic Sea already finds itself hosting one of the largest dead zones in the world. The area is much more sensitive to the anthropogenic shifts in our global climate and local pollutants.

Polish artist Marta Krześlak uses seascapes as social commentary. Krześlak's main body of work includes site-specific installations in existing spaces, altering the function of the space in a way that brings attention to how the forces of nature encounter human activity.[8] Her 2019 solo exhibition *Party at the Artists' Club*, curated by Marcin Polak at the U-jazdowski Castle, Center of Contemporary Art (Warsaw), was a room filled with homemade corals and reefs of recycled materials, mimicking an underwater seascape. This fantastical scene was the artist's response to her interactions with the works made by Polish artists working in communist Poland, and in fact, the reefs were made collaboratively with several artists who were active during communism, who Krześlak consulted for this project.[9] To aid with the authenticity of the response (in relation to communist Polish aesthetics) Krześlak and Polak worked with stage designer Maciej Jasiński and set designer Bogdan Mozer; Jasiński was instrumental in designing stages for galas and festivals, often televised from the Baltic coast, and Mozer is known for his fantastical and kitschy sets on cult films.[10] The significance of these aesthetics is a generational connection with Polish artists engaging with the coast within different contexts: forced beautification and aestheticization by a regime, versus, freedom to point out environmental policy hypocrisies.

The sea is used as an aesthetic backdrop while highlighting the regime shifts and former 'propaganda of the sea' (the fishing industry, coastal retreats, using the seascape to instill national pride). This installation of absurdity is lavish, celebratory, but in using plastic and recycled materials, also makes commentary on the current global issues of climate change. The hyper-stylized waterfront festivals and galas of communist Poland did not consider the damage being done to the sea's ecosystems, while current scientific research makes for anxious policy change requirements. The combination of opulent celebration with recycled realities of our plastic consumption (displayed in an under-the-sea tableau) creates an uncanny reality of geopolitical and historical shifts in climate change priorities. Political systems are affected by climate change (and vice versa) and their own "interpretive choices"[11] shape how domestic and international systems address specific climate issues. Studies have found that regime types are fundamental in these issues: a country that is undemocratic and heavily saturated with state-sponsored nationalism may use climate fears to deflect any criticism onto foreign leaders, halting important discussions on policy shifts. Using Russia as an example, political science professor Peter Haldén states that if the country became weakened by climate change, especially in the Arctic regions: "then we can imagine a 'pause' in militarization as the country deals with urgent domestic economic and political problems. Alternatively, more aggressive policies may be pursued by the Russian leadership to deflect domestic tensions and to compensate for the country's weaknesses."[12]

On the other hand, more democratic nations with leaders who are not afraid of accountability and in turn, govern a strong civil society that allows for public pressures, are then able to create actions that tackle environmental issues.[13] Keeping in mind these interconnected geographies and governments, Haldén further emphasizes that "the level of hostility or readiness to cooperate between Russia and the EU's member states can become decisive for how well the affected populations are able to deal with the impact."[14]

Regime shifts in such a concentrated zone (The Baltic Basin) play large roles in how the sea's ecosystems are affected; from war-time concerns and pollutants, the Soviet Union, independent nations and EU legislations, the Baltic is 'co-parented' by a variety of nations, each with their own needs, laws and futures involving the Baltic and its resources (predominantly fish, clams and shrimp). The Baltic Sea is surrounded by a basin that includes countries that do not border its shores (such as Belarus and even Ukraine), and so any activity within those basin borders (melting Northern glaciers or Polish in-land farming policies), does and will have a direct impact on the ecological identity of the sea's waters.[15] In this sense, the Baltic Sea as both seascape and landscape is much larger and much more interconnected to global anthropogenic issues than it seems. Global rising sea levels create unfortunate consequences for the Baltic's ecosystem; if the level of rising continues, or worse, accelerates, larger volumes of oceanic saltwater will enter the sea through the shallow Danish straits, resulting in higher salinity, which will affect the distribution of nutrients.[16] Unfortunately, governing the Baltic Sea is a serious challenge, and to successfully manage the care for its waters is complicated given that it directly borders nine nations and five states. Further complications can arise when considering the Sea's influence on the other bodies of water and ecosystems of a few non-bordering nations that are considered part of the larger Baltic Basin and connected to the Baltic proper through smaller waterways. Historically speaking, various empires have used the Baltic Sea for trading or fighting wars, becoming "a sea of tensions, a border between two very different kinds of society, which conveniently have often been labelled 'East' and 'West'."[17] Eventually, the East (former Soviet nations) and the West (Nordic Nations and [West] Germany) became reluctant participants of Europeanization (still in 2021, not every Eastern European nation is in the EU), working together as best as possible, despite political and cultural differences, to ensure the longevity of the Baltic Rim. The geopolitical reality of the region is that "the Baltic Sea is a common resource that is subject to high demands, from diverse user groups, and geographically shared among"[18] many nations with unique political agendas and environmental laws. Since the 1970s, attempts have been made to help regulate various pollutants entering the sea, such as agricultural drainage, placing "the Baltic among the most intensely managed marine regions in the world,"[19] and luckily, relations between the Eastern and Western European nations bordering the Baltic have warmed since the Cold War.

One festival that speaks about this diverse stewardship and co-parenting of this specific waterscape is the Baltic Sea Festival, which in recent years has taken on the role of acting as "a musical protest against the damage being done to the Baltic Sea and to all of the world's oceans."[20] Seven festival days of music and conversations (lectures) bring together experiences and perspectives from Denmark, Latvia, Finland, Sweden, Lithuania, Estonia, and the Aland Islands (an autonomous region), to explore how "culture, politics and science should work together to create a sustainable future for the Baltic Sea region"[21]. The 2019 edition saw participants performing and discussing in various Baltic cities, and the diverse presentations highlighted a mosaic of artistic, activist, scientific, sustainability, economic and geo-political discussions about the Baltic region, with topics ranging from the Nord Stream 2 Pipeline[22] to Indigenous environmental activism[23], a performance of climate operas, and panel discussions, asking: "Can culture and music help create awareness about one of the most pressing issues of our time? Can we actually save the Baltic Sea through the emotional power of music and cross-border collaboration?"[24] The eco-futurist[25] climate opera, *NeoArctic* (2016-ongoing) produced by Danish performance collective Hotel Pro Forma and composed by Andy Scott (British), Krists Auznieks (Latvian) and Sjón (Icelandic), is a transnational understanding of the collaborative nature of various waters; the effects of one body of water on another. With an increase in warming temperatures all over the planet, but especially in the North and in considering the rivers that connect larger waterscapes, the opera creates a contact zone between the Arctic waterways and the Baltic Sea through the Anthropocene opera and visual eco-performance art. The opera's timeline begins in the Anthropocene, and the visual supports of traditional and electronic paintings incorporate imagery related to our current geological era of "climate change, soil erosion, urbanization, the digitization of all aspects of life, and the dramatic loss of biological species that characterize this new age."[26] The performers are dressed in shrouds, chanting as computer-generated images of melting glaciers, abstract colors and shapes, as well as aerial images of ice flows superimposed on top of each other are projected onto them and their background. They are interconnected with the imagery, symbolically mimicking the dependence of humans on nature, but also the destructive force we exert over it.

The importance of Indigenous voices and presence in ecological protection (or eco-defense) and activism was also brought on stage, with Sofia Jannok (Sámi) and Johan Kuylenstierna (Swedish). Both Kuylenstierna and Jannok focus on the future of climate change and activism in different ways; Kuylenstierna is a geographer, geologist and paleo climatologist, working in academia and with policy makers to ensure proper climate laws are made and monitor their implementation. Jannok is an Indigenous Sámi musician from the Arctic Gällivare town in Sweden, and works in cultural, artistic and grassroots activism to ensure not just the Baltic Sea, but all lands and waters are sustainable and still livable on or around in the next generations. The Indigenous concept of 'Seven Generations', where we must consider our impact on the environment in relation to seven generations ahead of us, is a concept of accountability in sustainability, and is a philosophy that Jannok and Kuylenstierna address as being opposed to Western, capitalist concerns which only go so far as each quarterly economic period.[27] Where Kuylenstierna bases his observations on research, Jannok bases similar facts around centuries-long community observations on the shifts in the Baltic Sea and the relationships with the lands around it through legends; different methodologies, similar findings.[28] Jannok has been very active in global Indigenous climate activism, having been at Standing Rock in solidarity with Indigenous eco-activists and land protectors. Jannok's Sámi heritage provided another layer of context in the understanding the damage done not just to the Baltic Sea, but to the lands of the Baltic Basin, where "the Sámi indigenous peoples are resisting a number of environmental grievances from the forest industry, damming and mining."[29] During the presentation, Jannok states that "we are one with our surroundings and in this crisis that we are in now, I feel that I want to use the platform that I have, when I have the microphone, I want to say something that matters"[30]and in using her Indigenous Sámi teachings and her activist work with other Indigenous eco-protectors, Jannok highlights how her music is a medium from which these ecological issues and global Indigenous connections are expressed creatively.

Though the focus of the discussion and the festival at large, is on the Baltic Sea itself, Kuylenstierna states that it is also about "its surroundings and all the people that live in this region"[31] to which Jannok replies, "you have to see where you come from to know where you are going,"[32]making a comparison to her Indigenous knowledge with Kuylesnstierna's geological interests, showing a partnership between Indigenous land and sea knowledge and how a partnership with mutual respect from scientists can create possibilities in saving the future of the planet; specifically in this case, at the moment, the future of the Baltic Sea. This sea is unique because of its interconnectivity with land and other bodies of water; the Baltic Sea is bordered by landmasses with various geographies and ecosystems, and the sea flows out towards the Atlantic Ocean, first merging into the North Sea. It is a shallow sea, both old (with ancient, million-year-old coral reefs dotting coasts) and young (with dynamic shifts since the last Ice Age in terms of water levels, coastal borders and human and fauna migration around these considerations).[33] Jannok knew of the stories of her ancestors moving with the reindeer after the last Ice Age, following the birth of the Baltic Sea, while Kuylenstierna contextualizes and supports this oral story with scientific knowledge of human and reindeer migration patterns around the Baltic Sea after the Ice Age.[34]

Migration is a common theme in cultural works surrounding the Baltic coast, whether through forced displacement, following food or traversing the waterways with goods and people. Finnish performance artist Antti Laitinen explores the human limitations that are present when faced with natural elements such as land and sea in his projects *It's My Island* (2007) and *Bark Boat* (2010). The former project is a man-made island of two-hundred sandbags that he floated on in the Baltic Sea, while the latter is the artist's documentation of his voyage across the Baltic on a raft made of bark which he scavenged from a Finnish forest floor. Documentation of these ephemeral eco-performances was featured in the 2015 exhibition *Future Fossils* curated by Yulia Topchiy and Tess Thackara at the Dutton Art Gallery in New York City. This exhibition brought the local context of the Baltic issues to a global discussion among artists from Wales, Canada, Japan and Turkey, to name a few, where artists worked with various topics, such as the afterlife of objects in the Anthropocene, demonstrating "an environmental consciousness, imagining a more symbiotic relationship between human and environment."[35] Laitinen especially imagines this symbiotic relationship in *It's My Island*, where over a period of three months, the artist physically dragged two hundred sandbags from the coast and into the water. The artist documented the performance in both photographs and video, and viewers can see the physical strain of this forceful encounter with the water and harsh waves, until slowly, the island begins to appear over the Baltic seascape.[36] Through this action, the artist is not just experimenting with the relationship of human and environment, which he documents in his photographs showing how the seascape can easily shift from idyllic to foreboding, but also with the concept of nation and nationalities; in building his own "independent micro-nation inhabited by a single citizen"[37] Laitinen is questioning deeper issues of citizenship and identity (a topic, which is not unique to the Baltic, but is also explored by artist duo SIMKA), and in some cases, specific cultural imagery related to Finnish masculinity and cultural imagery[38], contextualized through nature. His 2010 continuation of this dialogue with the Baltic Sea also builds upon cultural imagery, but in *Bark Boat* it is through the lens of childhood and storytelling from the context of cultural geography. Laitinen launched his boat, made from ancient pine bark, in the Finnish peninsula of Porkkala in the Gulf of Finland, across to the island of Naissaar north of Tallinn, Estonia. Even the decision in locating his work primarily within the Gulf of Finland, is a specific geo-cultural expression, as Laitinen is expressing his unique perspectives on relationships with nature from his location along the Baltic, unique to artists whose works are situated in Latvia, Poland, Denmark or Sweden. This solo journey refers to childhood wonder, of toy and paper boats being gifted to the sea and imagining what adventures they may encounter. Laitinen is living this childhood fantasy while also "pushing the boundaries of his physical endurance and braving the natural elements, to engage with the world in a collective mission to stage [personal] mythologies"[39] through transitory travel between larger landmasses, islands, and his make-shift transportation, and when considering his other work, *It's My Island*, "Laitinen points to the incongruity between an individual's performance and circumstances and how it grows into a cultural metaphor"[40] of migration and human-environmental relationships.

The Swedish artist duo Karin Lind and Simon Häggblom have been collectively known as SIMKA since 2003. Their 2014 community collaborative installation *Floating Trunks* similarly looks at the migratory nature of the communities surrounding the Baltic Sea specifically, as "a metaphor for flight across the Baltic Sea and dreams of another life."[41] The work is made up of "multicultural"[42] trees from various habitats supported on lifebuoys, creating a similarly man-made island as Antti Laitinen had done, though in this case, more natural elements are being used and the trees are planted back into the land after use. Chance encounters with diverse people travelling across the waters create this transnational sea contact zone where you can find "various languages beyond the national borders in human exchange across the sea"[43] interconnecting people under a common interest (the sea). The port cities of Umeå (Sweden), Riga (Latvia) and Pori (Finland) were chosen for this installation, due to their importance as transit stations along the coast, attracting urban development from their strategic placement for shipping goods. In such coastal cities, SIMKA states that "it is here that the urban meets the sea and the fresh water flows into the Baltic Sea…[t]he sweet meets the salt lake and the brackish water typical of the Baltic Sea is created."[44]Just like the differing waters unite to form a cohesive sea, the artists used trees from the aforementioned port cities as well as other locations along the Baltic, uniting different landscapes, trees, waters, and residents[45] together over a shared seascape. Though trees are especially important symbols in Nordic cultures, the use of them in this eco-installation shows the importance of trees and forests within the entire Baltic Basin, and it provides a common element shared between various nations. In a transnational sense, "the sea is both locally characterized but also very international with areas not owned by any state as well as all traffic passing between all the world's ports"[46], with international and local transportation passing over the waters, providing food sources for diverse global communities. As such, it is important, according to the artists, to save the sea, as it also saves us not just in a literal sense, but also as a "free horizon for our minds to explore or contemplate"[47] and that it is necessary to explore and respect close relationships with this shared sea area.

Interconnectivity between nations but also inland waterways is crucial to keep in mind, as the Baltic Basin is a very co-dependent ecosystem. Rivers also need to be considered when thinking about climate activism and saving the Baltic Sea. From the large mass of the Arctic circle to the small flow of inland rivers, all these elements add to the growing shift in the Baltic's environmental 'DNA'. Nordic and Sámi connections to the environment are very literal, with Sofia Jannok even stating "I am nature"[48], highlighting her people's interconnectivity with natural elements around them, a point that SIMKA also tries to make. Jannok explains her statement, one that is repeated in global Indigenous communities, as a contextualization to the strong connections to environmental defense Indigenous communities have. Jannok does not sing about nature, she *sings* nature; it is tied to her identity. For Sámi people, the Baltic Sea is part of their ancestral home (there once were Sea Sámi), but colonial Swedish geo-politics forced the Sámi into more Northern lands, isolating them away from most of the coastal contact zones and creating one of the first instances of climate violence, denying Sámi their connection to these lands, which they had been stewards of for centuries. And yet, Jannok's statement emphasizes that we cannot just look at one area as a unique area, but a circle; everything is connected, and any crisis along the Northern Baltic coast, will impact Northern Sámi land.[49] Reindeer do graze along the Baltic Coast in the winter months, and

Baltic waters can affect rivers and land quality, so in fact Sámi do still have this ancestral connection to the sea, and should be involved in discussions and policy-making around the sustainability and future of this unique body of water[50]. SIMKA's work, though not directly referencing Sámi involvement, still echoes Jannok's sentiments, where *Floating Trunks* "becomes with its location [Baltic Sea] a link between the river and the sea which leads on to an international context."[51] The trunk installations float along the waters and change shape between each port city they are harbored in, and it is not just the sea these trunks meet, but the sweet river mouths, bringing with them particles and pollutants from inland, that clash with the salt water. The concept of interconnectivity between the unique landscapes and waterways continues, the trees acting like long-distance conversations; the trunks were part of "corresponding installations across the sea [which] tied them together and also brought us the viewers closer to one another."[52] The trees travelled in this altered state, within the realms of altering waterways, intersecting at these meeting points of trade, transportation and cultural exchange.[53] This particular representation of movement in the Baltic waters brings back to mind the aforementioned issue of 'dead zones' in the sea, which are direct results of human-impacted events and lifestyles during the Anthropocene era. These zones are not easily visible above water, but the hypoxia which affects the ecosystems deeper in the water, feel the grave impact. Both flora and fauna are not immune to this crisis; animals who can move, such as fish, will still suffer from the effects of hypoxia and lower their abilities to reproduce, while slow moving or non-moving animals, such as shrimp and clams, respectively, are even more at risk.[54] This then negatively impacts fisheries and coastal livelihoods, adding economic intersections to the list of Baltic issues.

Similarly, to SIMKA, cultural and scientific intersections are also found in the exhibition *Mare Balticum* (2016) and the Baltic Pavilion at the 15th Venice Architecture Biennale (2016). *Mare Balticum* was curated by Torum Ekstrand (Swedish) at the Kumu Art Museum in Tallinn, Estonia and included work by Swedish artist Åsa Stjerna in collaboration with the scientific EU LIFE+ project Baltic Sea Information on the Acoustic Soundscape (BIAS). It was an artistic exploration and interpretation of the underwater Baltic soundscape which played soundbites taken during a 2014 to 2015 scientific investigation by BIAS throughout the exhibition space. The work is an extensive "sonic map"[55], where previously, senses of sight, touch and smell were the primary ways of interacting with the Baltic, but through these sound experiments, scientists can now understand how noise pollution also affects the well-being of the sea. The audio data collected spanned a substantial section of the seascape, from the northern Bothnian Sea to the southern Öresund, and reaching as far east as the Estonian coast and as far west as the edge of the Danish archipelago, creating a "synchronized portrait"[56] of temporality and spatiality from these diverse yet vicinal spaces. Human, animal and natural noises are present in this 'multilingual' aqueous conversation. What is pertinent about this work in relation to the multicultural and multisensory experience of the sea, is that thirty-eight hydrophones were recording the sea's every breath, movement and interference at the same time, every hour of each day for one whole year.[57] The work creates a choreographed symphony of audio-solidarity between various points in the sea, creating one voice out of many experiences, adding agency to the body of water. This concept of agency on bodies of water is not new (as seen in the 2017 case where the Whanganui River in New Zealand was granted personhood status), and during their Baltic Sea Festival discussion, Jannok and Kuylenstierna wonder: "how the Baltic Sea would be treated, or how would we use the Baltic Sea if we gave the Baltic Sea rights?"[58] so that rather than seeing nature as a resource to exploit, we look at it as a relative or neighbor to support. Solidarity among neighbors in this age of the Anthropocene was the key theme of the 2016 Baltic Pavilion at the Venice Architecture Biennale, where explorations of man-made spaces intertwined with social understandings of land relations and resource use. In planning future infrastructure in the Baltic States (Estonia, Latvia and Lithuania), architects considered the options of working harmoniously across national borders, creating a "shared space of ideas...in light of the Anthropocene"[59] making sure any developments in the region are not just in conversation with geopolitical policies, but in consideration of the sea itself too.

By facing the anthropogenic crises of the Baltic Sea, whether it be cultural, scientific, geopolitical or economical, instead of ignoring the realities, the artists and projects presented in this essay are actively speaking *with* and working *with* the water, landmasses, animals and ecosystems associated with the Baltic. In this sense, Indigenous ecological philosophies and theories support this type of engagement, whether it be Sofia Jannok, who has direct experiences with the Baltic, or environmental philosopher Dr. Kyle Whyte (Potawatomi) and anthropologist Dr. Zoe Todd (Métis/otipemisiw), who are critical of the 'Anthropocene' as a concept, and instead promote reminders of the importance of local, Indigenous knowledges[60] and that place, history and stories are important nuanced factors[61] that shape the complexities of environmental theories and actions. Though what Donna Haraway would call 'staying with the trouble'[62], which was used as the main theoretical anchor for the show *Human Free Earth* (2019) (part of the larger *Plasticity of the Planet* project at U-jazdowski in Warsaw) by curators Jarosław Lubiak (Polish) and Michał Grzegorzek (Polish), is more widely known in academic circles, the words of Jannok, Whyte and Todd also support the actions of the artists and projects mentioned in this essay. Haraway's words ask us to remain aware of the obvious problems in our environment, and instead of running away from them, take care of what is left, since ignoring the situation at hand will prove "insoluble"[63]. *Plasticity of the Planet* compromises of multiple exhibitions, film screenings and published essays, and along with *Human Free Earth*, follow more so the philosophy of Jannok (rather than Haraway), who only a few paragraphs prior questioned what giving autonomy to the Baltic would do in terms of our relationship with it. The project at U-jazdowski came to the "realization that nature has ceased to be a stable, neutral backdrop for human activity"[64] and nature in this state is both defenseless and reciprocal, being both damaged by our actions but also capable of causing us damage in return; nature is fighting back after we have refused dialogue with its needs. In this sense, the ability for the sea to 'respond' to our actions harkens back, again, to Jannok and Kuylenstierna's conversation of the sea's agency. Jannok believes that "music is a fantastic way to reach other people that did not know they wanted to be reached"[65] and she speaks about how her songs are not just about nature as a whole, but about specific creeks, rivers or hills, who to her, are living ancestors, which prompted Kuylenstierna to speak about the movement of giving autonomy and legal rights to bodies of water, landmasses or other natural elements, such as the Whanganui River in New Zealand[66], or the 2014 case of the Lake Erie Bill of rights, granting the lake legal rights of a human being in order to help with the drinking water crisis in Toledo, Ohio.[67] Culturally and personally, Jannok sees natural elements as living ancestors; perhaps the future of the Baltic Sea then lies in Indigenous consultation and methodologies, as well as instilling legal policies that could give it personhood?

For Lubiak and Grzegorzek, "both catastrophism and techno-optimism are no more than futile escapism,"[68] meaning, we cannot rely on wallowing in despair over the state of the Earth and should not hope or think that technology is the only viable solution. As Jannok has previously stated, the importance is in respecting the sea and land as interconnected ancestors, or in considering Antti Laitinen's body of work which "harks back to an era where humans had yet to conquer nature with technology, instead working with and struggling against it for their survival"[69], the relationship with the sea was much more respected, knowing the limitations and boundaries of sea use, while now, the sea is merely a resource to exploit. Through our anthropogenic actions, we have rendered the Earth in a state of destruction, where some ecosystems cannot return to their original states, but at least through climate activist action and policy shifts, the destruction may not be so much reversed, as it could be transformed. If we continue at our current course through this Anthropocene era, in turn, it will be the Earth that enacts destructive transformations of plasticity, in reference to Catherine Malabou's argument that "plasticity is destructive in principle, and in some cases can even mean the annihilation of all form"[70], which, as the exhibition suggests in both name and concept, will result in a 'human free earth'. French-Polish artist Angelika Markul's work "Memory of Glaciers" (2017) is one of the featured pieces of *Human Free Earth*, examining interconnectedness through catastrophic shifts in climate. In recent scientific papers, it was found that "anthropogenic activities in the 20th century, such as the widespread usage of fertilizer, have caused coastal ecosystem changes that are unprecedented during the last millennium"[71] which further includes other agricultural activities, deforestation and wetland ditching. Also, in a geopolitical context, the way different nations change their use of the land "will most likely influence the coastal zone before possible effects are registered in the open Baltic Sea"[72] which will need to be studied more carefully to monitor these shifts. Geopolitical issues (whether environmental policy changes across bordering nations or regime shifts) increased as "the onset of these ecosystem changes is site-dependent and reflects the local history and geography"[73] of the polluted areas. Markul features images of Patagonian icefields melted due to human activity, but what the artist focuses on are the blackened glaciers, falling apart into the water. The glaciers appear infected, gangrenous, like amputated limbs becoming "a metaphor for the illness that is devouring planet Earth...the human-induced ailment – perhaps incurable."[74] Also, in the exhibition, American-Canadian artist Tom Sherman looks at antibiotics in fish and the dangers of new bacteria in our warming waters in his work *Playing With Fire Underwater* (2012), reminding us that there are many other lives, non-human, that are affected in this climate crisis. Though Sherman's work is in specific reference to Norwegian and Chilean fishing farms, the anxieties of food industry pollutants are just as high in the Baltic Sea, especially regarding the large dead zone that kills or limits the breeding of fish, clams and shrimp. The artists participating in this exhibition consider the future and impact of plastic use on our Earth, and the implications these physical pollutants have on both the sea and its flora and fauna, bringing the global anthropogenic context into a dialogue with local Baltic concerns.

In fact, all the artists and projects access their own local histories and environmental concerns to, as it were, co-parent to Baltic and the concerns around its waters. Multiple drainage systems connect to the sea, such as Lulealv in northern Sweden through the Bothnian Bay, the Szczecin Lagoon and Gulf of Gdansk in Poland, the Latvian Gulf of Riga, the Curonian Lagoon bordering Lithuania and Russia, as well as the Russian Neva Estuary. A near semicircle of diverse coastal ecosystems, provides freshwater and nutrient loads in the Baltic Sea proper, but also, any agricultural or industry runoff through the riverways.[75] The difficult histories of the 'Western' and 'Eastern' nations surrounding its waters go back centuries (Sami forced displacement, The Great Northern War, both World Wars and Soviet colonization, to name a few). The inland agricultural and mining actions of even non-bordering nations, and rising sea levels of presumably distant oceans have also been touched upon in this essay to highlight just how interconnected the global anthropogenic issues are to this very localized body of water. Regime shifts in such a concentrated zone also play large roles, from War Time concerns and pollutants, the Soviet Union and its agricultural and natural resource-focused industries, independent nations, and European Union legislations; the geopolitical reality of the Baltic Sea makes for difficult policy regulations and environmental protection. In making art around these layered issues, the artists in this essay create works and projects which are, “produced according to an ‘internal’ logic of lineages and referents, but also by way of innumerable external social pressures, technical innovations, and geopolitical transformations that also shape the spatial tactics and operative strategies of contemporary art practice.”[76]

All these lineages and referents are prevalent in works made about the Anthropocene and climate-based projects, as there are multiple factors to consider when examining and dissecting the genealogy of an ecosystem's interaction with climate change and pollutants. The anxieties of maintaining and studying the Baltic waters with, not just geopolitical, but cultural and scientific, interconnected realities, are very much real, and it will not be until there is full participation and solidarity from all surrounding nations that the future of the Baltic waters will start to look bright.

The Baltic Sea is like an ecological time machine, showing the possible fate of other bodies of water, even oceans, if the rate of pollution and climate change continues. The irony of the Baltic Sea is that it “is the most polluted sea in the world today, and it is located in one of the richest regions of the world”[77] meaning there is a heightened responsibility, and obligation to work towards shifts in policy to turn that around, or else the Baltic Sea will no longer be a time machine into the future, but a grim reminder of what could have been done. Success can only then come from collaboration and expression of these concerns to local and global governments, policymakers, corporate investors and daily citizens of the coast. The Baltic Sea can also be used as a case study for hopeful reversal of anthropogenic traumas to other bodies of water: “in the Baltic Sea, some negative trends caused by major regional pressures have now peaked and have been partly reversed, a progression that has led to the improvement of overall ecosystem status”[78] with recovery of fish stocks and tighter regulations. Artists, activists and scientists from all over the Baltic Basin and the coastal borders are making work that brings anthropogenic concerns to global and local attention, acting as ambassadors and translators to the sea's plight as witnessed on the shore.

Notes

[1] Dipesh Chakrabarty, “Anthropocene Time”, *History and Theory*, 57.1 (2018): 9.

[2] “The 2019 Baltic Sea Festival brings together the Baltic countries with cross-border music and conversations”, *news.cision.com*, April 24th, 2019 https://news.cision.com/berwaldhallen/r/the-2019-baltic-sea-festival-brings-together-the-baltic-countries-with-cross-border-music-and-conver,c2796889

3 "The 2019 Baltic Sea Festival brings together the Baltic countries with cross-border music and conversations," *news.cision.com.*
4 Chakrabarty, "Anthropocene Time," 9.
5 Jan Zalasiewicz and Colin Waters, "The Anthropocene", *NERC Open Research Archive* (2015): 11, http://nora.nerc.ac.uk/id/eprint/513436/1/The%20Anthropocene_for%20NORA.pdf.
6 Zalasiewicz and Waters, "The Anthropocene," 11.
7 Ibid.
8 "About", *martakrzeslak.com,* http://www.martakrzeslak.com/about.html, accessed March 1st, 2020.
9 "Party At Artist Club", *www.martakrzeslak.com,* accessed March 1st, 2020, http://www.martakrzeslak.com/party-in-the-artists-club.html.
10 "Party At Artist Club."
11 Peter Haldén, "Geopolitics in the changing geography of the Baltic Sea Region: the challenges of climate change," *Global Affairs* 4, 4-5 (2018 543.
12 Haldén, "Geopolitics in the changing geography of the Baltic Sea Region," 546
13 Ibid., 543.
14 Ibid., 542.
15 Baltic Sea Festival, "TALK - JOHAN KUYLENSTIERNA (SE) AND SOFIA JANNOK (SE)", August 31st, 2019, Berwaldhallen Hall, Stockholm, Sweden, online film, 45:00, https://www.berwaldhallen.se/en/balticseafestival-2019/saturday-august-31/
16 H.E.M Meier et al, "Impact of accelerated future global mean sea level rise on hypoxia in the Baltic Sea", *Climate Dynamics,* 49 (2017): 164.
17 Nils Blomkvist, "The Baltic: From European Sea of Troubles to Global Interface", *Forum of Public Policy* (2006): 14.
18 Thorsten B. H. Reusch et al., "The Baltic Sea as a time machine for the future coastal ocean", *Science Advances* 4 (2018): 5, https://advances.sciencemag.org/content/advances/4/5/eaar8195.full.pdf
19 Reusch et al., "The Baltic Sea as a time machine for the future coastal ocean," 5.
20 "The 2019 Baltic Sea Festival brings together the Baltic countries with cross-border music and conversations", *news.cision.com.*
21 "The Baltic Sea Festival presents seven personal talks on sustainability, the environment and music", *news.cision.com,* June 26th, 2019, https://news.cision.com/berwaldhallen/r/the-baltic-sea-festival-presents-seven-personal-talks-on-sustainability--the-environment-and-music,c2850593
22 Baltic Sea Festival, "TALK - TATIANA LANSHINA (RU) AND JOCHEN LAMP (DE)", August 30th, 2019, Berwaldhallen Hall, Stockholm, Sweden, online film, 45:00, https://www.berwaldhallen.se/en/balticseafestival-2019/friday-august-30/
23 Baltic Sea Festival, "TALK - JOHAN KUYLENSTIERNA (SE) AND SOFIA JANNOK (SE)."
24 "The 2019 Baltic Sea Festival brings together the Baltic countries with cross-border music and conversations", *news.cision.com.*
25 A personal term used to describe the futurist aesthetics used in the opera.
26 Opera de Montreal, "NeoArctic", accessed June 7th, 2020, https://www.operademontreal.com/en/events/neoarctic
27 Baltic Sea Festival, "TALK - JOHAN KUYLENSTIERNA (SE) AND SOFIA JANNOK (SE)."
28 Ibid.
29 Undisciplined Environments, "Weaving musical spaces of indigenous resistance for environmental justice", *undisciplinedenvironments.org,* March 16th, 2017, https://undis

ciplinedenvironments.org/2017/03/16/weaving-spaces-of-indigenous-resistance-through-music-an-environmental-justice-perspective/

[30] Baltic Sea Festival, "TALK - JOHAN KUYLENSTIERNA (SE) AND SOFIA JANNOK (SE)."

[31] Ibid.

[32] Ibid.

[33] Ibid.

[34] Ibid.

[35] "Press Release", *soniadutton*.com, accessed March 1st, 2020, http://www.soniadutton.com/exhibitions/future-fossils/selected-works?view=slider

[36] "ANTTI LAITINEN: It's My Island", *nettiehorn.com*, accessed March 1st, 2020. http://www.nettiehorn.com/It%27s%20My%20Island.htm.

[37] Ibid.

[38] Ibid.

[39] Ibid.

[40] "ANTTI LAITINEN: Bark Boat."

[41] SIMKA (eds), *Floating Trunks*, (Latvia: Finborg Graphic, 2015): 5.

[42] Lars Göran Karlsson, "Floating Signs That Engraft and Prune," in *Floating Trunks*, SIMKA (eds), (Latvia: Finborg Graphic, 2015), 75.

[43] SIMKA, "Baltic Sea – Floating Trunks", *simka*.se, accessed March 1st, 2020, http://www.simka.se/blog/baltic-sea-floating-trunks.

[44] Ibid.

[45] Pui-Yi Kong, "A Floating Forest In The Baltic Sea", *popupcity.net*, January 18th, 2016, https://popupcity.net/observations/a-floating-forest-in-the-baltic-sea/.

[46] SIMKA, "Baltic Sea – Floating Trunks."

[47] Ibid.

[48] Baltic Sea Festival, "TALK - JOHAN KUYLENSTIERNA (SE) AND SOFIA JANNOK (SE)."

[49] Ibid.

[50] It is somewhat ironic then, that young Swedish climate activist Greta Thunberg is given space and praise, while Sámi climate activist Sofia Jannok, is relatively unknown outside Indigenous climate activist circles.

[51] NOASS, "Baltic Sea – Floating Trunks", *vecs.noass.lv*, accessed March 1st, 2020, http://vecs.noass.lv/baltijas-jura-peldosie-koki-tuvojas-rigai/into/en/.

[52] Maria Hirvi-Ijäs, "Aesthetic Nets Put Out In The Baltic Sea – On SIMKA and The Project Floating Trunks", in *Floating Trunks*, SIMKA (eds), (Latvia: Finborg Graphic, 2015): 35-36.

[53] SIMKA (eds), *Floating Trunks*, 5.

[54] Michelle McCracken, "The Dead Zones", *Baltic Eye*, 2017, https://balticeye.org/en/eutrophication/elemental/dead-zones/.

[55] "Mare Balticum, "An artistic exploration of the underwater soundscape of the Baltic Sea", *echogonewrong.com*, accessed March 1st, 2020, https://echogonewrong.com/mare-balticum-an-artistic-exploration-of-the-underwater-soundscape-of-the-baltic-sea-at-kumu/.

[56] Ibid.

[57] Ibid.

[58] Baltic Sea Festival, "TALK - JOHAN KUYLENSTIERNA (SE) AND SOFIA JANNOK (SE)."

[59] "The Baltic Pavilion", *balticpavilion.eu*, accessed March 1st, 2020, https://balticpavilion.eu/.

[60] Kyle Whyte, "Indigenous science (fiction) for the Anthropocene: Ancestral dystopias and fantasies of climate change crises", *Environment and Planning E: Nature and Space,* 1.1-2 (2018): 226.
[61] Caroline Picard, "The Future is Elastic (But it Depends): An Interview with Zoe Todd", *BadAtSports,* August 23rd, 2016, http://badatsports.com/2016/the-future-is-elastic-but-it-depends-an-interview-with-zoe-todd/.
[62] Donna J. Haraway, *Staying with the Trouble: Making Kin in the Chthulucene* (Durham: Duke University Press, 2016).
[63] Jaroslaw Lubiak, "Human-Free Earth" - as part of the project *Plasticity of the Planet* (Warsaw: Ujazdowski Castle Centre for Contemporary Art, 2019), 2.
[64] U-jazdowski, "Plasticity of the Planet: About the project", *u-jazdowski.pl,* https://u-jazdowski.pl/en/wydarzenia/plastycznosc-planety?tid=program. Accessed March 1st, 2020.
[65] Baltic Sea Festival, "TALK - JOHAN KUYLENSTIERNA (SE) AND SOFIA JANNOK (SE)."
[66] Ibid.
[67] Savitri Jetoo, "An Assessment of the Baltic Sea Action Plan (BSAP) Using the OECD Principles on Water Governance", *Sustainability* 11, no. 3405 (2019), https://www.mdpi.com/2071-1050/11/12/3405/htm.
[68] Lubiak, "Human-Free Earth," 3.
[69] Julie Baumgardner, "Nine Artists Respond to Climate Change", *artsy.net,* September 22nd, 2015, https://www.artsy.net/article/artsy-editorial-nine-artists-respond-to-climate-change.
[70] Lubiak, "Human-Free Earth," 3.
[71] Wenxin Ning et al., "Anthropogenic and climatic impacts on a coastal environment in the Baltic Sea over the last 1000 years", *Anthropocene* 21 (2018): 77.
[72] Lena Norbäck Ivarsson et al., "Baltic Sea Coastal Eutrophication in a Thousand Year Perspective", *Frontiers in Environmental Science* 7, no. 88 (2019): 2.
[73] Ivarsson et al., "Baltic Sea Coastal Eutrophication in a Thousand Year Perspective," 13.
[74] Lubiak, "Human-Free Earth," 17.
[75] Dennis Swaney, "Text Box 3.14. Regional variation of nutrient dynamics in the Baltic Sea", in *Coastal Fluxes in the Anthropocene,* C.J. Crossland et al (eds), (Berlin: Springer, 2005), 136.
[76] Heather Davis and Etienne Turpin, "Art and Death: Lives Between the Fifth Assessment and the Sixth Extinction", in *Art in the Anthropocene: Encounters Among Aesthetics, Politics, Environments and Epistemologies,* Heather Davis and Etienne Turpin (eds), (London: Open Humanities Press, 2015), 15.
[77] Baltic Sea Festival, "TALK - JOHAN KUYLENSTIERNA (SE) AND SOFIA JANNOK (SE)."
[78] Reusch et al., "The Baltic Sea as a time machine for the future coastal ocean", 10.

V.

Woven Imaginations: Stories of fluidity and fixity in coastal Louisiana

Catherine Bonier

Carleton University

Abstract

This essay takes the waters of coastal Louisiana as its starting point, considering the webs of living things, systems, and structures that exist below, above, and within the Mississippi Delta's moving edges. This mobile coast is the ground for all life and livelihood in Southeastern Louisiana -- the source of cultivation and extraction, celebration and settlement. The region is characterized by the impossibility of straight lines, the daily loss of land, and the devastating failures of rigid engineered water-control structures. If water underlies all life in this region, the violent legacy of slavery, racism, white supremacy, and social injustice permeates the networks that bind human and non-human life and health in this complex terrain. The stories, cycles, living beings, and material practices that connect the vastly disparate scales and shifting edges of the Louisiana coast are bound together by relationships that are difficult to visualize, hydraulic and social dynamics that were partly submerged long before climate change was recognized as an existential threat. Questions of vision and imagination -- how to see, understand, and protect coastal Louisiana -- have been undertaken with greater urgency over the decade and a half since Hurricane Katrina. With a focus on infrastructural and socioenvironmental history, this essay critically evaluates the ways particular lenses and logics contribute to the escalating vulnerability of the Mississippi River Delta and Louisiana's Gulf Coast. Inspired by the thought and work of Anuradha Mathur, Dilip da Cunha, and Monique Verdin, this essay argues for future imaginations rooted in the complex and nuanced understandings of the communities most closely interwoven with ephemeral coastal ecologies.

Keywords: Louisiana Gulf Coast, New Orleans, the Mississippi-Atchafalaya River Basin, wetlands, coastal resilience, the Great Mississippi Flood of 1927, water control structure, ecological infrastructure, engineered vulnerability, infrastructural racism, critical visualization

***

Doubled Terms of Engagement

The ephemeral coast of Louisiana is a phrase that presents a paradox. Both nature and culture of Southeastern Louisiana are rich, heavy, and deep-rooted, far from the fragility and lightness that we normal associate with the word "ephemeral." Coastal Louisiana is hardly lightweight, shimmering, or delicate. Its coast winds and involutes, it churns with sediment and seeps with everything spit out by the Mississippi River. In fact and in reputation, coastal Louisiana, stretching to include New Orleans and the Mississippi and Atchafalaya Deltas, is a richly interwoven place, with human and non-human ecologies bound or knitted together by threads of water and oil. It is a region in which complex webs have been made and unmade over the past four centuries. As a place of focus, it condenses many of the factors that create "disappearing" coastlines: rich ecosystems, dense industry, massive geotechnical modifications, and sociopolitical systems that favor short-term economic gain over stable, inclusive socioecological development. Yet the material conditions that contribute to the ephemerality of the lines between land and water are far more straightforward than the distorted epistemological frameworks that prevent action to value and protect vulnerable ecologies and communities.

This essay begins with the author's own lenses, personal epistemological frameworks shaped from lived experience and disciplinary training. A background in the social histories of infrastructure, environment, science, and cities – all conducted with a focus on water – could only partially prepare me for several years spent living and teaching in Southern Louisiana. A migrant academic, relocated from the privileged, rocky, high ground of New England, I realized right away that I did not have sufficient knowledge or experience to understand the place I had landed, and questioned whether I had the right to participate as an active agent. The feel, the smell, the sounds, the language, the earth, air, and water were all wildly unlike the Atlantic coast of my experience. In addition, socioeconomic relationships based on painful histories and shifting geographies seemed immensely powerful and immediately palpable yet were only made intelligible through anecdotes and exchanges beyond the scope of this essay. As an introductory disclaimer, having now made my home far north in Canada, my view is still partial and now more distant despite continued research partnerships in Louisiana. I encourage the reader to take my arguments as tentative, and to trust more fully in the words and wisdom of those who experience the murky fragility of Louisiana's Gulf Coast as a matter of daily living and family history.

In this essay, I hope to share and explain some of my own struggles to understand Louisiana's current state of fragility, reframing it not as a simple matter of infrastructure and environment, but rather re-viewing it as a socially constructed crisis resulting from a history of structural injustices, violent displacements, and attempted erasures directed simultaneously at Black Americans and at coastal and riparian zones. I begin with the word "ephemeral," using it as a portal to invite readers into the paradoxes of Southern Louisiana. The original double meanings of ephemerality provide a clue to unknot the visions and vocabularies that have turned a region so visceral and viscous, muddy and mobile, into a place that may be as vulnerable as the tiny gnats or transitory fevers caused by "corruption of the Ayre" that the word ephemeral was invented to describe.[1]

The first English use of the word *ephemeral*, now obsolete, was decidedly negative and born in the context of medicine, at the time an integral category of natural philosophy. Sixteenth-century medical texts used *Ephemerall* to describe the pathology of a fever that lasted only one day. Thomas Newton's translation of Levinus Lemnius (1505-1568), for instance, describes the "Ephemerall Ague" or "Sweating Sicknesse" as a passing fever brought about by corrupt air. He uses the term *Ephemera* to describe the "miasmas" or smelly, humid exhalations then believed to emanate from swamps and unimproved land.[2] What is important for the purposes of this essay is that this original notion was based on an ignorance of the viruses, bacteria, and parasites that had not yet been identified as disease vectors. Prior to advances in optical technologies and in scientific approaches to determining disease etiologies, the mysterious appearance of fevers near marshy areas validated fears of mosquito-filled wetland ecologies. In the early modern era, the origins of ephemeral fevers were seen as environmental, with "corruption" understood to be dangerously and primordially connected to soft, swampy zones. Even though we now understand that wetlands are ecologically rich and environmentally resilient, human brains may still harbor a deep-rooted bias against the smells of damp, decaying organic matter. I would speculate that this fundamental revulsion probably still lingers behind development efforts to drain and fill wetland areas.[3]

Coastal ephemerality is also the result of a partial blindness, with the distinguishing difference that this limited perspective is based on a willful refusal to see the deep social roots of ecotechnological damage. The colonial construction of large-scale earth-altering infrastructures, such as pipelines, railroads, canals, highways, and levees, has allowed the creation and connection of vast territories. Simultaneous to the collapsing of distances between resources, industries, and consumers, these physical structures have distanced the beneficiaries of extractive processes from the suppressed and ignored regions designated to bear the impact of ever-accelerating industry. It is only possible to believe that the coast of Louisiana is "suddenly" sinking by clinging to a shallow, short-term understanding of the centuries-long processes of infrastructural and industrial racism that have destabilized what was once by its nature rich, resilient ground.

Ephemerality has other more positive meanings that allow us to float above the murk of swamps and fevers. The word took on more uplifting meanings during the nineteenth century, coming to be associated with insects that live only briefly and then (more bitingly) by association to books, political movements, or ideas that flare up suddenly and disappear.[4] Gradually, the negative connotations of swamps, fevers, and faddish irrelevance were washed out of the word somewhat, so that it could become more firmly linked to magical images and fragile forms of life. By 1880, Gray's *Structural Botany* textbook could describe the short-lived "petals of a poppy" under the classification "Ephemeral or Fugacious, lasting for only a day."[5] The *Oxford English Dictionary* traces the evolution of this word through these examples, which seem to demonstrate that the word ephemeral comes from the swamps and then lifts up out of the ground to apply to things that are precious precisely because of their beautiful fragility.

Today the filth and fever have evaporated, and we can comfortably use the word "ephemeral" to describe beautiful visual phenomena like rainbows and sundogs. These colorful rings and arcs across the sky are caused by water and ice particles that behave as prisms – lenses splitting bright sunlight into translucent, transitory images. Again, the magic of the illusion is that its mechanism is hidden. I argue that Louisiana's disappearing coast relates to both the murky indeterminacy of its soft alluvial plains, and to the seemingly magical ways a refracting lens can dazzle our eyes. To use the word *ephemeral* as a label for this place is, in a sense, to acknowledge the prismatic lenses and optical illusions that mask deeper truths of systemic suppression and planned vulnerability. This essay argues that whether the bright color and sound – the weave of life - that lights up the night during Mardi Gras or the blinding winds and rains that beat the coast during hurricane season – and the war waged to defend against these disasters, either view of Louisiana amplifies a partial reflection, masking deeper histories of infrastructure-driven dislocations and disappearances.

The Louisiana coastline exists in dynamic tension; a finely woven mobile fabric of human and non-human relationships hold the coast together, but hardline industrial interruptions have pushed this vibrant, vital place to the edge of disappearance. The fundamental paradox of the ephemeral coast is, in the case of Louisiana and of many other such ocean edges, a matter of planned vulnerability. Future attempts to remediate the environment and improve infrastructures will only perpetuate a legacy of damage and discrimination if the shadow costs of coastal development are not seen and counted. Imaginations must be knitted and knotted together to protect space for water, weather, and life in ways that may challenge prior definitions of use and ownership. After four centuries of envisioning economic progress as the primary system into which all other phenomena can be folded, today's disappearances – of coastlines, of species, and of populations – demand more complex visions and policies.

Many modern infrastructures have been constructed based on a perspective of defending property and commerce, while interrupting or erasing local ecologies and communities. Situated, grounded conditions of negotiation, exchange, and fluctuation have been "fought" in an imagined war. Most basically and obviously, concrete levees and petrochemical pipelines cut through mud, through water, and through plant, animal, and human life. Since the Great Flood of 1927 and the insertion and improvement of levees, spillways, and other control structures, the Mississippi River Delta has lost nearly 5,000 square kilometers (1,930 square miles) of ground.[6] Sociotechnical systems built to contain and control now contribute to coastal vulnerability. Simultaneously, reverence for these systems excludes and occludes the views and relationships they cannot contain or calculate. Unlike most imaginations and plans, the idea of "development" -- of land, of resources, of property -- rarely includes concrete strategies to for its own eventual reduction or termination.[7]

Contemporary coastal vulnerability coincides with legacies of colonization and extraction, but also derives from the geographical and environmental factors that once made port cities the pulsing nodes of empires. New Orleans, as a meeting point of a powerful river, ocean trade routes, and a booming chemical-industrial economy, offers an accelerated picture of the excess optimism and impending failures of 17th to 20th-century approaches to infrastructure, industry, and ecology. Canada and the United States share different versions of this still unfolding history, but the vast efforts to control the Mississippi River and to perpetuate a race-based division of labor (and of safety, security, stability, autonomy, and opportunity for a privileged class) across the Mississippi Delta brought a unique scale and complexity to systems of eco-social exploitation. Southeastern Louisiana's contemporary fragility grows out of the brutal violence and systemic legal and social controls constructed to categorize Indigenous and Black[8] bodies as obstacles or resources – first within the plantation system, and then within segregated economic and physical landscapes.

That the entire landscape of the Mississippi River Delta was radically reshaped through agricultural practices dependent on chattel slavery is uncontested fact. What is less well known is that the Mississippi River might not have been controlled without the labor of Black workers conscripted and, in some cases, held at gunpoint following the Great Flood of 1927[9]. A century of reinforced levees still leaves the most vulnerable citizens, many of them Black or Indigenous, at greatest risk of loss. The exclusion of Indigenous and racialized people from the 'safe zones' and desirable socio-geographical positions claimed and occupied by white bodies is foundational to the escalating manipulation of the Louisiana coastline, and to a national blindness to the seriousness of the danger. The material support of the veins and arteries of commerce – especially roads and bridges – gains more devoted support in the United States Congress than either environmental or human relief. To make any real change, the vocabularies we use to debate policy and allocate funding must be radically altered. It will be necessary to undertake a revised critical understanding of singular, supposedly neutral terms like *progress, infrastructure,* and *development* to imagine a new story of the coast.

In an essay that seeks to sort out such complex dynamics, I am consciously using doubled terms to acknowledge how historical efforts to fix a firm coast and to remove resources have a shadow side, a double barely held at bay. The exclusion of that shadow from maps, from laws, and from speech has allowed the redefinition of lives and ecosystems as resources to be eaten up in service of progress. Whether coastal life, forested wetlands, or Indigenous people and racialized communities, living ecologies not factored into plans and maps and not seen by ethical or legal systems have been transmuted into what might cynically (and morbidly) be called "buried costs" or in military terms "collateral damage."

Weave

A revised vocabulary and vision for Louisiana's ephemeral coast can be built on many stories, which, bound together, have shaped the fixed and fluid relationships along the Louisiana Gulf Coast and Lower Mississippi Delta. I will begin with a pair of common epistemological frameworks applied to Louisiana, which I've titled *Weave* and *War,* not to diminish their seriousness, but to make clear their basic terms of operation. The first of these stories describes Louisiana according to its rich mobility of matter -- as a vital mix of living things, a roiling and raucous world of layers and thresholds that are hard to see and difficult to define. Southeastern Louisiana evades easy survey in part because the land, the rivers, and the ocean do not meet at a sandy beach or a rocky cliff; salt and freshwater mesh and mix within the porous ground and in natural and manmade bayous, diversions, and channels. The coast itself is a series of feathery edges that protrude into the Gulf of Mexico, each one part of a past meander of the Mississippi River. The 1944 Fisk survey produced one of the most compelling and colorful visualizations of the great river snaking back and forth across the lowlands, over eons building the coastline of rich sediment in cycles of flood, deposition, and subsidence.[10] The rainbow layers of thousands of years of interwoven, serpentine paths create a pattern that is both beautiful and ominous, suggesting that this moment may soon be buried in a bright new layer, an unknown path.

In the past fifty years, the edge between land and water has become even more indeterminate, making the connections between living systems more tenuous and unpredictable. Climate change has amplified and imbalanced transpiration and precipitation cycles, making a crisp blue and green map with a strong coastal dividing line impossible to draw. Increasingly powerful summer and fall hurricanes coming from the Gulf and higher spring runoffs coming from the Mississippi's vast drainage basin draw into question the possibility of defining flood as a time when water escapes its "normal confines." To define normal edges to water in Louisiana has always been, at best, aspirational. In this first perspective of the estuary's complex weave of land, life, and water, typical systems of mapping and engineering and other tools for documentation, prediction, and control are challenged by the region's innate complexity and volatility. The force and volume of the river and the softness of the ground mean that the coast can shift overnight, in the blink of an eye in comparison to the geomorphological timescales associated with rockier shores.

Coastal Louisiana is a place dense with life and each group settled within the fingers of land between bayous has developed its own unique allegiances and cultures. What unifies human life with animal, plant, and other natural systems is that they are all losing both firm ground and clean water. For anyone near the coast, this means the potential loss of homes, streets, churches, schools, hunting, fishing, business, and agriculture that once supported self-determination, autonomy, safety, and stability. In January of 2016, federal funding ($48 million USD) was allocated to relocate an entire community, Isle de Jean Charles. The drowned island was largely inhabited by members of the Biloxi-Chitimacha-Choctaw tribe, who in effect became the first formally-recognized, federally-funded climate refugees in America.[11] Flooding is not unexpected to anyone with a deep knowledge of the river and the coast, but exponentially stronger storms and coastal erosion have taken a violent toll in the constrained and vulnerable locations to which Indigenous communities were pushed during the latest in a long history of relocations.

The snaking, swelling river is known to be deceptive, due to its sinewy flow and cycles of flooding, but also to the fact that its sheer volume allows it the appearance of a slow meander, even though it is an avalanche of water powerful enough to control anything in its path. As of this moment, its flow passing Baton Rouge is recorded at 331,000 cubic feet per second (9,373 cubic meters per second).[12] This combined power and deceptiveness – and the resulting illegibility to outsiders despite many readings – underlies some of the legends of Louisiana and New Orleans. In 1543 a member of Hernando de Soto's expedition witnessed a flood that he claimed covered the land of the Mississippi basin for twenty leagues (almost 100 kilometers or 60 miles). Most of New Orleans was brackish marshlands and cypress swamp at the time of European colonization, except for the natural levees from the river's regular flooding and sediment deposition along its banks.

Louisiana was a center for Indigenous peoples who constructed earthen and shell mounds along the Mississippi River Delta, locating those mounds in some cases on natural levees allowing them to find safety in high water, and to take advantage of the watery travel routes and biodiversity of the "terrestrial-marine interface."[13] These mounds, some hundreds of feet high and wider at their base, also housed buildings related to craft, ritual, and rulership. Jayur Mehta and Elizabeth Chamberlain's recent study of mound construction and ceramics along the Lafourche Subdelta finds evidence that one mound site was occupied between the 12th to 14th centuries, but was abandoned by the Grand Cauillou community as that path of the Mississippi River began to decline and shift to its present meander belt.[14] Dr. Mehta's research demonstrates the socially complex efforts that must have been involved in the construction of these mound sites, which were vast monumental landscapes constructed in major phases over hundreds of years.[15]

Because of the history of the decimation and dispossession of Indigenous peoples and their forced relocation from their land, the long history of complex Indigenous societies in this region is less well known today than are other narratives. Most of the stories that are transmitted beyond the boundaries of the state are of violent dispossession and dislocation of Indigenous people from the places and ecosystems fundamental to preserving traditional knowledges and practices. The forced relocation of Indigenous peoples to smaller territories has pushed many groups to regions that are beyond and outside of safe ground, and more vulnerable to climate change and sea-level rise.[16] Today, many of the southernmost coastal parishes are home to Indigenous people, including the Biloxi-Chitimacha-Choctaw Tribes, and citizens of the United Houma Nation.

Layers of colonization began with the voyage of Hernando de Soto, who died of a fever along the banks of the Mississippi River (either in Louisiana or Arkansas) in 1542. What followed were French, Spanish, and American efforts to control the coast and the valuable port of New Orleans.[17] Settler-colonial land occupation here as elsewhere was enabled through the violent displacement or enslavement of Indigenous people, the use of African chattel slavery, the violent suppression of vulnerable communities, and attempts to annihilate difference through forced acculturation. In addition, the port of New Orleans was a doorway that welcomed new waves of immigrants from the Caribbean, South and Central America, and the rest of the world.

In fiction and in fact, the winding bayous and impenetrable swamps of coastal Louisiana have allowed threatened populations to resettle in areas that were not easily found or traversed prior to the age of engineered bridges and highways. A variety of different cultures are rooted in this swampy separateness from the cities along the Mississippi River as well as from the distinct and separate culture of Northern Louisiana. In areas removed from the industrial and economic main channel, different displaced people came to settle in swampy regions further from the control of the government and (for a time) outside the reach of the U.S. Army Corps of Engineers. Cajun territory falls in this watery zone, primarily west of the Atchafalaya River. The city of Lafayette is a center of French-speaking culture for the Acadiens (Cajuns) who were exiled and dispossessed of their land in today's Canadian Maritime Provinces during the French and Indian War (1754-1763), at a time known as the Grand Dérangement. The language, food, and music along the Atchafalaya River reflects a mixture of Acadian tradition with new American influences, as well as the impact of free Black communities that settled in the region. While each group brought with them aspects of the places they left behind, Cajun and Creole culture took on a unique form in the richness and heat of the Mississippi-Atchafalaya Basin.

To the east of the Atchafalaya Basin is the mélange that is New Orleans: a city whose history, art, food, music, and entire physical fabric and infrastructural framework were to a large part created by chattel slave labor and by waves of colonial settlement. Immediately south of New Orleans in St. Bernard Parish were communities descended from Canary Islanders (Isleños) who settled during the late 18th-century Spanish occupation. Both Lafayette and New Orleans as well as smaller cities in the lower Mississippi River Delta are imbricated in the coast and have been inflected in different ways by creolization - the process by which different cultures and languages mix and mutate, often creating something bigger and richer than their separate parts.

New Orleans is both culturally and geographically entangled with the coast. The port is now further from the ocean than it was when first colonized. It is 160 kilometers (100 miles) from the city to the Gulf of Mexico by the river's path, but its position both below sea level and adjacent to the recently closed Mississippi River Gulf Outlet (MR-GO) make it a coastal city. The MR-GO Canal was opened in the late 1960s to provide a more direct route than the river from the port to the ocean. It quickly became a brackish inlet, with salinity reaching above 20 parts per thousand (ppt) in 2006. Notoriously, oysters have been found along its course, clinging to the blackened skeletons of bald cypress trees killed by the water's elevated salinity. The channel eroded and degraded wetlands, killed cypress swamps, and made the heart of the city more subject to flooding and storm damage. The Industrial Canal (Inner Harbor Navigation Canal), which cuts off the Lower Ninth Ward from the city, intersects with MR-GO; the two together funneled destructive storm surges into the Lower Ninth Ward during Hurricane Katrina.[18]

The perspective framework that defines Southern Louisiana as a place of complex layers and intermingling is empirically true and socioecologically important but can also create an epistemological distortion that allows and even excuses outsiders for failing to see, interpret, or engage with local conditions accurately. With so many waves of colonization and brutalization, as well as so many woven stories and lives brought together in this place, it seems almost a natural defense that Louisiana's social and political structures are inextricably linked to unspoken notions of family, place, and history. The complex weave of allegiances based on unique local histories, languages, and knowledges deters easy entry even by other groups of Louisianans to any circle or setting in which important decisions are made. Yet it is also true that the dense weave of relations cannot be truly impenetrable to ethical and ecological logics.

War

> "It is a great battle against the oncoming rush, and in every home behind the battle line there is apprehension and anxiety. Every night's reading of the water gauges is telegraphed to the remotest parts of those states – a sort of communiqué of the progress of the impending, threatening invasion of an enemy. It is a great battle which the engineers are directing."[19]
>
> Herbert Hoover, April 30, 1927

The second major framework of understanding that has shaped contemporary understanding and industrial management of Southeastern Louisiana's coast is one of active control, of a military battle against Nature. Herbert Hoover was not the first to declare war on the Mississippi, but his first national radio address to the nation, which declared the engineers' battle against the "threatening invasion" of the flood was significant. As John Barry documents in *Rising Tide: The Great Mississippi Flood of 1927 and How it Changed America*, this was a turning point that would permanently transform the battle against the river into a matter of federal control.[20] The broadcast took place April 30, 1927, the day after the levee at Caernarvon was intentionally dynamited, allowing the river to flood Saint Bernard Parish. This destruction and dispossession of residents turned out to be unnecessary for the survival of New Orleans, but was deemed important by local bankers, businessmen, and politicians to maintain the faith of distant investors. Hoover's mention of the telegraph indicates that this battle against the river was also a war of public relations. At the time Hoover was coordinating President Calvin Coolidge's response to the Great Flood and wanted favorable press reports to bolster what would become his successful campaign to succeed Coolidge as President. So, just as in today's series of non-binding slow-motion national commitments to "combat" climate change, the matter of environmental control was intricately bound up with projecting an aura of safety to corporate and industrial interests.

It is now generally understood that the war against nature waged by the U.S. Army Corps of Engineers, and vividly described in John McPhee's 1989 essay *Atchafalaya*, has its own shadow. McPhee shares a section of a Corps of Engineers training video that declares the entanglement at the root of infrastructural and economic warfare: "We are fighting Mother Nature. … It's a battle we have to fight day by day, year by year; the health of our economy depends on victory."[21] Efforts to control the Mississippi – to make it a predictable, fast, clear, fixed channel and to drain and fill the land around it have in fact destabilized the Louisiana coastline for over a century, despite their economic rationale. Unfortunately, this has set a path that is difficult to redirect, even though members of the Corps believed even thirty years ago that they would eventually lose this war.[22] A faith in industry and in the power of scientific and infrastructural management that led to radical changes to land and water during the 19th and 20th-centuries is not unique to Louisiana. The mark of systematic management is stronger here, however, because the intransigence of ground and water offered a powerful excuse for heroic and violent efforts to enforce dominant technosocial systems of progress, solution, and division.

The malleability of water-soaked wetlands made them more vulnerable to engineered devices and diversions. These systems – especially cutoffs, canals, levees, and the draining of land in service of industry and agriculture – have interrupted the complex and thick protective weave of hydrodynamic ecosystems along the lower delta and Gulf Coast. This is a regional riparian version of manifest destiny, rebooted to pin the construction of extractive economic and infrastructural systems to narratives of survival. Very often, coastal ecologies have been posed against human systems and weighed based on cash value or the attainment of escalating standards of human comfort and consumption. In this contest, complex ecologies have been excised or contaminated by a century of oil drilling and chemical production on and off the Louisiana coastline.

War has been waged in a way that has undermined elements of Louisiana's woven coast. The fine fabric of relationships that weaves together salt and fresh water with life and soft land has been consistently and intentionally cut through in Louisiana, a battle waged with an intentional blindness towards the lives and livelihoods of Indigenous and racialized people. John Barry's *Rising Tide* documents the ways in which the Great Flood gave birth to the modern management of the river and simultaneously eroded the independence of Black workers and families in its wake. As the spring flood swelled during April of 1927, creeping from north to south along the Mississippi River, many white residents were evacuated in cars or on dedicated trains and barges and shifted to higher ground. Documents Barry unearthed show that white landowners, the National Guard, and deputized white civilians prevented the evacuation of Black sharecroppers and their families to avoid losing their workforce, using guns, whipping, and other violence to manage work crews.[23] In this moment, latter-day overseers were not only denying free people their autonomy, but also robbing those families of the opportunity to join the ongoing Great Migration to the North. 'Concentration camps' with inadequate shelter, food, and water sprung up on the top of the levees, as John Barry documents in *Rising Tide*, holding thousands of Black citizens under armed guard. In certain locations, receipt of Red Cross rations was conditional upon working to offload supplies and to rebuild following the devastation.[24]

After the flood, the wartime framework for disaster management meant that there was no true reparation for damages done to poor sharecroppers and small landowners. Some of the delta's most powerful men would be in the room when the terms were set that placed the river under the permanent control of the U.S. Army Corps of Engineers. It would have a lasting relevance that white politicians, bankers, industrialists, and landowners argued that there should not be federal financial relief for flood victims; they feared that this request might slow down the passage of what would become the Flood Control Act of 1928 and might provide a bad precedent. In a flood that would put thirty feet of water above a territory inhabited by close to a million people, there is no question that the refusal of freedom, autonomy, and compensation to racialized people was essential to "fighting" the war on the river and to the long-term modification of the geomorphology of the delta.[25]

Engineered Vulnerability

> "In an average year, some two hundred million tons of sediment are in transport in the river. This is where the foreland Rockies go, the western Appalachians. Southern Louisiana is a very large lump of mountain butter, eight miles thick where it rests upon the continental shelf, half that under New Orleans, a mile and a third at Old River. It is the nature of unconsolidated sediments to compact, condense, and crustally ink. So the whole deltaic plain, a super Himalaya upside down, is to varying extents subsiding, as it has been for thousands of years."[26]
>
> John McPhee, *Atchafalaya*, 1987

It is not irony or accident that strengthened levees have led to more flooding in Southern Louisiana; it is a logical, if unforeseen, result of operations that have imagined solid lines on maps and strong defenses against nature. Once these lines are drawn, operations are mobilized to pump undesirable water out of the areas marked "land" and into the areas marked "water." Through canalization, land "reclamation," and swamp drainage, Louisiana and other delta zones have been reconstructed to approximate the lines on a map and to allow agriculture and industry to operate. As wetlands are filled, cut, or poisoned, not only are ecosystems decimated and carbon sequestration reduced, but also human settlements lose a valuable barrier against coastal erosion, storm surges, and sea-level rise.

The technical reasons for the vulnerability of New Orleans and the Louisiana coastline are well known.[27] Like many deltaic zones, the slope of the land is minimal, so the topography offers little resistance to global sea level rise. In addition, the Mississippi River has been mechanically altered from a fluctuating water course to a channel that is rigidly contained and managed. This containment has cut off the river from the wetlands around it and has interrupted the processes of flooding and sediment deposition which would typically build land and raise ground level.[28] For cities and settlements hovering close to sea level, pump systems must constantly eject precipitation beyond the levees, further compressing the ground as moisture is removed. So, the southern coastal regions of Louisiana are faced with eustatic sea-level rise and rapid anthropogenic subsidence.

Bureaucratic imaginations also have a part to play in the planned degradation of this and other coastlines.[29] It remains a failure of imagination to suppose that water in Southern Louisiana could or should fall within its current constraints. In Annex I, the Glossary to the 2019 Intergovernmental Panel on Climate Change (IPCC) Special Report, "flood" is defined as "The overflowing of the normal confines of a stream or other water body, or the accumulation of water over areas that are not normally submerged."[30] The increased ferocity of flooding in Louisiana's estuary is due to an engineered vulnerability, the logical result of two things: a short-term, opportunistic understanding of the river and ocean waters, that imagines flooding in this low-lying region to be "abnormal" despite thousands of years of evidence to the contrary, and the anthropogenic interruption of the river-driven systems that once deposited sediment and the shoreline landscapes that stabilized the coast against drowning.

Prior to the damming of many tributaries and the containment of the river delta by levee walls, the Mississippi would have conveyed sediment from the entirety of its watershed (2,980,000 sq. km.). At times of high water, such as spring rains and snowmelts, it regularly flooded its banks, dropping sediment and building up the delta's quaking prairie with its offerings. As a research team at Louisiana State University and University of Minnesota explain it, the mighty river has been contained and turned into a "superefficient pipeline channel."[31] It cannot build the land, but it conveys watershed nitrogen and agricultural and urban waste directly into the ocean. This jettisoning of excess nutrients and runoff creates an algal bloom that consumes oxygen as it decomposes, creating the Gulf of Mexico Hypoxic Zone or Dead Zone every summer.[32] According to the U.S. Department of Commerce, the hypoxic (deoxygenated) zone spanned 6,334 square miles (16,405 square kilometers) in 2021.[33]

The massive geotechnical undertakings that contain the swelling, snaking Mississippi inside concrete walls have had the most devastating effects on the communities already most marginalized by operations of land dispossession and racialization. The shifting of work and risk to racialized communities prevails and impacts health outcomes today; environmental injustice pairs exposure to toxins with lack of access to power in Southern Louisiana and in many coastal areas most vulnerable to techno-social manipulations of ocean and river edges.[34] The tragedy of the devastation of New Orleans following Hurricanes Katrina and Rita – as has been documented in detail since the event – was not just a failure of infrastructure in the face of destructive storms, it was also a failure to adequately survey the damage, stabilize neighborhoods, listen to community-members, and to fund remediation in a timely manner. It cannot be overemphasized that these failures were exacerbated by the attitudes of politicians and developers who saw the destruction of the Lower Ninth Ward as an opportunity to rid the city of poverty by removing the poor (Black) residents of this neighborhood.[35]

The burden of petrochemical extraction also falls on working coastal communities. After the explosion of the Deepwater Horizon in 2010, British Petroleum created a program called "Vessels of Opportunity" that hired fishermen and other workers across the southern coast of the United States to use their bodies and their boats to assist with the cleanup.[36] Their legal claims for ensuing health problems due to exposure to chemical dispersants continue to be processed within a slow-moving, byzantine system that places much of the burden for medical and legal expenses on the victims.[37] This is a dramatic example of the environmental degradation that has been a constant process since the discovery of on and off-shore oil in Louisiana.

The truth of engineered ephemerality is perhaps most easily understood through the experiences of residents of Louisiana's Gulf Coast, even though their voices seem to have limited impact on political decision-making. Residents of the parishes south and west of New Orleans have been especially harmed by coastal land loss, industrial encroachment, and by the BP spill, as well as by smaller-scale spills and dumping of toxic waste by other petrochemical companies. On the national and international stage, generalized epistemological frameworks have been constructed largely through the work of journalists and historians. There is a gap between these disseminated stories of land loss and environmental disaster and the work of local documentary filmmakers, artists, and others whose knowledge and imagination are more directly rooted in deep histories and ground conditions. This region has no shortage of visionary thinkers and knowledge-keepers, who have gathered oral histories from the people and communities most effected by hurricanes, failed infrastructure, toxic oil spills, and destruction of the cypress swamps.

Filmmaker, educator, and artist Monique Verdin's documentary *My Louisiana Love* is a powerful work that tells some of her own story as a citizen of the United Houma Nation and a resident of Saint Bernard Parish.[38] She powerfully relates interwoven stories of her connections to family and her identity as a cultivator of the coast.[39] Verdin has also participated in collaborations, such as the *Cry You One* project, which captures the voices of the people of Southeastern Louisiana, sharing their stories of sadness and joy as they imagine the future of a sinking coastline.[40] Verdin, in particular, jumps scales and connects frames in a way that shows clearly the relationship of the local to the global, and that also reveals possibilities of positive change rooted in practices that are embedded in the lives of the people who have seen drastic environmental changes within their own lifetimes. Film and interviews with her grandmother, father, lover, and other family members reveal adaptations that unfold within strategies of care. Despite unfathomable damage, Verdin celebrates efforts to plant, create, record, heal, and rebuild. Unfortunately, the voices and visions of the artists and activists whose imaginations are deeply woven into the fabrics that sustain ephemeral coastlines are rarely the perspectives that shape national debates.

Disaster

War is a powerful and simple framework that constrains imagination by starting from the point of view that the river and the Gulf must be fought at any price. It is a dominant perspective, because it is easy to understand and conveys the danger and immediacy of the problem as well as the need for sacrifice and effort. It also removes responsibility from civilians, shifting the weight to infantry, experts, and hidden bureaucracies. Unfortunately, the war metaphor may similarly deprioritize local communities even as the idea of "battling" or "tackling" climate change becomes more popular. It requires more patience and effort to understand and undertake processes that involve collaboration, negotiation, and accommodation. While weaving, knitting, planting, nourishing, cultivating, and other metaphors are more apt to contribute to real, long-term resilience, *disaster* is the contemporary lens (or metaphor, or framework, or story) that shapes commonly shared understandings of Southern Louisiana. The lens of disaster validates continued and unequal sacrifices, despite the dawning understanding that fighting the climate is like fighting a cloud, an unwinnable battle. There are real dangers that may come from the dual narrative of climate change and human disaster. The most obvious risk is that just as the narrative that declares a war on nature has excused forced labor, relocation, and the oppression and relocation of poor and Black citizens, a battle against climate change could replicate and even accelerate discrimination and the disenfranchisement of communities at risk.

Southern Louisiana's tenuous environmental state and recalcitrant political conditions have been constructed and sustained through legal, social, and carceral systems designed to constrain definitions of personhood. Today poor, Indigenous, and racialized people bear the brunt of engineered disasters, and may continue to absorb this violence in the face of sacrifices to come. Had there not been sharecroppers and others pinned to this muddy ground to face the Great Flood of 1927 over sixty years after the Emancipation Proclamation, the river might never have been held to its course. With reliance on a hostage workforce, the real costs of infrastructure have never been counted or accounted for, and even today, Louisiana holds the nation's highest per-capita percentage of legally unfree labor in its prison systems.[41] In the next fifty years, with individual states determining the use of recently approved federal infrastructural funding,[42] it is likely that the displacement of the costs of development to the most vulnerable communities will continue.

To those who have never seen the Louisiana coast and never survived a flood, on a national and international level the delta projects a powerful cultural identity that may make it seem impervious to loss. The power of local connections and the possibility of finding liberation, corruption, or chthonic horror back in the bayous have been celebrated and exaggerated both in fiction in film. Whatever their artistic quality, swamp-gothic stories have amplified the reputation of Southeastern Louisiana as an exotic and unintelligible place -- with the lingering mystique of a former French colony, the magic imported from the Caribbean, and the sorrow and hope of blues and jazz. While all these imaginations are lingering stereotypes that were always only partly true, they remain essential to marketing and tourism. I would argue that the linking of coastal Louisiana to stories of magic, admixture, and depredation (with a charming post-colonial patina) also contributes to a fetishization of suffering, an outsourcing of resilience, and an ethical detachment from the grounded realities and challenges of people living along the Gulf and delta.

In a time when national and global cooperation is needed to reorient priorities and change environmental policies, there is a way in which Louisiana's traditional mystique along with its seasonal appearances in flyover disaster footage may contribute to a strange political paralysis regarding its future. If the two connected stories of *weave* and *war* can be reframed as being about vision (seeing and caring for the coast as a rich weave of relations) and of value (the single-minded calculation of what can be used, burned, extracted, bought, and sold) – today's continuous disaster narrative mashes the two together and accelerates a cycle of fascination and fear, which I would argue may both amplify and dull public interest in the fate of the coast.

While the structures that pin environmental control to systemic oppression are not new, the 24-hour news cycle and satellite-driven imagery have created new possibilities of titillation and dehumanization. During Katrina, television networks broadcasted images that were shocking to viewers, promoting the easy equation of human suffering and environmental disaster with conditions of poverty, rather than with the very real infrastructures, controlled by the U.S. Army Corps of Engineers, that had ruptured, destroying the majority of the Lower Ninth Ward. Black, suffering bodies would become the emblem of this disaster, pushing into the background the history of infrastructural racism that created the situation.[43] Award-winning journalist Matthew Power noted that local New Orleans newspapers were forced to debunk the sensationalistic stories spread by cable news. He points out that "it was the *Times-Picayune* – weeks after the anchormen had gone chasing after Rita and were again tying themselves to telephone poles in the wind -- that methodically debunked the rumormongering and speculation of widespread murder, rape, and anarchic violence that had colored much of the early television coverage with shades of racial hysteria and served to slow the pace of relief efforts."[44] The deluge of images even led to the imagination that New Orleans was not a part of the United States, but rather a fragment of an "underdeveloped" nation lodged somehow at the base of the continent. Fox News reported that the United States would be 'forever scarred by Third World horrors unthinkable in this nation until now.'[45]

As global infotainment slides away from ethical responsibility and further towards high-stakes entertainment, viewers may be watching CNN and Twitter, guiltily hoping that they will witness a moment of tragic excitement, even if what they are seeing has devastating consequences for real people and other living things on the ground or in the ocean and marshes. The possibility of shock-watching from a safe distance has only expanded beyond the bounds of terrestrial vision with more advanced methods of coastal surveillance. In August of 2021, anyone with a computer and internet connection could click into the National Oceanographic and Atmospheric Administration's website to find current satellite views of Tropical Storm Ida pummeling the coast. NOAA's Geostationary Operational Environmental Satellite (GOES) updates every five minutes, allowing viewers to zoom in to see images that include "Nighttime Microphysics," "Air Mass RGB" and other custom views. To get a deeper and at the same time extra-terrestrial view, you could also pull up the "Potential Storm Surge Flooding Map" to see a satellite's-eye vision of a vast area of intertidal estuarine wetland marked as a sea of grey that surrounds New Orleans' little island of levee systems (Figure 5.1).[46] Shifting over to the United States Geological Survey (USGS) website would provide real-time flood-height data from one of their many sensors pinned around the coast.[47] Beautiful, colorful swirls and real-time flood readings are visually captivating, but can convey nothing of the experience of a Louisianan on the ground, let alone of the other living things that make Louisiana's Gulf Coast their home. These aerial disaster views contribute to the idea of inundated coastlands as a matter of passive statistics, rather than of active negligence.

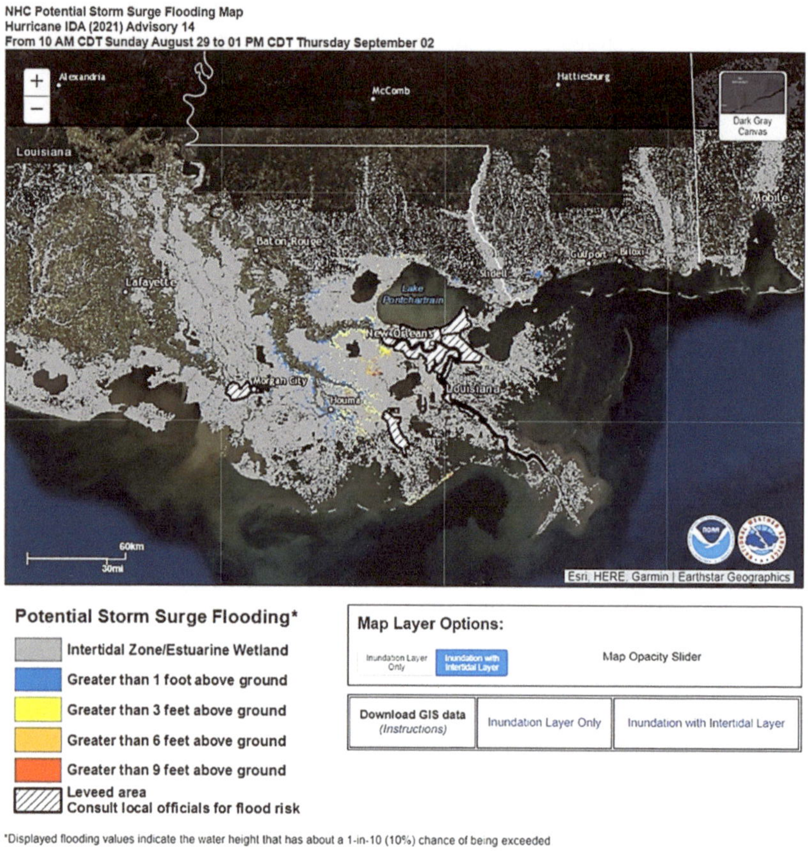

Figure 5.1: National Oceanographic and Atmospheric Administration (NOAA) – NHC Potential Storm Surge Flooding Map, Tropical Storm Ida, 29 August 2021.

While the danger of the land disappearing into the ocean seems most pressing, it is also quite likely that the Mississippi River will one day leave its current course and violently rearrange the geomorphology, and economies, and social bonds of Southern Louisiana. The channelization of the Mississippi River Delta was an aggressive leap of imagination and the main strategy to win the war on nature and avoid disaster. Despite improvements and modifications, the fluctuating river may not remain captive forever. It is recognized that this river turned artificial pipeline, ever lengthening as it shoots sediment further into the waters of the Gulf, can only last so long. The river has other routes to follow that are steeper and faster to the ocean, namely the Atchafalaya River, which takes 30% of the Mississippi's lateral flow at the Old River Controls. This percentage is arbitrary, fixed to levels measured by the U.S.A.C.E. in 1950. One of the control gates nearly failed during the flood of 1973, leading to the construction of a second, larger "Auxiliary Structure," which is 442 feet across, with six massive gates, each 62 feet wide. (Figure 5.2.) Between three control structures working together at Old River, discharge may reach up to 700,000 cubic feet per second (19,822 cubic meters per second).[48] If any failure should occur at the Old River control structures, and the Mississippi escape its path to find a faster route to the Gulf via the Atchafalaya, the existing Mississippi riverbed would become a shallow, marshy channel, eliminating all industry and port activities as well as the region's source of drinking water. It seems that this technological solution, made more robust over the twentieth century, may one day fail catastrophically, erasing or abandoning the traces of modern progress.

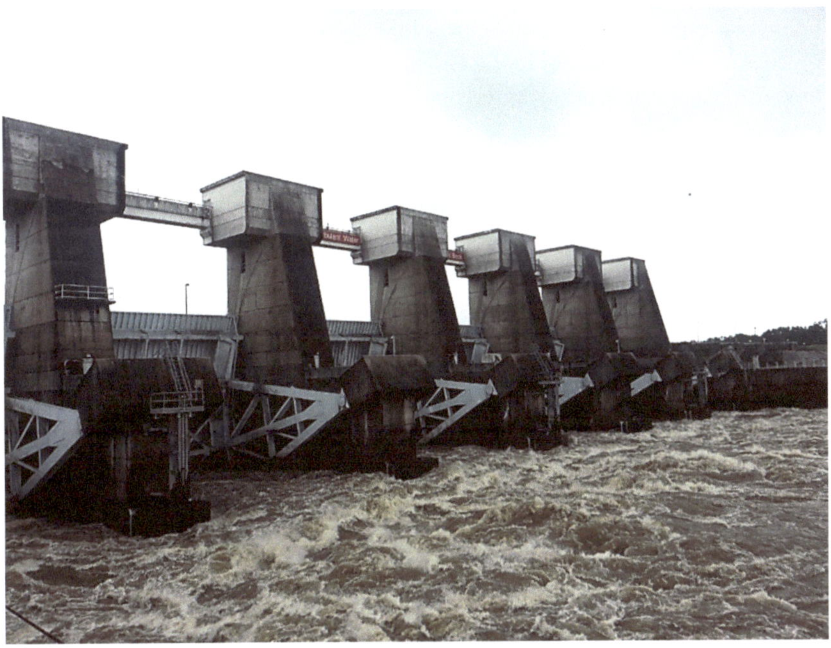

Figure 5.2: Auxiliary Structure, Old River Control, Louisiana. Photo and permission by C. Bonier, 15 April 2015.

Progress

The imaginations that officially document and define coastal Louisiana have been streamlined and sharpened for battle to negate and perforate rich layers of life and relations. Abstract ideas like development have been treated as fixed orientation points, while human dignity, autonomy, and safety have been treated as a fluid realm, contingent on and secondary to "progress" imagined as a duplicate of national identity. Progress may be the most powerful lens turned towards coastal ephemerality; in Louisiana and elsewhere, technological optimism continues to shape understandings of coastal challenges as well as frameworks for action. John Gast's oil painting of 1872 titled *American Progress* (Figure 5.3) might still serve as an emblem of the stubborn and short-sighted vision that allows the expansion of the petrochemical industry and the neglect of coastal communities in the face of contamination and land-loss.

I would argue that Gast's commissioned image of post-Civil War expansion and colonization accurately predicted the unifying faith that would rise to the center of divided American life, displacing other beliefs and even now fueling self-cannibalizing national hopes that technological advancement and economic expansion will squeeze out enough benefits to trickle down and provide "equity" to the most vulnerable people and places. At the center of this famous image Columbia, an enormous, angelic white woman intended as a female personification of the Americas – a sort of blond Godzilla – drifts serenely westward, her feet hovering above the ground. She is holding a book marked "common school" in one hand, and stringing telegraph lines behind her with the other to symbolize the unity of the nation through education, information, and industry. Counterposed against her are a family of Indigenous people fleeing the frame and escaping the promise of progress. Their brown bodies are angled as they run, looks of horror turned back towards the soft, untroubled face of their pursuer. Bison, bear, stag, and other living things sorted into the category of "wild" and therefore expendable, also flee into the dark and clouded west. This image was widely circulated by George Crofutt, a publisher and promoter of westward settlement, and distributed after 1873 as a chromolithographic print insert within his publications.[49]

Initially, when Gast's painting was reproduced, it was an advertisement meant to entice white American and European settlers to move west. Because she hovers placidly in the air, quite literally ungrounded, Columbia doesn't need to see or consider the differences and difficulties of human experience or wade through the deep, muddy ground and shifting torrents of the Mississippi River. In fact, at that time the dirty battle to contain and control the Mississippi River to serve a network of ports and plantations was already underway. The bodies of Black, Asian, enslaved, and other racialized people were not depicted, pushed outside the margins of view despite the centrality of their labor to infrastructural, agricultural, industrial, and geotechnical enterprises. Plantations, oil wells, coal mines, and polluting factories certainly existed in 1873, but fell beyond the borders of this rosy and partial picture. Today, the image and imagination of progress still often erases the people, work, and waste that both propel it forward and follow in its wake.

American Progress remains a picture of ignorance masquerading as innocence, a lens deeply embedded in the structures of the United States, allowing a perpetual and willful blindness to the decimation of communities and contamination of ecologies. Airy, expansionist Columbia continues to claim territory with her technological, educational, and human entourage. In the original image, the path was lit by a star on her brow, which Crofutt called the 'Star of Empire.'[50] This same ungrounded technosocial optimism still often guides American environmental policy, today following other bright and shiny lights. The myth of progress has become an all-encompassing and distorting lens that now guides the direction of development well beyond the borders of North America. It is a defactualized perspective that allows a constant reaching towards one counter-rational goal: to push development only forward, with no planned reduction or termination to that motion, and no care regarding its toxic and disruptive effects.[51] There is a danger that this naïve vision will continue as the mainstream and measure, the metastatic standard by which everything else is judged. If global commercial interests continue to undermine the ground and poison living things and air and water while planting trees and buying carbon offsets, there will be no end to the cycle. [52]

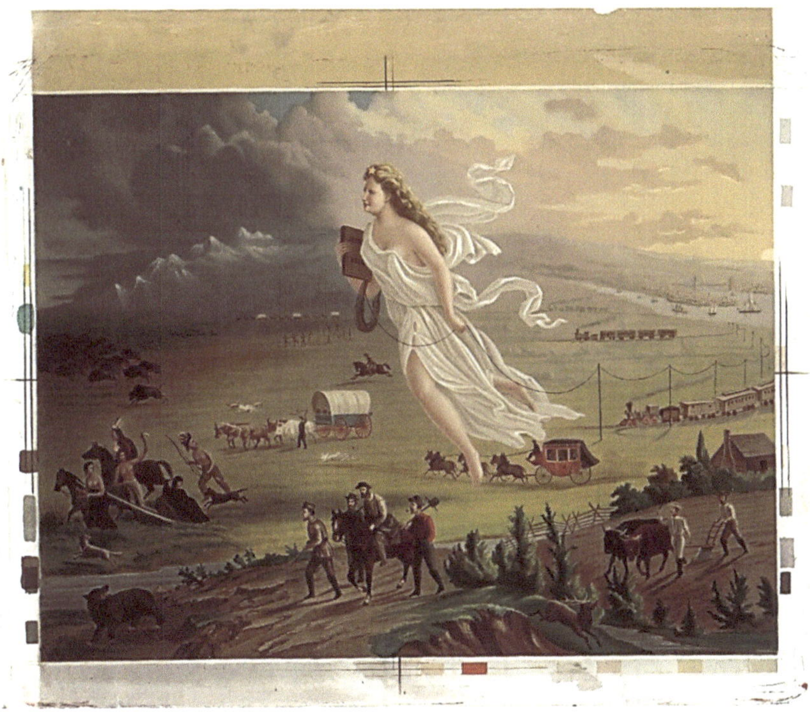

Figure 5.3: George A. Crofutt, *American Progress*, 1873. Chromolithograph. Reproduction of a painting of the same title by John Gast, 1872. Courtesy of the United States Library of Congress.

Critical Visualizations

How can an area so comprehensively controlled and surveilled, and so central to mythologized progress, be allowed to disappear? Louisiana politics is a complex game, and with oil and natural gas contributing (by industry estimates) an average of $68 billion dollars annually to the state's GDP,[53] the prevalence of short-sighted anti-human, anti-ecological thinking makes sense. This disjunction between short-term financial logic and contemporary socioecological awareness is also in part a function of which living things and communities are shown and seen -- or hidden and unseen -- by historical and contemporary methods of mapping, planning, and designing.

For the past several decades, architects and landscape architects have studied the epistemologies that underlie certain systems of survey and visualization, and the ways in which colonial methods of mapping, drawing, and planning have suppressed and (unsuccessfully) erased vulnerable systems, communities, histories, and bodies. Most notable among these theoretical and visual studies is the work of Anuradha Mathur and Dilip da Cunha.[54] From *Mississippi Floods* (Yale Press, 2001) to *The Invention of Rivers* (University of Pennsylvania Press, 2018), Mathur and da Cunha have looked at the ways in which the mapping of the lines between land and sea has in fact allowed the invention of rivers, and of flood. As da Cunha says regarding the lines that define the desired path and feared overflow of rivers, from the Mississippi to the Ganga, "... the line transgressed is not simply a line drawn; it is a line imposed. Furthermore, this line does not simply separate water from land; it creates water and land on either side of it as entities that can be commodified and as such coveted, made scarce, and violated."[55] Mathur and da Cunha have re-seen edges and recovered the indeterminacy that characterizes watery cities from New Orleans to Mumbai, using text as well as experimental forms of visualization, including drawings, paintings, silkscreens, and of course, writing. In a recent series of visual works titled "Ocean of Rain," they explain: "We pursue the stain. It begins another nature and infrastructure, one that holds, absorbs, intercepts, and celebrates wetness in a multitude of ways."[56]

To greatly simplify their complex ideas, Mathur and da Cunha argue that the "colonizing eye," whether of Alexander the Great or the British in India or of modern-day surveyors who continue to practice colonial methods and mindsets, view the land and survey it not in the time of monsoon or flood but with the imagination that dry land is the "normal" condition of things. With this reversal of thousands of years of accommodation and negotiation, flood and monsoon were redefined as violations of boundaries arbitrarily fixed and infrastructurally reinforced to ensure conditions of stable possession.

To the eye that sets a hard boundary on appropriated land, neglecting vernacular methods of living with water, the seasonal cycles characterized by what da Cunha and Mathur call "ubiquitous wetness" are enemies.[57] To the eye that sees solid, graspable land as property and progress, natural hydrological cycles constantly transgress and violate what was from the start an arbitrary edge. Mathur and da Cunha demonstrate, through an examination of historical writings, maps, and drawings, as well as from an analysis of pre-colonial myth, design, and practice, that "rational" colonial survey and engineering practices in fact obliterated and overwrote traditional methods of capturing, slowing, absorbing, and accommodating water in all its various places, phases, and forms.

Other imaginations of the Louisiana coastline have followed the path of Mathur and da Cunha by placing water at the center and using design, mapping, and drawing to uncover connections between past improvements and contemporary conditions. *Petrochemical America* (Aperture, 2012) combines Richard Misrach's evocative photography and Kate Orff's critical drawings and cartography to visually theorize the occupation of Louisiana's river and ocean edges by near infinite systems of petrochemical extraction, chemical processing, and waste transportation and storage.[58] Orff famously graphically documents the overlay of a stretch of the river called "Cancer Alley" with a constellation of chemical plants run by multinational corporations and collages images that convey the diversity of people and wildlife impacted by toxins in air, earth, and water.[59] What might be taken as romantic, desaturated images of misty marshes crisscrossed by pipelines and rail bridges take on a new power and sharpness because they are accompanied by Orff's team's analytical text and layered visualizations that trace the networks of extraction, processing, contamination, and transport beyond the boundaries of this region. Orff's constellation-like images are beautiful and informative, but also paralyzing, since they show this ephemeral coast tangled in powerful global economic networks that easily evade local regulation.

A question that comes with design explorations and critical visualizations arising in academic settings is whether they have any demonstrable value or measurable impact on the world. Following Hurricane Sandy's devastating hit on New York City in October of 2012, designers Catherine Seavitt Nordenson and Guy Nordensen obtained funding from the Rockefeller Foundation to launch the *Structures of Coastal Resilience* design research project.[60] This initiative invited teams from landscape architecture programs at various universities to work directly with the U.S. Army Corps of Engineers North Atlantic District to imagine visionary design strategies for several locations on the eastern seaboard. Teams of designers were selected from four programs: Harvard, Princeton, Columbia, and the University of Pennsylvania. All the participants, including Mathur, da Cunha, and Orff, share an ethical orientation towards teaching and practice, and have been deeply invested in inventing new ways of seeing and understanding coastal histories and possibilities. It is hopeful that these critical perspectives may continue to inspire real work towards building coastal resilience. Orff has opened offices in New York and New Orleans and constructed imaginative projects, including artificial barrier oyster reefs off the coast of New York City.[61]

Of course, there are groups in Southern Louisiana working on just these types of projects as well, such as the *Coastal Protection and Redevelopment Authority* (CPRA), Louisiana State University's *Coastal Sustainability Studio* (CSS), and the Baton Rouge *Water Institute of the Gulf.* Louisiana's coastal resilience groups often involve large partnerships of coastal scientists, engineers, biologists, geophysicists, landscape architects, architects, planners, local businesspeople, and others. New Orleans generated an ambitious master plan, *The Greater New Orleans Urban Water Plan,* which was inspired by the Dutch Dialogues, a collaborative workshop between the design firm Waggonner & Ball and designers from the Netherlands that took place in 2014.[62] A challenge for all of these teams, despite their brilliance, ambition, dedication, and shared local knowledge, is that they must find ways to operate within financial and political systems that stress the separation of science and economy from past and present issues of colonization, racialization, and discrimination. In effect, this allows work to continue at its smoothest when researchers embrace the false premise that infrastructural and natural systems somehow exist outside of, and separate from, human social and legal constructions. In more recent years, with a growing awareness of the embeddedness of violence and racism in socioenvironmental systems, organizations have found more support to take on the frictions that accompany structural change, even as a detached, retrograde politics seeks to undermine those efforts.

Conclusion

> "A characteristic of human action is that it always begins something new, and this does not mean that it is ever permitted to start *ab ovo*, to create *ex nihilo*. In order to make room for one's own action, something that was there before must be removed or destroyed... and things as they were before are changed. Such change would be impossible if we could not mentally remove ourselves from where we are physically located and imagine that things might as well be different from what they actually are."[63]
>
> Hannah Arendt, *Lying in Politics*, 1972

Hannah Arendt's essays describe the ways people and governments separate themselves from the truth of the world and the fact of suffering by submitting themselves, consciously or unconsciously, to systems that speak of progress and enact violence. In the excerpt above, Arendt explains that this relinquishment of ethical decision-making begins with the same fundamental imaginative impulses that make all action possible. In "Lying in Politics," she observes that the wartime "image-making" of the U.S. Pentagon, severed from what she calls "factual and given reality" resulted in a gradual and complete detachment from the world, with fantasies spiraling in a closed semantic loop that rejected any outside interruption or interpretation.

The double-edged sword of imagining a future for coasts that appear to be flickering and disappearing is that any new picture, new policy, in short, any new vision must become airborne, to an extent leaving behind what was there before in an imaginative act that is both hopeful and fantastic. This creative leap by which we "mentally remove ourselves from where we are physically located" can be a practice that returns again and again to ground, to water, to communities of people and other living things, or it can be an act of brute force that insists on a solitary path to victory, abnegating and erasing the rest of reality. Arendt's essay "Lying in Politics" was not an indictment of totalitarianism, but an observation regarding the everyday functioning of modern bureaucracies and governments. She wrote it in response to the 1971 release of the Pentagon Papers, the self-audit of military decision-making during the United States war in Vietnam. She describes the failures of a closed group – "men of great self-confidence" – who converted an aggressive marketing strategy, a series of lies told to maintain the reputation of the United States, into a message that they came to believe. In their pursuit of unmoored problem-solving, they sequestered themselves in "an entirely defactualized world" of their own invention.[64] In this simultaneous process of marketing and self-hypnosis, they echoed the founding ethos of European colonialism and American progress – and presaged the current double-speak of American politicians across the political spectrum, who promise industry-friendly environmental conservation, or "green development." In short, they proceeded by a serious of rational steps and calculations, based on an entirely faulty, insular, and uncontestable epistemic framework.

In this essay, I have attempted to pick up and examine several lenses, considering them separately though they are, in fact, closely connected. This effort was undertaken to better understand the frameworks of *weave, war, disaster,* and *progress* – and to put forward the ideas of *engineered vulnerability* and *critical visualization* as responses that point towards more grounded, synthetic understandings. Fundamentally, this effort comes from my concern that contemporary efforts to solidify ephemeral coasts may perpetuate the harm that has come from narrow, battle-based visions and metaphors made real. In Southern Louisiana, as in many other places, ecological vulnerability was not the first cause that engendered social vulnerability as a secondary byproduct. I have revisited various histories to explain the ways environmental ephemerality was constructed from a position of fear and a perspective of white supremacy. Once this distorted periscope was fixed in place, it warped and limited possible viewpoints. Or more exactly, a distorted view was co-constructed through the maps, laws, institutions, infrastructures, and boundaries that suppressed, divided, and relocated poor communities, particularly those of Black and Indigenous people. The same hubris that sought to erase people also drew a solid line dividing land from water and imagined that line to be permanent. These coevolving segregations were both based on limited sight and shallow understanding.

If environmental remediation continues to be framed outside of the imaginations of communities most affected by climate change and continues to rely on frameworks that classify socioenvironmental impacts as secondary to techno-economic optimism, then damage and violence will continue to be absorbed by those deemed "outside" of the path of progress. In classifying vulnerability or ephemerality as a sudden and recent problem, there is a danger of misidentifying the deep, intentional ruptures that lie beneath it. Kathryn Yusoff explicitly connects this dangerous trick of recategorization to the geospatial enterprises that continue to alter the planet. I would argue that this procedural un-imagination of Black bodies operates similarly whether in service of extraction or of remediation. In *A Billion Black Anthropocenes or None* (2019), Yusoff explains the ways the "innocence" and incompleteness of the "planetary analytic" of the Anthropocene fails to acknowledge that "the human and its subcategory, the inhuman, are historically relational to a discourse of settler-colonial rights and the material practices of extraction, which is to say that the categorization of matter is a spatial execution, of place, land, and person cut from relation through geographic displacement (and relocation through forced settlement and transatlantic slavery)." Through this epistemological process, Yusoff explains, slavery is practiced, and Blackness constructed by excising people from the category of human, and relocating them to the category of passive matter, "activated through the mastery of white men."[65] In relation to Louisiana, we can apply Yusoff's analysis, that liberal arguments often focus on infrastructures, politics, rights, and other aspects of "material political economy," ignoring factors "prefigured through a racialized geosocial matrix."[66]

Designers, activists, and artists construct images and stories of what might be otherwise and have the power to challenge commonly accepted categorizations and definitions. In particular, the work and imaginations of Monique Verdin and Anuradha Mathur and Dilip da Cunha take on a variety of functions, including documentation, education, critique, argument, and inspiration. Their radical, yet grounded rethinking provides new lenses with which to see more clearly. Other planners and designers, such as Kate Orff as well as numerous

Louisiana collectives and agencies, attempt the slow work of integrating between new imaginations and existing bureaucracies.

Imaginations can float above the ground, or they can ground deeply in the knowledge of communities and the complexities of life. The great difficulty in advancing new modes of care, protection, and reparation in firmly knotted socionatural imaginations may be how to refuse any environmental, professional, political, or economic discourse that treats non-human ecologies as entirely separate and different from affected human communities. In this difficult balancing act, environmental remediation has the possibility of prioritizing the protection of corporations and wealthy property-owners over vulnerable habitats and communities. The neutrality of industry and infrastructure is and always has been a lie; simple engineered structures like roads, levees, and dams have been deployed to preference some groups and to dislocate and push others into more dangerous ground. "Marginalization" means a shoving or shifting into the borders, out of sight, away from the center of action, far from the "mainstream." If the epistemological frameworks that have relocated coastal damage out of view as acceptable casualties in a perceived war against water, then Louisiana's coastal ecologies and communities will remain paradoxically fixed at both the margins and the frontline, even as that edge wavers and recedes.

Notes

1 *Oxford English Dictionary.* "Ephemeral" adj. meaning 1.a.

2 Levinus Lemnius, *The Touchstone of Complexions Generallye Appliable, Expedient and Profitable for All Such, as Be Desirous & Carefull of Their Bodylye Health,* https://quod.lib.umich.edu/e/eebo/A05313.0001.001?view=toc, 101–2.

3 Mary Douglas, *Purity and Danger* (London: Routledge & K. Paul, 1966), as well as Ivan Illich's *H2O and the Waters of Forgetfulness: Reflections on the Historicity of "Stuff"* (Dallas: Institute of Humanities and Culture, 1985) remain essential references on the histories of disgust and their transformation in the modern era.

4 *Oxford English Dictionary.* "Ephemeral" adj. meanings 1.b. and 2.b.

5 Asa Gray, *Structural Botany; or, Organography on the Basis of Morphology,* 6th ed. (New York, American Book Co. 1879), 243.

It is interesting that "Fugacious" is derived from the Latin root *fugere,* to fly. This pairing of floating petals with ephemeral flight marks the beautiful uplift of the word ephemeral – out of the swamps and into the sky.

6 Y Xu, Nina Lam, Kam-Biu Liu, *Resilience and Sustainability of the Mississippi River Delta as a Coupled Natural-Human System.* Water. (Basel, Switzerland: MDPI, 2018), 2.

7 Rosanna Xia, Susanne Rust, and Anita Chabria. "California's Offshore Oil Rigs Are Decades Old, and Industry Resists Decommissioning Them," *Los Angeles Times,* October 10th, 2021. https://www.latimes.com/environment/story/2021-10-10/californias-offshore-oil-rigs-decades-old-industry-resists-plugging-them.

The most recent oil spill off the coast of California sparked another round of news stories about the many ancient oil wells still operating, because it is cheaper for companies to keep them going than to safely decommission and cap the wells. In the current U.S. landscape, corporations have achieved the level of legal personhood for the purposes of political donations as "free speech," but bear little responsibility for the entirely predictable results of their negligence.

[8] I will typically use the term "racialized" for categories of people who have been labeled as non-white within systems designed to exclude them from protection or power. The term "Black" has real meaning in Louisiana, however, as a powerful historical and social identity claimed and shared by people of African descent whose ancestors were kidnapped, transported, and sold into chattel slavery in America, and whose histories and experiences are still shaped by that reality. Therefore, in this essay both terms are used.

[9] John M. Barry, *Rising Tide: The Great Mississippi Flood of 1927 and How It Changed America*, (New York: Simon & Schuster, 1997), 200.

[10] H. N. Fisk, "National Geological Map Database: Geological Investigation of the Alluvial Valley of the Lower Mississippi River." *U.S. Army Corps of Engineers*, 1944. https://ngmdb.usgs.gov/Prodesc/proddesc_70640.htm.

[11] Coral Davenport, and Campbell Robertson, "Resettling the First American 'Climate Refugees," *The New York Times*, May 3, 2016, sec. U.S. https://www.nytimes.com/2016/05/03/us/resettling-the-first-american-climate-refugees.html

[12] US Geological Survey, "USGS Current Conditions for USGS 07374000 Mississippi River at Baton Rouge, LA." https://waterdata.usgs.gov/usa/nwis/uv?site_no=07374000 (Its maximum recorded flow at Baton Rouge was 948,000 cubic feet per second in 2010.)

[13] Jayur Madhusudan Mehta, and Elizabeth L. Chamberlain. "Mound Construction and Site Selection in the Lafourche Subdelta of the Mississippi River Delta, Louisiana, USA," *The Journal of Island and Coastal Archaeology* 14, no. 4 (October 2, 2019): 453–78. https://doi.org/10.1080/15564894.2018.1458764.

[14] Mehta and Chamberlain, *Mound Construction.*

[15] Mehta Jayur M. Mehta, "Mound Building and Summit Architecture at the Carson Site, a Mississippian Mound Center in the Southeastern United States," *North American Archaeologist* 40, no. 2 (April 1, 2019): 67–98. https://doi.org/10.1177/0197693119863975.

[16] Justin Farrell, Paul Berne Burow, Kathryn McConnell, Jude Bayham, Kyle Whyte, and Gal Koss. "Effects of Land Dispossession and Forced Migration on Indigenous Peoples in North America." *Science* 374, no. 6567 (n.d.): eabe4943. https://doi.org/10.1126/science.abe4943.

[17] The territory was first claimed by France (1682), then transferred to Spanish administration (1762), briefly returned to French control (1803), and then sold to the United States (1804).

[18] John Lopez, Paul G. Kemp, and Amanda Moore, "MRGO: The Road to Recovery." White Paper, October 1, 2020. https://mrgomustgo.org/wp-content/uploads/2020/09/MRGO-White-Paper-10-01-2020.pdf.

[19] Herbert Hoover, April 30, 1927

[20] Barry, *Rising Tide*, 280.

[21] John McPhee, "Atchafalaya." *The New Yorker*, February 15, 1987. http://www.newyorker.com/magazine/1987/02/23/atchafalaya.

[22] McPhee, *Atchafalaya*, 1987

[23] In places like Mounds Landing, Mississippi, a National Guard Lieutenant commanding the efforts to stack sandbags and prevent the levees from crevassing (as a violent storm raged) explained that 'It became necessary for the civilian foreman and my detachment to force the negroes to the break at the point of guns.' Barry, *Rising Tide*, 200.

[24] Barry, *Rising Tide*, 311–17.

[25] Ibid., 285, 309–14, 389–401.

[26] McPhee, *Atchafalaya*, 1987

[27] Chris Paola et al., "Natural Processes in Delta Restoration: Application to the Mississippi Delta," *Annual Review of Marine Science* 3, no. 1 (2011): 67–91, https://doi.org/10.1146/annurev-marine-120709-142856.

See also Kelly M. Henry and Robert R. Twilley, "Soil Development in a Coastal Louisiana Wetland during a Climate-Induced Vegetation Shift from Salt Marsh to Mangrove," *Journal of Coastal Research* 29, no. 6 (2013): 1273–83.

[28] Paola et al., "Natural Processes in Delta Restoration," 67–73.

[29] Southern Louisiana is imagined as solid ground and drawn on maps as the solid, iconic "boot" shape, but in truth that land is composed of the eroded remains of prior delta fans -- traces of past courses of the Mississippi River. If you imagine the mighty river not as a fixed path, but as a perforated garden hose, its many past courses snake and twine around each other within a wide plain bordered by a wedge of uplands that spread apart south of Baton Rouge to the east and Lafayette to the west. These two cities are about 80 kilometers apart as the crow flies and have ground heights of 15 to 17 meters above sea level, but the land between them hovers just above or just below sea level. The Mississippi River at Baton Rouge is well above sea level - 5 meters above and hemmed in by large concrete levees and booming port and petrochemical terminals. It's easy to forget that rivers have slopes, and the Mississippi still has 370 kilometers (230 miles) to go before it reaches the Gulf of Mexico. The low-lying region west of Baton Rouge includes the Atchafalaya National Wildlife Refuge and the Atchafalaya River. South of Baton Rouge spread across the soft remnants of past river deltas are New Orleans, Morgan City, Houma, and other smaller settlements. All of these lie in locations that "are not normally submerged" only if judged within what is in geophysical terms a very short and recent time span.

[30] In Intergovernmental Panel on Climate Change, "Climate Change and Land: An IPCC Special Report on Climate Change, Desertification, Land Degradation, Sustainable Land Management, Food Security, and Greenhouse Gas Fluxes in Terrestrial Ecosystems," 2019. https://www.ipcc.ch/srccl/. 686.

[31] Paola et al., "Natural Processes in Delta Restoration," 68.

[32] https://www.noaa.gov/news-release/larger-than-average-gulf-of-mexico-dead-zone-measured

[33] US Department of Commerce, National Oceanic and Atmospheric Administration (NOAA), "Happening Now: Dead Zone in the Gulf 2021." Accessed October 28, 2021. https://oceantoday.noaa.gov/deadzonegulf-2021/.

[34] Leona F. Davis and Mónica D. Ramírez-Andreotta, "Participatory Research for Environmental Justice: A Critical Interpretive Synthesis," *Environmental Health Perspectives* 129, no. 2 (February 16, 2021): 026001. https://doi.org/10.1289/EHP6274.

[35] Dan Baum, "The Lost Year," *The New Yorker*, August 13th, 2006. http://www.newyorker.com/magazine/2006/08/21/the-lost-year.

[36] National Commission on the BP Deepwater Horizon Oil Spill and Offshore Drilling, "National Commission on the BP Deepwater Horizon Oil Spill and Offshore Drilling | The Gulf Spill." N*ational Commission on the BP Deepwater Horizon Oil Spill and Offshore Drilling,* 2014. http://www.iadc.org/archived-2014-osc-report/media/. Accessed October 28, 2021.
[37] Richard Thompson and David Hammer, "Eight Years Later, BP Oil Spill Clean-up Workers Await Their Day in Court as Medical Questions Linger," *The Advocate,* 2018. https://www.theadvocate.com/acadiana/news/business/article_5a5f8874-e47a-11e8-9b6d-3b7b9ecf811a.html. Accessed October 30, 2021.
[38] https://www.moniqueverdin.com
[39] Monique Verdin, *My Louisiana Love | American Documentary,* https://www.amdoc.org/watch/my-louisiana-love/. Accessed October 29, 2021.
[40] ArtSpot, Monique Verdin, *The Cry You One Documentary @ Cry You One.* http://www.cryyouone.com/people/detail/3/Monique-Verdin
[41] National Public Radio, "How Louisiana Became the World's 'Prison Capital.'" *NPR,* June 5, 2012, sec. National. https://www.npr.org/2012/06/05/154352977/how-louisiana-became-the-worlds-prison-capital.
[42] Zolan Kanno-Youngs and Madeleine Ngo, "Racial Equity in Infrastructure, a U.S. Goal, Is Left to States," *The New York Times,* November 16, 2021, sec. U.S. https://www.nytimes.com/2021/11/16/us/politics/racial-equity-states-government.html
[43] I refuse the word "environmental racism," because it can lead to the entirely false impression that racialized communities simply "ended up" in neighborhoods that are repeatedly flooded, or filled with industrial toxins that poison soil, air, and water. All of these conditions are the result of human racism, often channeled through municipal, state, and federal governments that manage infrastructural placement and industrial zoning. It seems clearer to identify "infrastructural racism," or "industrial racism," than to allow the loose sense of causality that the phrase "environmental racism" implies.
[44] Matthew Power, "Immersion Journalism: Panning for Ratings Gold in New Orleans," *Harper's Magazine,* December 1, 2005, https://harpers.org/archive/2005/12/immersion-journalism/, 75.
[45] Dan Baum, "The Lost Year", *The New Yorker,* August 13, 2006, http://www.newyorker.com/magazine/2006/08/21/the-lost-year.
[46] US Department of Commerce, NOAA, "NOAA GOES Geostationary Satellite Server," Accessed October 28, 2021. https://www.goes.noaa.gov/.
[47] US Geological Survey, "Flood Event Viewer," Accessed October 28, 2021. https://stn.wim.usgs.gov/FEV/#2021TropicalCycloneIda.
[48] US Army Corps of Engineers, New Orleans District, "Old River Control," 2009.
[49] Michael H. Hunt, *The American Ascendency: How the United States Gained and Wielded Global Dominance* (UNC Press, 2007), 11. From Samantha Rothenberg, *Beyond American Progress: The Legacy of John Gast* (ProQuest, 2013), 41.
[50] Bryan F. Lebeau, *Currier & Ives: America Imagined* (Washington: Smithsonian Institution, 2001), 121 in Samantha Rothenberg, *Beyond American Progress: The Legacy of John Gast* (ProQuest, 2013), 42-43.
[51] I borrow the term "defactualized" from Hannah Arendt. In her essay "Lying in Politics," Arendt described the Pentagon's damaging self-deception during the war in Vietnam as the result of "men of great self-confidence," sequestered in "an entirely defactualized world" of their own invention. (Arendt, *Crises of the Republic,* 1-48.)

[52] Or the end may be Jeff Bezos' grand vision, of shifting polluting industries to space, while humans on earth are riven by climate change and battles for resources. Justine Calma, "Jeff Bezos Eyes Space as a New 'Sacrifice Zone," *The Verge*, July 21, 2021. https://www.theverge.com/2021/7/21/22587249/jeff-bezos-space-pollution-industry-sacrifice-zone-amazon-environmental-justice.
[53] Louisiana Mid-Continent Oil and Gas Association, "Economic Impact." LMOGA, Accessed October 28, 2021. https://www.lmoga.com/benefits-of-the-industry/economic-impact.
[54] https://www.mathurdacunha.com
[55] Dilip da Cunha, *The Invention of Rivers: Alexander's Eye and Ganga's Descent.* Penn Studies in Landscape Architecture (Philadelphia, Pennsylvania: University of Pennsylvania Press, 2019).
[56] Anuradha Mathur and Dilip da Cunha, "Ocean of Rain", *Mathur / da Cunha.* Accessed October 28th, 2021. https://www.mathurdacunha.com/ocean-of-rain.
[57] da Cunha, *The Invention of Rivers*, 10.
[58] https://www.scapestudio.com/projects/petrochemical-america-book/
[59] Kate Orff and Richard Misrach, *Richard Misrach & Kate Orff: Petrochemical America* (New York: Aperture, 2012).
[60] Catherine Seavitt Nordenson, Guy Nordenson, and Julia Chapman, *Structures of Coastal Resilience* (Island Press, 2018).
It seems at the same time disappointing and perhaps ironic that this grant and collaborative effort with USACE would move forward after a hurricane that was both less deadly and less costly than Katrina, and that its efforts would target the wealthier mid-Atlantic coastline, engaging only with ivy-league universities.
[61] Klinenberg, "The Seas Are Rising. Could Oysters Protect Us?"
[62] Louisiana Coastal Protection and Redevelopment Authority: https://coastal.la.gov/
LSU Coastal Sustainability Studio: https://css.lsu.edu/
Water Institute of the Gulf: https://thewaterinstitute.org/
Greater New Orleans Urban Water Plan: https://livingwithwater.com/
[63] Hannah Arendt, *Crises of the Republic: Lying in Politics, Civil Disobedience on Violence, Thoughts on Politics, and Revolution* (New York, Harcourt, Brace, Jovanovich, 1972), 5.
[64] Arendt, *Crises of the Republic*, 1–48.
[65] Kathryn Yusoff, *A Billion Black Anthropocenes or None* (Minn.: University Of Minnesota Press, 2018), 2–3.
[66] Yusoff, *A Billion Black Anthropocenes*, 13.

VI.
From Ongoing Nakba to a Palestinian Hydro-commons: Reading the Jordan River and the Dead Sea as Ecopolitical Refusal

Sherena Razek

Brown University

Abstract

What does oceanic heating and environmental degradation compounded by an ongoing colonial disaster mean for the Palestinians on the land and those forcibly estranged from it? What do these parallel catastrophes, endured by the human bodies and bodies of water in Palestine, disclose about the long-term machinations of settler-colonial regimes in the context of global climate crisis? And how does the question of Palestine, both in its specificity and its transferability to other Indigenous struggles for land reclamation and decolonization, complicate the reductive aspects of posthuman theories of the Anthropocene as they have been established in white-dominated academic spaces?

Keywords: Anthropocene, Palestine, Jordan Sea, decolonization, Indigenous, Nakba, water apartheid

***

My sheer delight in encountering the Dead Sea for the first time and my dad's visible dismay in returning to it marked my first meeting with this shoreline profoundly when we visited in late June 2019. Under the blaze of the afternoon sun, I waded barefoot into the waters. I remember the high salt concentration stinging my skin slightly, but not unpleasantly. The water was shallow and crystal clear on a quiet section of the beach where we stood in the sweltering heat at the disappearing shoreline of an ancient body of water.

My dad's experience at the shore that day was punctuated with unspoken memories, mine eager and consumed by nostalgia for a place I had never been.

There was a palpable intergenerational difference that materialized on this shoreline between my father, born in Burqa, a small village in what is now known as the West Bank, and myself, born in so-called Canada on unceded Haudenosanee land. This was where he grew up, but he had not been back to Jordan in thirteen years and to Palestine, where he was born, since an even longer absence of thirty-five years. At the shore of the Dead Sea so many years later, he seemed to oscillate between two positions: gazing apprehensively across the body of water to the Palestinian shores seized under Israeli occupation – now dotted with private beaches and tourist resorts, and back at the Jordanian shoreline where we stood. I tried to attune myself to his tangible grief and felt compelled to take a photograph where he looked (Fig. 1). He swore the shoreline had receded several kilometers since he had last been there. He repeated this refrain multiple times in disbelief. In so many words, and in noticeable distress, he told me that the Dead Sea and the river that feeds it were dying.

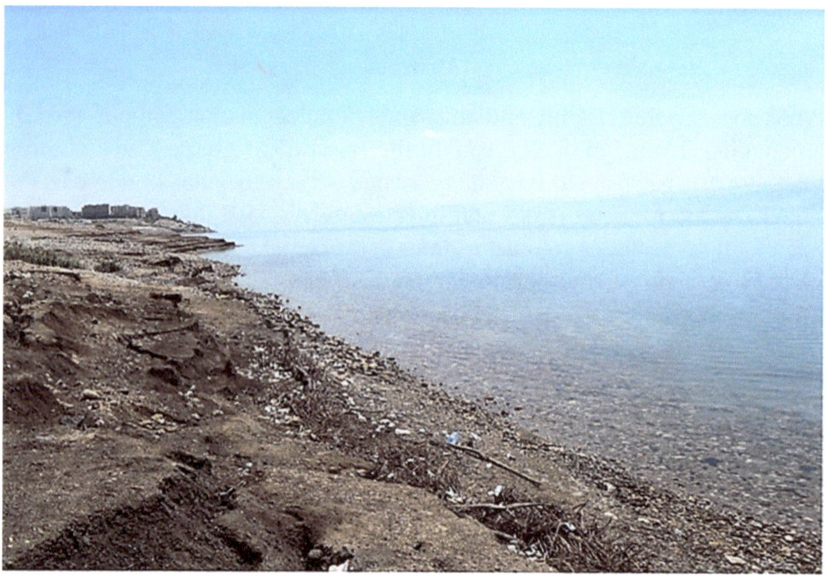

Figure 6.1: Photograph of the Dead Sea shoreline on the Jordanian side of the border. Photo taken by the author. Image courtesy of the author.

After witnessing my dad's reaction to the receding shorelines of the Dead Sea that day, I began reflecting more closely on the ways in which Palestinian lands and waters have been dispossessed and transformed under the concomitant effects of global climate change and the Israeli settler-colonial project that has exacerbated these effects. What does oceanic heating and environmental degradation compounded by an ongoing colonial disaster mean for the Palestinians on the land and those forcibly estranged from it? What do these parallel catastrophes, endured by the human bodies and bodies of water in Palestine, disclose about the long-term machinations of settler-colonial regimes in the context of global climate crisis? And how does the question of Palestine, both in its specificity and its transferability to other Indigenous struggles for land reclamation and decolonization, complicate the reductive aspects of posthuman theories of the Anthropocene as they have been established in white-dominated academic spaces?[1] What otherwise worlds become possible when decolonial and environmental repair are read together, as deeply implicated practices? In this essay, I attempt to unpack these questions through an engagement of the hydropolitics of two specific waterscapes: the Jordan River and the Dead Sea.[2] The former feeds the latter, and in the past several decades, both interconnected bodies of water have been subjected to severe depletion, settler-colonial occupation, and the de-diversification of human and non-human Indigenous ecologies resulting in the critical condition we find them in today. I will reflect on the ecopolitical phenomenon of the environmental *Nakba* that runs parallel to the human *Nakba*, the Arabic word for "catastrophe," used by Palestinians to describe the settler-colonial siege on Palestine that began in 1948 as a process of ongoing destruction. Focusing on the Jordan River and the Dead Sea as sites/sights of ecopolitical refusal I will read different and intersecting personal, photographic, archival, material, imaginative and literary engagements of these colonized bodies of water to render the urgency for environmental repair coterminous with Palestinian demands for decolonization and the right of return.[3]

When attending to the overlapping and often times contradictory layers of the ancient, contemporary, fabricated, concealed, and destroyed histories of Palestine, Edward Said proposes that in many cases, "one has to rely on landscape readings, because little else remains."[4] In dialogue with the field of postcolonial and critical ecologies, I consider "the inextricability of environmental history and empire building" [5] and the alternative material, imaginative, and discursive paths that emerge when these issues are read together with the possibility for human, and non-human, worldly watery sovereignty. By necessity, the essay takes to task the Eurocentric discourse prevalent in the "white public space" of the North American and European academy surrounding the Anthropocene, which as Zoe Todd argues, wrongfully assumes that "all humans are equally implicated in the forces that created the disasters driving contemporary human-environmental crises."[6] Subsequently, in the first section, I will discuss the Jordan River as a spatiotemporal threshold of Palestinian displacement and potential return following the natural course of the river to its mouth in the Dead Sea. The second section considers the ecological phenomenon of Dead Sea sinkholes as both metaphorical and agential registers that are crucial to understanding the convergence of ecopolitical refusal and Palestinian demands for decolonization and return. The final section of the essay speculates on how these bodies of water resist the unsubstantiated universalisms of the Anthropocene and the commons, both of which posit environmental crises as peripheral to the imperial regimes that have wrought constant destruction upon colonized lands and bodies. I problematize Astrida Neimanis's concept of the hydrocommons by placing it in tension with the theoretical and material contradictions that emerge in the context of Palestinian human and non-human bodies of water.[7] In reading the degraded environmental conditions, phenomena, and conditions expressed by the Jordan River and the Dead Sea as articulations of ecopolitical refusal, I attempt to engage in a process of unlearning the colonial severing of the relations between Palestinian lands, waters, and bodies and move towards the possibility of a repaired worldly hydrocommons.

The Jordan River as Threshold of Return

In *I Saw Ramallah* (1997), acclaimed Palestinian writer Mourid Barghouti describes his first encounter with the Jordan River after thirty years of exile on his way to return to his home village of Deir Ghassaneh.

> I was not surprised by its narrowness: the Jordan was always a very thin river. This ishow we knew it in childhood. The surprise was that after these long years it had become ariver without water. Almost without water. Nature had colluded with Israel in stealing itswater. It used to have a voice, now it was a silent river, a river like a parked car.[8]

At the banks of the dried-up Jordan River, a threshold many Palestinians dream of crossing back over since it is the site of their original displacement, Barghouti recalls the stories of other Palestinians who had breached its narrow shores and wept, evoking an image of salty tears soaking into the drying riverbank. He fluctuates between feelings of intimate proximity and unreachable unfamiliarity that often afflict those conditioned to life in the diaspora making partial returns to Palestine.

The Jordan River is 360-kilometres long and flows roughly north to south from Lebanon and Syria through the Sea of Galilee to its terminus at the Dead Sea on the border of what is known as the occupied Palestinian Territories in the West Bank and Jordan. Since the 1967 colonial expansion of Israel into the West Bank, East Jerusalem, Gaza Strip, as well as the Syrian Golan Heights and Egyptian Sinai Peninsula which Palestinians refer to as *al-Naksa*–Arabic for the set back–the Jordan River has stood in as a border marking this spatiotemporal displacement of Palestinians made into refugees. The Jordan River is a site where many underwent a derisive transformation from Indigenous peoples to refugees, and later, infiltrators when they attempted to return after their forced displacement in the decades following the Nakba.[9] The military invasion of 1967, which continues today in the form of a protracted and multifaceted occupation in violation of international law, saw the additional displacement of 300,000 Palestinians, approximately a third of who were already displaced in 1948.[10] Since then, the Jordan River has undergone its own form of settler-colonial displacement. Its waters have been severely depleted and redirected to Jewish-only settlements that perforate the West Bank. By consequence of these illegal settlements, and the unequal distribution of available water to the settlements, Palestinians in surrounding villages who have relied on the river for centuries now go without adequate access to water.[11][12] The river has been so drastically overused that, in Barghouti's words, it has become a river without water. His depiction of the depleted Jordan River is a metaphor for the "Palestinian national tragedy" which situates the Nakba in parallel with the environmental catastrophe and specifically its impact on the waters of Palestine.[13]

There are three bridges that cross the river and are under the jurisdiction of Israeli and Jordanian border authorities. The al-Karama /Allenby/King Hussein Bridge is a familiar passage for Palestinians in the West Bank who use this corridor to travel since they are not permitted to enter the Palestinian territories occupied in 1948, now called Israel, which prohibits them from international travel. Instead, to travel, Palestinians who hold West Bank identification cards must take a segregated bus over the river while tourists get ushered onto another; it is one of the more obvious signposts of Israeli apartheid and the first that I personally encountered.[14] For Palestinians returning to a homeland denied, we are reduced to unwanted visitors, and are subjected to this route also.[15] The river without water marks a threshold of intergenerational pain. We approach it with anxiety knowing how our parents and grandparents may have been forced over its transformative banks. We endure blatant racial profiling and rigorous and often humiliating security screening from the Israeli border agents in the process. We do this because we hope to make it across the narrow, dry, dying river because it is also a potential threshold of return to Palestine. Still, many are turned away at this point, like Barghouti's brother Mounif, who reached the threshold as many times as he was turned away, a profound disappointment that Barghouti says killed his brother in the end, since his untimely death followed soon after his denial of return. In this way, the fate of the river and the fate of the Palestinians are deeply implicated.

Photographic documentation of the mass displacement of Palestinians across the river in 1967 was made available via an online archive put together by the United Nations Relief and Works Agency for Palestinian Refugees in the Near East (UNRWA) and first exhibited in Jerusalem in 2013.[16] The photographs are a testament to the reconsolidation of the Jordan River as one of the sites of the categorical imposition of "refugee," "stateless person," and "infiltrator" on Palestinians being forced out of their shared world and banished from return.[17] Children and the elderly alike are pictured carrying items in large sacks over their covered heads as they cross the demolished bridge and leave their entire world behind.[18]A small child carries his even smaller sibling on his back with wet boots soaked in the river water where the bridge has been partially submerged. Another image shows the extent of the damage to the bridge. Military officers are seen perched at the highest point of the damaged structure supervising the dispossession of the Palestinians crossing the bridge below them. In this series of UNRWA archival photographs we witness the forced disappearance of the Palestinians and the river together in the same frame. For many of those displaced, who remain in the diaspora, denied their right of return across generations, this would be their last physical encounter with the river and with Palestine. The photographs capture the disruption of Indigenous bodies and bodies of water, rendering visible what Eve Tuck and Kevin Wang describe in the context of settler colonialism in North America as "a profound epistemic, ontological, cosmological violence…not temporally contained in the arrival of the settler but… reasserted each day of occupation."[19]

The profound violence of this rupture, captured in the UNRWA photographs of this moment of displacement should be understood correspondingly as an ongoing image of settler colonial violence, flowing like a river, rather than fixed in a closed historical or archival event. The photographs that show the second phase of mass displacements that took place in 1967 must be understood as an unfinished process of continuous environmental and human *Nakba* that are inextricably intertwined. Ruba Salih and Olaf Corry make the convincing argument that the violent separation of nature and culture, as captured in the archival photographs of Palestinians forced over the banks of the Jordan, works to ensure that the deep enmeshments of Indigenous life worlds are unraveled so that a settler-nature counterfeit relation can take its place.[20] Consequently, "given that power and politics are at the very core of the ways in which nature and humans become enmeshed or forcibly separated, only when these inequalities are conceived, and then foregrounded, is there a possibility of recognizing a common or global vulnerability."[21] In the wake of this violent separation, Palestinians across historic Palestine have been left deprived of their daily, ancestral, traditional, and future interactions with the land and water as well as with each other. The profound violence of displacement has ecological implications evident in the critical condition of the Jordan River. The photographs of the Palestinians' turned refugees are also photographs of the Jordan River being consolidated as an imperial border.

This transformation is one among many wherein the profound diversity of the human and natural worlds and their inherent overlaps in Palestine have undergone immense colonial transformation in order to legitimize the founding of a new imperial regime on Palestinian soil.[22] The Nakba therefore continues materially, politically, and epistemically through the "Zionization," seizing, enclosure, destruction, renaming, appropriating, and uprooting of the land.[23] The tactics used by Israel are not new however, nor are the machinations of Israel's colonization of Palestine exceptional, which is not to say that this particular case is without its distinctions. Like other settler-colonial regimes, Israel shares an interest in forcibly appropriating the lands and bodies of water home to the Indigenous peoples living in the territory prior to the settler state's foundation. It is through this unremitting plunder of the lands and waters that the ethno-nationalist settler project of Indigenous elimination[24] and settler futurity reconfigures the landscape sacred and essential to their original caretakers into natural resources, or rather, into commoditized property primed for extraction, profiteering, and/or the further perpetuation of the settler colony.[25] As Yousef Abu-Safieh, chairman of the Environmental Quality Authority of Palestine contends, "nowhere is the relationship between environmental protection and social justice displayed more clearly than between Israel and the Occupied Palestinian Territory (oPT)."[26]

If, as I have tried to show, the entangled conditions of displacement endured by both human and non-human bodies of water in Palestine are irrevocably intertwined, what would this mean for reformulating an understanding of the capaciousness of the Palestinian right of return? Rashid Khalidi has observed that for Palestinians, acknowledging and attending to the crimes instigated by the *Nakba* means that "the wrong done… can only be righted, and the disasters ended, through a return to the homeland."[27] The right of return is an incommensurable step towards the repair of Palestine and yet, despite the UN General Assembly Resolution 194[28] that sanctified this universal right of return for the Palestinians made refugees in 1948, it has never been mobilized beyond its status as a "recommendation."[29] The concept of return instead has more often been limited to the dogmatic schema of human rights rhetoric and takes as its starting point the validity and perpetuation of nation-state formations. This limiting interpretation has accordingly continued to fail Palestinians because of the ways in which these international human rights frameworks and nation-state forms limit the radical possibilities of return to a colonial system of legality.

The same logic that shapes the human rights framework is also operative in the Israeli "Law of Return," which in dialogical opposition to the Palestinian right of return, grants to any Jew in the world birthright citizenship in Israel no matter where they or their ancestors come from.[30] The law was passed unanimously by the Knesset, Israel's parliament, in July 1950 and has ensured the continued influx of new settlers to Palestinian lands since. It has legalized a future cleansed of generations of Palestinians and in their absence, normalized their replacement by a constant influx of settlers. In an elaborate revision of history, this evidently settler-colonial cycle of ongoing displacement of the native Palestinians, land encroachment, settlement development, and deeply institutionalized violence has been reoriented in Zionist historical narratives to be viewed as an anti-colonial Jewish national liberation movement against the British Mandate wherein the native Palestinians have been rendered entirely absent. Such repackaging of imperial crimes into sanctified legal norms or of Jewish history into colonial Zionist mythology has therefore worked to reframe the colonization of Palestine by white Europeans[31] as a decolonial return of the ancient dispersed Jews who have been re-oriented as the new modern Jews or Israeli citizens.[32] Edward Said calls this reductive Zionist revision of Jewish history and identity "retrospective teleology."[33] The Jordan River has its part in this narrative too as a site of possible reversal of settler teleology.

Palestinians, who are intentionally disappeared in this Zionist framework are likewise made to be already absent in the human rights context that forecloses the reparative means of return to an abstract articulation of international law rooted in colonial conceptions of the world which sees Palestinians as inevitably always already displaced. Neither structure leaves room for an understanding of return that would untether the lands, bodies, and waters of Palestine from the ongoing tragedies of ecological and imperial violence. The profoundly settler-colonial nature of the foundation of Israel by way of the dissolution of Palestine continues to be refracted in the deep waters of ideological and imperial violence that have led to the rupture of Palestinian society and history and the denial of the right to return in favor of the law of return. These spatial, temporal, and tangibly settler colonial forms of violence have consequences that impact both Palestinian human bodies and bodies of water. The magnitude of the violence enacted on both resonates in the ways in which the Jordan River has come to represent a border separating between the history of Palestinian's mass displacement and the possibility of Palestinian return. The river mediates between a spatial and temporal threshold, and as we can infer from its reduction to barely a trickle, attests to the dire ecological impact of such disjunctions of indigenous bodies and bodies of water.

The photographs of the Palestinians forced over the Jordan River in 1967 therefore exceed the temporal and interpretive parameters of the UNRWA archive. These images do more than document an event of mass displacement in a chronicle of catastrophes wrought against Palestinians. Though they do this too, they also allow for an engaged reading of the Jordan River's degraded and exploited condition as a staging of ecopolitical refusal. The photographs contribute to this reading a locatable site/sight of a crime that did not necessarily begin, but was consolidated, with the forced separation of the

Palestinians from the river that has sustained the diversity of local life worlds for centuries. There is a legible synchronicity between the river's refusal to flow and the Palestinian refusal to relinquish the right of return, neither to the oppressive settler state that has worked to prohibit and punish this right nor to the reductive limits of return rooted in nation-state validating laws and concessional international politics. Miraculously, and devastatingly, in the absence of the Palestinians forced over its banks, the Jordan River refuses to flow. And as the mouth of this river closes, no longer sourcing the Dead Sea below it, further ecological impacts are literally shaking the ground upon which these cycles of catastrophe are maintained.

The Dead Sea Sinkholes as the Land's Revenge

The Dead Sea is located at the lowest terrestrial point on Earth, 430 meters below sea level.[34] It is a hypersaline lake known for the restorative and healing properties of its mineral saturated water and mud. Since the 1980s, due to a negative water balance, the shores of the Dead Sea have receded by approximately one meter every year and they continue to dissipate at this rate.[3536] The degradation of the Dead Sea shoreline therefore renders legible the impact of Palestinian absences, which can be quantified in the calculus of years and meters of receding shoreline. I witnessed my father count his years of absence from the sea in the meters of exposed beach that day in July as we stood at its shores. Such shoreline reading practices, in the context of settler colonial occupation, wherein the imperial tools of choice have been land enclosure and Indigenous dispossession, entails, as Said has contended, that we must take seriously the stories, agency, and expressions of the Palestinian landscape.[37] In *Culture and Imperialism,* Said argues in greater depth that:

> If there is anything that radically distinguishes the imagination of anti-imperialism, it isthe primacy of the geographical in it. Imperialism after all is an act of geographical violence through which virtually every space in the world is explored, charted, and finally brought under control. For the native, the history of colonial servitude is inaugurated by the loss of locality to the outsider; its geographical identity must thereafter be searched for and somehow restored . . . . Because of the presence of the colonizing outsider, the land is recoverable at first only through imagination.[38]

In other words, the Palestinian landscape registers as both a site and a sight of memory making, for the Palestinians, and historical erasure for Israeli hegemonic state narratives and requires speculative and imaginative readings that can attend to "the loss of locality" Palestinians have endured for over seven decades. This essay is an exercise in anti-imperial and restorative landscape reading of bodies of water that are deeply implicated in human and non-human ecologies that have at different moments sustained or drained them.

In his comprehensive study of hydro-politics and hydro-hegemony in Israel/Palestine, Mark Zeitoun studies the phenomenon of the collapsing Dead Sea shoreline.[39] As the shoreline of the Dead Sea continues to recede, subterranean caverns caused by groundwater erosion have started to form under the surface of the exposed beach where the salt and mineral rich lake water used to be. The receding water has resulted in the collapsing of the bared shoreline into thousands of sinkholes that began to form in the 1980s and range in size from as large and as a deep as a city block to as small as a footprint.[40] The sinkholes, Zeitoun argues, are one of many detrimental environmental effects caused by Israel's hydro-hegemony and systems of water apartheid, which explicitly deprives Palestinians of access to water.[41][42] Israeli geologists have struggled to predict and control the spreading of the sinkholes, which have caused massive damages to settler properties and settler-only roads illegally located in the West Bank causing substantial losses in revenue to Israeli spas and tourist beaches around the Dead Sea, some of which have been abandoned because the exposed shorelines around them have already collapsed or threaten to collapse at any time.[43] No one has been seriously injured by the sinkholes, which seem to expressly target settler-owned tourist properties, which, Zeitoun argues, "may intimate Nature's capacity for defiance."[44] Taking this interpretation further, Zeitoun mentions that many of his Palestinian interlocutors, some of whom are now living in exile on the Jordanian side of the Dead Sea, have accordingly referred to the sinkholes that have swallowed Israeli-only apartheid roads and Israeli resorts on land stolen and occupied since the 1967 *Naksa*, as the 'land's revenge.'[45]

Reading the sinkholes as part of the land's revenge for the environmental *Nakba* requires an understanding of the profound place that the landscape holds in Indigenous Palestinian social, cultural, and political imaginations and practices. In a special issue of *Science for the People*, on "Science Under Occupation," Mazin B. Qumsiyeh and Mohammed A. Abusarhan attest that, "Humans and nature have been intertwined in Palestine for thousands of years, and the continuing loss of biodiversity irreversibly damages Palestine's cultural and natural heritage, threatens endangered species, and harms agriculture and environmental sustainability."[46] Salih and Correy recount that in many of the oral narratives they collected from Palestinian elders – now scattered in refugee camps in surrounding Arab countries – they reminisced on life prior to the rupture of 1948 as the "'natural life' (haya tabi'ie) (Salih, 2017 and forthcoming), a cosmological notion encompassing human and non-human rhythms."[47] Palestinian artist Jumana Manna contends that as a result of the *Nakba*, which ruptured these traditional ways of Palestinian "life guided by cross-species care," "Palestinian society at large is now becoming detached from its historical intimacy with the land, which only two or three generations ago was a central part of Palestinian life."[48] These modalities of sustainable and restorative life based in "cross-species care," and connected to the land are not, however, irretrievably lost.[49]

Dene scholar Glen Coulthard's concept of "grounded normativity," provides an important language with which to articulate the radical potential of reconnecting Indigenous bodies and practices with Indigenous lands, and in this case, the shores, coasts, and river banks that comprise Palestine.[50] For Coulthard, grounded normativity centers "the modalities of Indigenous land-connected practices and longstanding experiential knowledge that inform and structure our ethical engagements with the world and our relationships with human and nonhuman others over time."[51] The destruction of Indigenous homelands has been a central tenet of settler-colonial Anthropocentric violence for centuries on Turtle Island and in Palestine and continues today. In the case of Palestine, grounded normativity has been brutally interrupted by the Zionist project of colonization, which is predicated on the removal of Palestinian presence on the land and the rupture of traditional Palestinian land-based intimacy to undermine these deep ecological entanglements. Therefore, for Palestinians who have been forcibly displaced from their homelands, the ecopolitical phenomenon of the Dead Sea sinkholes registers as the land's refusal of the ongoing catastrophe or *Nakba* of mass displacement and environmental degradation.

Leanne Betasaomsake Simpson advocates similarly to Coulthard, for a reconfiguring of Indigenous epistemology that foregrounds the land as pedagogy, rooted in Anishinaabe grounded normativity. Simpson asserts that attempts at studying, protecting, conserving, tending, foraging, and harvesting on the land – all crucial components of Anishinaabe and Palestinian life respectively – "inevitably means coming face-to-face with settler colonial authority, surveillance and violence because this practice places Indigenous bodies in between settlers and their money."[52] For Palestinians, it has also meant that the foraging of culturally significant herbs and plants like za'atar and akkoub have been rendered illegal under so-called preservation laws such as the "National Parks, Natural Reserves, and National and Memorial Sites Law of 1998."[53] These thinly veiled settler laws that are framed as environmental conservation are really meant to alienate Palestinians from the land and traditions that have sustained diverse and entangled human and non-human life worlds for centuries. When Palestinians continue to be on the land and return to the land, it is "an act of both survival and anti-colonial resistance."[54] Every attempt to reclaim grounded normativity is thus a practice of refusal. And if we read the sinkholes as an inversion of this concept – an ungrounding of colonial normativity – we might understand the spectacular phenomenon of subterranean cavities and unmitigated sinkholes emerging underneath the occupied shores of the Dead Sea as both an environmental *Nakba* and a form of ecopolitical refusal.

In the winter of 2020, Palestinian artist and photographer Rehab Nazzal travelled to the Dead Sea to photograph its receding and collapsing shores. In a conversation I had with Nazzal, during which she showed me these photos, she recounted that upon arriving to the areas around the Dead Sea, now fenced in and deemed a "Closed Military Zone" or "closed nature reserve" she was immediately confronted by an Israeli Occupation Forces military jeep that sped towards her.[55] The heavily armed soldiers that emerged from the jeep ordered her to leave, claiming that she, an Indigenous Palestinian woman, was trespassing. This was not the first time that Nazzal has faced reprisal for her artistic practice by the Israeli Occupation Forces;[56] every time she points her camera she is perceived and treated as a threat, her body positioned radically and vulnerably between settler soldiers and the land a century of colonization has turned ethno-racially prescribed Jewish property.[57] Nonetheless, Nazzal was able to photograph the Dead Sea and the sinkholes around its shores despite, or rather, in spite of this confrontation. Nazzal's photographs of the Dead Sea are therefore taken from the precarious position of a Palestinian photographer made infiltrator, or "trespasser," according to the language of the signage posted on fences that wrap around the seized lands around the Dead Sea.[58] They are resistance photographs of a resistant landscape.

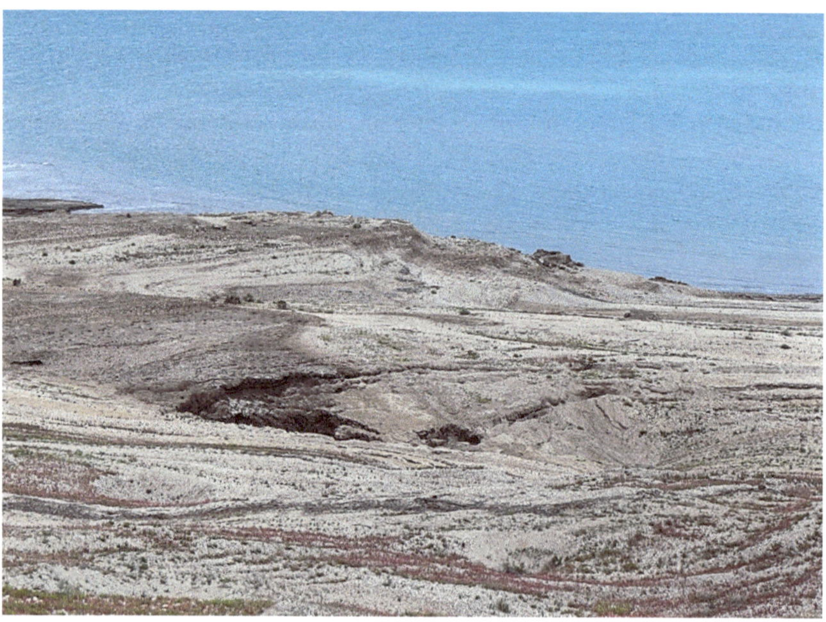

Figure. 6.2: Rehab Nazzal, West Bank, Dead Sea Sink Holes, near Ein Fashi, Feb. 2020. Photo courtesy of the artist.

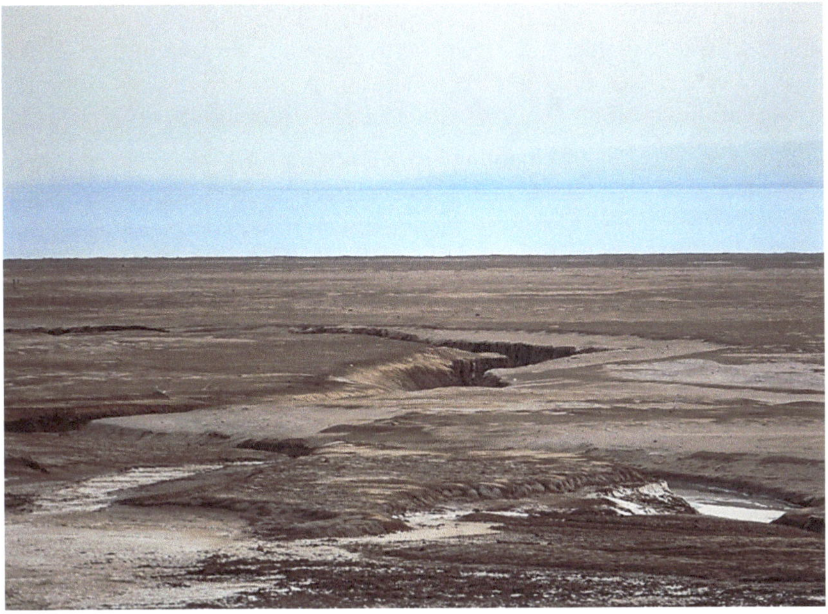

Figure 6.3: Rehab Nazzal, West Bank, Dead Sea, near the only Palestinian surviving salt factory in the area, January 2020. Photo courtesy of the artist.

The first photograph, taken in the West Bank near the Palestinian village of Ein Fashi in February 2020, shows a massive sinkhole near the sea's edge (see figure 6.2). The collapsed shoreline occurs in a slight dip of the ground. The astonishing blue of the water stands in stark contrast to the sandy taupe of the land between the photographer and the sea, which is dotted with bright burgundy and green vegetation. Another photograph by Nazzal taken a month earlier in January captures another sinkhole that looks slightly more sinister and cavernous (Fig. 6.3). It is located near the last surviving Palestinian Dead Sea salt processing factory where Nazzal also visited. The calm hazy blue of the sea and sky above the reddish shores of the beach again stands in distinction against the menacing sinkhole in the middle ground of the frame. In addition to the ethereal and ominous beauty of the photographs, they also demonstrate a moment of concomitant refusal between a displaced Palestinian returned to the landscape with photography acting as the mediator of this encounter. The images allow for a multifaceted reading of the landscape of the Dead Sea and the deep implications of the imperial conditions under which the photographs and sinkholes are co-constitutively made. The photographs are documents of the environmental Nakba but also exceed the frame of the documentary. They are a testament to the ongoing violence of the Israeli settler-colonial system of simultaneous environmental and human *Nakba* and a moment of potential repair between Palestinian bodies and bodies of water. More than simply capturing the sinkholes, Nazzal's photographs and the conditions under which they were taken, shared, and shown, between her camera and my screen and now yours, are part of a markedly Palestinian process of unravelling the colonial distinction between human and natural catastrophe.

Reframing ongoing and looming ecological disaster as ecopolitical refusal reaffirms the deeply entangled relations of Indigenous human and non-human entities in Palestine. It restores agency to Palestinians and the lands and seascapes of Palestine and the relations between these indiscrete bodies. Reading the sinkholes as the Dead Sea's staging of ecopolitical refusal reaffirms the deeply entangled relations of Indigenous human and non-human life in Palestine. The interconnected conditions of the river and the sea and all other human and non-human bodies of water that shape and define Palestinian life intersect and converge in deeply relational systems. The sinkholes rupturing the shorelines around the Dead Sea demonstrate that when these relations are disrupted, entire systems can collapse. Nazzal's photographs are both a testament to and disruption of this collapse. They document a moment of possible, reparative grounded normativity between the photographer, sea, and viewer, amidst the enforcement of colonial systems of destruction that far exceed the limited scope of climate catastrophe alone. Even more than articulating "the land's revenge," the Dead Sea sinkholes offer an opportunity to reckon with the intertwined catastrophes of the parallel environmental *Nakba* and ongoing human *Nakba* imposed on Palestinian lands, waters, and people. It is the remarkable phenomenon of a Palestinian shoreline that refuses its colonization in parallel with the ongoing resistance of the Palestinian people.

Decolonizing the Anthropocene: A Palestinian Hydrocommons

On the relation of human and non-human bodies of water, post-humanist feminist scholar Astrida Neimanis, makes a case for an ontological recalibration of the "interbeing of bodies of water."[59] In her essay "Bodies of Water, Human Rights, and the Hydrocommons" (2018), Neimanis attests that, because of the profound interpermeability of our largely water-constituted bodies with other bodies of water, water is an inherently social, cultural, and political entity that is irreducible to the individualistic logic at the nexus of neoliberalism, capitalism, and human rights rhetoric and structures. Neimanis asks: "What might shift if we more overtly acknowledged our bodies, not only as objects of enclosure, but as agents and tools of resistance, as gestational matter for the commons to come?"[60] This question opens the discursive and radically material potential of our watery bodies in relation to other human and more-than-human bodies of water. There are, however, limits to the viability of this framework when the bodies of water in consideration are differentially governed.[61] The colonized bodies of water that comprise the occupied Palestinian hydrocommons pose obstacles to the abstract posthumanist feminist theory of the potential recuperation of the commons, or our shared world, as a hydrocommons that is indivisibly interconnected. For over 70 years, Palestinian bodies of water have been striated under an apartheid regime forged under settler-colonial occupation. From centuries of Ottoman rule to the British Mandate, to the Israeli State now, Palestinian bodies of water have been increasingly restricted from the interpermeability Neimanis claims as a universal virtue of the commons to come. There can be no discussion about a hydrocommons in Palestine that does not first reckon with the colonial commons that defines Indigenous Palestinian and Israeli settler relations with the lands and waters and Others whose inter/impermability are structured by protracted colonial enclosures.

Neimanis's concepts of interpermeability and the hydrocommons are nonetheless interesting propositions to think about in tension with the hydro-political hegemony of Israel over Palestine. The waters that sustain both geopolitical communities, like the communities they sustain – are in the same place but governed differentially. It is common to talk about Israel and Palestine as entirely separate entities, and indeed the two geopolitical realities are very different in many ways, but nonetheless have been bound together over decades of colonization. Israeli settlers and Palestinian natives inhabit the land together across the different enclaves and open-air prisons Israel has imposed over the decades. This mutual existence is not defined by interpermeabilty, but rather by vastly different relations of power and subsistence that legitimize Israel's systems of institutional, environmental, and military violence and delegitimize Palestinian existence. Literature on the commons as an anti-colonial and pre-capitalist form of community practice and relationality to the land that predates the enclosures of modernity points to the irreconcilability of different Indigenous practices of the commons versus the imposition of colonial commons and property regimes[62] which Neimanis does not contend with in her postulations on bodies of water. Both colonial and precolonial systems of land tenure continue to exist in Israeli law[63] and Palestinian customs respectively, but they point to vastly different futurities.

In *Potential History: Unlearning Imperialism* (2019), Ariella Aïsha Azoulay introduces the concept of "worldly sovereignty" as a remedial term that mediates between the imposed and unqualified universalism of colonial world systems of domination and the life worlds that were destroyed in order to impose these new world regimes.[64] Worldly sovereignty exists both before and in constant opposition to the imperial sovereignty of nation-states and settler-colonial regimes across the world, which imposes a differential body politic that prioritizes one governed group over the others and "refers to the persisting and repressed forms and formations of being in the world, shaped by and through intimate knowledge of the world and its secrets, of its multiple natural, spiritual, political, and cosmological taxonomies preserved and transmitted over generations and shared among those entitled and invested to protect them."[65] Unlearning the universalisms of concepts like sovereignty, the commons, and the Anthropocene together creates the conceptual space necessary to imagine what a repaired hydrocommons situated in the worldly multiplicities of different modalities of agency, community, and care requires and could mean. Unlearning the colonial assumptions that render these terms self-explanatory or unilaterally applicable to all forms of life makes possible an alternative understanding of the temporal and spatial trajectory of diverse Palestinian ecologies. These ecologies have existed and continue to exist beyond the eco-political violence of the environmental and human *Nakba*. A repaired Palestinian hydrocommons is imaginable, but only when situated in and as a practice of worldly sovereignty that reaches beyond and before the violent imposition of imperial sovereignty that recalibrated our bodies of water as conquerable and divisible. It makes possible the imagining of a Palestinian hydrocommons rooted and reclaimed in decolonial practices of reparative human and non-human relations.

The case of Israel/Palestine takes Neimanis's limited conception of the hydrocommons to the limits of its applicability in a world maimed by imperial violence. Not all watery bodies are perceived equal under the systems of racial capitalist and settler-colonial violence that categorizes some bodies as worthy of life and others as disposable. Some bodies are made more porous, attenuated, or impermeable than others. The impenetrability of the colonial, carceral, and border regimes that govern Palestinian lives complicates the question of the Anthropocene beyond a reductive human-nature binary. For this reason, the hydrocommons requires further recapitulations of unlearning. When on July 3rd, 2021, Palestinian political prisoner Ghadanfer Abu Atwan escalated his hunger strike against his hold in Israel's system of uncharged and untried administrative detention to also include refusing water, he engaged in a form of ecopolitical refusal parallel to the other resisting bodies of water in Palestine.[66] Observing individual and collective hunger strikes and in escalated circumstances, refusing water, is a common form of individual and collective protest staged by Palestinian political prisoners. Leveraging the gross disparities of the colonial hydrocommons and courts, Abu Atwan and other imprisoned Palestinians like him have won better conditions, access to healthcare and release from confinement by subverting the "universalizing paradigm" of the Anthropocene[67] broadly, and the hydrocommons more specifically. As Abu Atwan's embodied protest demonstrates, to reach the potentially radical materiality of bodies of water/our watery bodies in the hydrocommons, we must engage in multiple rehearsals of unlearning and dismantling the colonial commons which forcefully encloses and separates Indigenous bodies from their lands and waters. Concepts like the Anthropocene also require unlearning because they have come to homogenize and obscure the origins of planetary violence, which have traceable roots in the destructive systems of capitalism and imperialism that continue to ensnare Indigenous lands and bodies in perpetual catastrophes. After 10 months of imprisonment without charge, and in critical physical health, Israel's Supreme Court was forced to release Abu Atwan from untried colonial captivity.[68] The use of water strike is a lesson in reclaiming the hydrocommons through embodied refusal. Abu Atwan's refusal is accordingly mirrored in the protests of the collapsing shores of the Dead Sea and drying banks of the Jordan River and all other bodies of water that comprise the Palestinian landscape. In deeply interconnected ways, these watery bodies and bodies of water are staging concurrent forms of ecopolitical refusal.

To begin to move towards a worldly watery sovereignty based in principles of reciprocity and care would mean reimagining these watery bodies beyond the carceral and colonial systems that impose differential material conditions on Palestinian lands, waters, and bodies. The ongoing ruination of Palestinian bodies and bodies of waters and the ancestral relations between them teaches us that environmental devastation is not just an effect of some abstract Anthropocentric era of the human but emerges from nameable imperial crimes and systems that arrange natives and settlers and land and property in violent hierarchal systems based on the nature-culture divide, race, class, and gender. These systems are proving themselves to be entirely unsustainable on local and planetary scales. As the curators of *Postcolonial Ecologies*, Joud Al-Tamimi, Firas Shehadeh, and Reem Marji attest, to begin to repair the colonial commons we must take seriously "as our point of departure that the pursuit of modalities based on interdependence, reciprocity and mutual aid is not a luxury, but rather, a matter of collective survival."[69]

The Dead Sea sinkholes and the draining of the waters of the Jordan River are telling signs of a ruptured hydrocommons caused by the ongoing Nakba against Palestinian lands, waters, and bodies. These crises are inscribed in the photographs of the Palestinians fleeing over the Jordan River, Rehab Nazzal's photographs of the collapsing shoreline around the Dead Sea, and the human and non-human testimonies of these intersecting catastrophes. If we attune ourselves to the stories that the drying river and dying sea tell, it becomes exceedingly apparent that the current settler-colonial regime is ruinous to all the human and non-human life forms and ecological entities that have been continuously dispossessed under colonial rule and imperial order. Reading these photographs, materials, landscapes, and testimonies together reflects the intimate entanglement of the life worlds represented and attended to by them.

Reading the concurrent catastrophes of the human and environmental Nakba together furthermore presumes that in the context of global climate crises, the Palestinian *Nakba* is not a Palestinian burden alone. The ecopolitical forms of refusal staged by the Jordan River and the Dead Sea against the multifaceted *Nakba* exist in tandem with multitudes of other forms of resistance. Reaching and repairing the hydrocommons, with the urgency of knowing it is a matter of collective survival, requires attending to these environmental crises in chorus with the testimonies of the photographs of these bodies of water and the cross-generational experiences of Palestinians both on the land and displaced from it and denied their rightful return. There is no path to the hydrocommons that does not contend with ending the environmental and ongoing *Nakba* that these bodies of water intimate. The hydrocommons requires a radical embrace of worldly watery sovereignty, which would be incomplete without the decolonization of all Palestinian lands and waters and the return of the Palestinians forcibly dispossessed from them.

Notes

[1] Zoe Todd, "Indigenizing the Anthropocene," in *Art in the Anthropocene: Encounters among Aesthetics, Politics, Environments and Epistemologies*, ed. Heather Davis (Open Humanities Press, 2015), 243.

[2] There is much to be said also about the Mediterranean Sea and the coastal life of the Palestinians who lived there in vibrant cities now settled by Israel and depopulated of most of the Palestinians who lived there, though many remain within Israel's borders under second-class citizenship. The Mediterranean features prominently in Palestinian political imaginaries, arts, and culture, but for the purposes of narrowing the scope of this study and paying attention to less-studied bodies of water, I will focus specifically on the Dead Sea and the Jordan River.

[3] Friends of the Earth International, *Environmental Nakba: Environmental injustice and violations of the Israeli occupation of Palestine* (September 2013), https://www.foei.org/wp-content/uploads/2013/10/06-foei-palestine-report-eng-lr.pdf.

[4] Edward Said, "Palestine: Memory, Invention, Space," in *The Landscape of Palestine: Equivocal Poetry*, ed. Ibrahim Abu-Lughod, Roger Heacock, and Khaled Nashef (Birzeit: Birzeit University Publications, 1999), 12.

[5] Elizabeth M. DeLoughery and George B. Handley, "Toward an Aesthetics of the Earth," in *Postcolonial Ecologies: Literatures of the Environment*, ed. Elizabeth M. DeLoughery and George B. Handley (New York: Oxford University Press, 2011), 10.

[6] Todd, *Indigenizing the Anthropocene*, 244.

[7] Astrida Neimanis, "Bodies of Water, Human Rights and the Hydrocommons," *Topia: Canadian Journal of Cultural Studies* 21 (2018).

[8] Mourid Barghouti, *I Saw Ramallah* (New York: Anchor Books, 2003), 5.

[9] Nadera Shalhoub-Kevorkian, "Infiltrated intimacies: The Case of Palestinian Returnees," *Feminist Studies* 42, no. 1 (2016): 166-193, 171.

[10] Zena Tahhan, "The Naksa: How Israel occupied the whole of Palestine in 1967," *Aljazeera*, June 4, 2018, accessed June 15th, 2021, https://www.aljazeera.com/features/2018/6/4/the-naksa-how-israel-occupied-the-whole-of-palestine-in-1967.
[11] Zayneb Al-Shalalfeh, Fiona Napier, and Eurig Scandrett, "Water Nakba in Palestine: Sustainable Development Goal 6 Versus Israeli Hydro-Hegemony," *Local Environment* 23, no. 1(2018): 118.
[12] According to Zayneb al-Shalalfeh, et al in their article on the "water Nakba," Israel now pumps an unsustainable 600 million cubic meters of water from the Jordan every year to service illegal settlements in the West Bank.
[13] Hannah Boast, ""A River without Water": Hydropolitics and the River Jordan in Palestinian Literature," *Journal of Commonwealth Literature* 51, no. 2 (2016): 277.
[14] Hagai El-Ad, "We are Israel's Largest Human Rights Group – And we are Calling this Apartheid," *The Guardian*, January 2021. https://www.theguardian.com/commentis free/2021/jan/12/israel-largest-human-rights group-apartheid.
[15] Depending on citizenship status, Palestinians who hold privileged passports like mine, which is Canadian, can also choose to fly through the Tel Aviv airport, but the level of surveillance and security is known to Palestinians in the diaspora as being worse there so many opt for the more arduous route through Jordan.
[16] Isabel Kershner, "Photographs Tell a History of Palestinians Unmoored," *The New York Times*, November 28, 2013, https://www.nytimes.com/2013/11/29/world/middleeast/photographs-tell-a-history-of-palestinians-unmoored.html#:~:text=Together%2C%20 they%20immortalize%20the%. 20Palestinian,history%2C%20identity%20and%20 collective%20memory.
[17] Ariella Azoulay, "The Imperial Condition of Photography in Palestine: Archives, Looting, and the Figure of the Infiltrator", *Visual Anthropology Review* 33, no.1 (2017): 9.
[18] Isabel Kershner, "Photographs Tell a History of Palestinians Unmoored," *The New York Times*, November 28, 2013. https://www.nytimes.com/2013/11/29/world/middleeast/photographs-tell-a-history-of-palestinians-unmoored.html#:~:text=Together%2C%20 they%20immortalize%20the%
[19] Eve Tuck and K. Wang Yang, "Decolonization is Not a Metaphor," *Decolonization: Indigeneity, Education & Society*, vol. 1, no. 2, (2012): 5.
[20] Ruba Salih and Olaf Corry, "Displacing the Anthropocene: Colonisation, Extinction and the Unruliness of Nature in Palestine," *Environment and Planning E: Nature and Space*, 0 (2021), 15.
[21] Ibid, 16.
[22] Joseph Andoni Massad, *The Persistence of the Palestinian Question: Essays on Zionism and the Palestinians* (New York: Routledge, 2006), 38.
[23] Fatma Kassem, *Palestinian Women: Narrative Histories and Gendered Memory* (London; Macmillan; New York; Zed Books, 2011; 2013), 15.
[24] Patrick Wolfe, "Settler Colonialism and the Elimination of the Native," *Journal of Genocide Research* 8, no. 4 (2006): 388.
[25] Brenna Bhandar, *Colonial Lives of Property: Law, Land, and Racial Regimes of Ownership* (Durham: Duke University Press, 2018), 120-121. Bhandar makes the case that one important distinction of Israeli settler colonialism is that ownership of the land is not driven solely by "appreciable economic value" as it is in the case of European settler colonialism. Configuring a Zionist historical memory and national identity were if not

always, often, driving factors in the colonization of Palestine and the justifications employed by Israel to shroud the colonization of the land in the aftermath.

[26] Yousef Abu-Safieh, "The Radical Transformation of Palestine's Environment," *Al Jazeera,* May 2, 2012, (https://www.aljazeera.com/opinions/2012/5/2/the-radical transformation-of-palestines-environment.

[27] Rashid Khalidi, "Observations on the Right of Return," *Journal of Palestine Studies* 21, no. 2 (1992), 30.

[28] "Universal Declaration of Human Rights," UN General Assembly, 13 (II) (Paris, 1948), http://www.un.org/en/universal-declaration-human-rights/.

[29] Salman Abu Sitta, *Palestine-Israel Journal of Politics, Economics, and Culture* 15/16, no. 4/1 (2008), 24.

[30] Massad, *The Persistence of the Palestinian Question,* 25.

[31] Noura S. Erakat, "Whiteness as Property in Israel: Revival, Rehabilitation, and Removal," *Harvard Journal on Racial & Ethnic Justice* 31, (2015): 71.

[32] Massad, *The Persistence of the Palestinian Question,* 25.

[33] Said, "Palestine: Memory, Invention, and Space," 14.

[34] Ido Sirota, Ali Arnon, and Nadav G. Lensky. "Seasonal Variations of Halite Saturation in the Dead Sea," *Water Resources Research* 52, no. 9 (2016), 7151.

[35] Ibid, 7152.

[36] Simone Popperl, "Geologies of Erasure: Sinkholes, Science, and Settler Colonialism at the Dead Sea," *International Journal of Middle East Studies* 50, no. 3 (2018), 431. The negative water balance of the Dead Sea is caused by the diversion of the Jordan River by the Israeli National Water Carrier. The Deganya Dam located just below the Sea of Galilee allows Israel to siphon 800 million cubic meters of water for Israeli usage, preventing this water from reaching its rapidly shrinking terminus in the Dead Sea.

[37] Said, "Palestine: Memory, Invention, and Space," 12.

[38] Edward Said, *Culture and Imperialism,* (New York: Vintage Books, 1994), 77.

[39] Mark Zeitoun, *Power and Water in the Middle East: The Hidden Politics of the Palestinian-Israeli Water Conflict* (London; New York; I.B. Tauris, 2008).

[40] Popperl, "Geologies of Erasure," 427.

[41] Mark Zeitoun, *Power and Water in the Middle East,* 155.

[42] Koek, Elisabeth, *Water for One People Only: Discriminatory Access and 'Water-Apartheid' in the oPT,* (Ramallah: Al-Haq, 2013), https://www.alhaq.org/cached_uploads/download/alhaq_files/publications/Water-For-One-People-Only.pdf.

[43] Eetta Prince-Gibson, "The Dead Sea is Dying," *Slate,* September 2013, https://slate.com/news-and-politics/2013/09/the-dead-sea-is-dying-how-sinkholes-habitat-destruction-and-low-water-levels-are-destroying-the-middle-easts-most-famous-body-of-water.html.

[44] Zeitoun, *Power and Water in the Middle East,* 156.

[45] Ibid.

[46] Mazin B. Qumsiyeh, and Mohamed A. Abusarham, "An Environmental Nakba: The Palestinian Environment Under Israeli Colonization," *Science for the People* 23, no. 1 (2020). https://magazine.scienceforthepeople.org/vol23-1/an-environmental-nakba-the-palestinian-environment-under-israeli-colonization/.

[47] Salih and Corry, *Displacing the Anthropocene,* 10.

[48] Jumana Manna, "Where Nature Ends and Settlements Begin," *E-flux* #113 (2020), accessed January 3rd 2021, https://www.eflux.com/journal/113/360006/where-nature-ends-and-settlements-begin/.
[49] Ibid.
[50] Glen Coulthard, *Red Skin, White Masks: Rejecting the Colonial Politics of Recognition*, (Minneapolis: University of Minnesota Press, 2014), 13.
[51] Ibid, 14.
[52] Leanne Betasamosake Simpson, "Land as Pedagogy: Nishnaabeg Intelligence and Rebellious Transformation," *Decolonization: Indigeneity, Education & Society*, Vol. 3, No. 3, (2014): 19.
[53] Manna "Where Nature Ends and Settlements Begins".
[54] Ibid.
[55] Rehab Nazzal, conversation with the author, March 29, 2021.
[56] "Artist Rehab Nazzal Shot in West Bank." *Canadian Art*, December 15, 2015. https://canadianart.ca/news/rehab-nazzal-shot-in-west-bank/. In 2015, while Nazzal was photographing demonstrations by Palestinian youth against the occupation and rapidly expanding illegal Jewish settlements in Bethlehem, she was shot through the lower leg by an Israeli sniper. The Palestinian ambulance and paramedics that came to her aid were then pummelled with tear gas by the occupation forces, which is a gross infringement of international law that nonetheless was violated with impunity.
[57] Bhandar, *Colonial Lives of Property*, 121.
[58] Rehab Nazzal, conversation with the author, March 29, 2021.
[59] Astrida Neimanis, "Bodies of Water, Human Rights and the Hydrocommons," *Topia: Canadian Journal of Cultural Studies* 21 (2018): 166.
[60] Ibid., 176.
[61] Ariella Aïsha Azoulay, *Potential History: Unlearning Imperialism* (London; Brooklyn, NY: Verso Books, 2019), 398.
[62] Silvia Frederici, *Re-enchanting the World: Feminism and the Politics of the Commons*, (Oakland, California: PM Press, 2019), 79. See also Allan Greer, "Commons and Enclosure in the Colonization of North America," *The American Historical Review* 117, no. 2 (2012): 365-386.
[63] Patrick Wolfe, *Traces of History: Elementary Structures of Race* (London;New York; Verso, 2016), 215-216.
[64] Azoulay, *Potential History*, 387.
[65] Ibid., 388.
[66] "Israel to release Palestinian prisoner on 65th day of hunger strike." *Middle East Eye*. July 8, 2021, https://www.middleeasteye.net/news/israel-palestine-prisoner-ghadanfar-abu-atwan-release-65-day-hunger-strike.
[67] Todd, *Indigenizing the Anthropocene*, 252.
[68] "Israel to release Palestinian prisoner."
[69] Joud Al-Tamimi, Firas Shehadeh, and Reem Marji, "Postcolonial Ecologies," curatorial statement, Darat al Funun, March 9, 2021, https://daratalfunun.org/wp-content/uploads/2021/03/2021_PCE_Statement_en.pdf.

VII.

Three Lines in Space: The Aesthetics of Data Visualization of Sea-level Rise in the Research-based Artworks of Andrea Polli, Timo Aho and Pekka Niittyvirta, and Paul Maher

Jakub Zdebik

University of Ottawa

Abstract

In this essay, I analyze the multidisciplinary media artist Andrea Polli's project entitled *N.* (2005), which is "a real-time online sonification and visualization of the Arctic", eco-artists Timo Aho and Pekka Niittyvirta *Coastline Paradox* (2020)—a virtual cartographic visualization of global sea-level rise by comparing it to the relationship between the unknown and data collection; and artist-researcher Paul Maher's art research project, *Visualising Coastal Erosion & Sea-level Rise* (2014), that brings together the aestheticization of data through community involvement to represent the effects of global warming. All these artists combine climate data research and the aestheticization of information to produce art as a form of knowledge. In order to articulate visualization strategies, in an aesthetic context, that can capture hyperobjects such as sea-level rise triggered by global warming, I will focus on Steven Shaviro and Peter Sloterdijk's respective concepts of emergence and explication; the graphic visualization angle of Morton's notion of the hyperobject; and Gilles Deleuze and Félix Guattari's concept of the smooth and striated space. Shaviro explains through emergence how environmental emergencies come to the foreground of thought while Sloterdijk's explication does the same in the case of environmental terrorism; Morton provides a concept that deals with the impossibility of apprehending the climate crises, in this case, applied to the ocean; and Deleuze and Guattari's theory of the smooth and striated is adapted to express the quantification of vast spaces such as the ocean. The works of these theorists will allow us to contemplate the interlacing of data and aesthetics needed to represent hyperobjects too vast to be effectively captured by the imagination. What is the purpose of theory at a time global warming?

Keywords: hyperobjects, cartographies, eco-art, sea-rise levels smooth and striated space

***

"Climate change in itself," writes J. Hillis Miller, "is invisible."[1] In his essay, "Reading Paul de Man While Falling into Cyberspace," in which he assesses the power of theory to uncover the invisibility of environmental degradation, or at least to bear witness to the irreversible loss, Miller takes stock of the state of environmental and historical conditions at the time he is writing: "When I worked on this essay in an earlier form in July and August, 2011, the United States was experiencing the hottest year on record."[2] He catalogues the heat, the Colorado fires, the droughts and tornadoes, the floods and the power outages. Miller also lists the irreparable Antarctic ice melt contributing to raising the sea-levels. The Arctic is also counted: a much faster than anticipated "sudden melting of the entire Greenland ice-cap surface was reported in 2012, to the amazement of scientists..."[3] 10 years later, 2021 is the hottest year on record. On the coast of British-Columbia, more than 1 billion sea creatures were 'cooked' to death in the hottest heat wave ever to affect Canada.[4] Texas saw a massive power grid shut down because the winter weather had been unprecedented.[5] The ocean literally caught fire after lighting struck a gas pipeline leak in the Gulf of Mexico[6]. What more will happen in the next ten years that we will forget the floods in Germany?[7] Or how forest fires that raged on the west coast affected almost the entire continent? Records keep being broken for the largest sheets of ice detaching themselves from the polar icecaps. Despite the emergency affecting the globe, it is at the local level that it is perceived. At issue is perception of time and distance.

Miller's theoretical strategy is to bear witness, through allegorical projective textual analysis, to show the invisibility of global warming, by reaching from the 21st century to the mid-twentieth and then forward to the future. Miller privileges text to provide evidence of the increase of global warming over time. But visual art also has the advantage to bear witness to spatial conditions of global warming. However, the problem is in the dimensions. Art dealing with global warming as a subject struggles to capture dimensions in a representational form. It is a problem Kant already brought attention to through the concept of the Sublime and that had been incorporated into visual arts since Romanticism. But currently, in the era of big data, objects that are too large to grasp are called hyperobjects by Timothy Morton. Sea-level rise; atmospheric degradation; and, global warming have be categorized under the concept of the hyperobject which is ascribed to "massively distributed entities that can be thought and computed, but not directly touched or seen".[8] This concept is at work in the invisibility of global warming described by Miller a decade ago. So how can visual art capture these hyperobjects such as global warming or the ocean in representational terms? Morton offers a solution - graphic visualization is a strategy with the potential to grasp these boundless entities.

To represent hard-to-frame phenomena such as sea-level rise and polar ice cap disintegration, artists have mobilized graphic visualization for aesthetic purposes and vice-versa. In this essay, I analyze the multidisciplinary media artist Andrea Polli's project entitled *N.* (2005), which is "a real-time online sonification and visualization of the Arctic", eco-artists Timo Aho and Pekka Niittyvirta's *Coastline Paradox* (2020)—a virtual cartographic visualization of global sea level rise by comparing it to the relationship between the unknown and data collection; and artist-researcher Paul Maher's art research project, *Visualising Coastal Erosion & Sea-level Rise* (2014), that brings together the aestheticization of data through community involvement to represent the effects of global warming. All these artists combine climate data research and the aestheticization of information to produce art as a form of knowledge. In order to articulate visualization strategies, in an aesthetic context, that can capture hyperobjects such as sea-level rise triggered by global warming, I will focus on Steven Shaviro and Peter Sloterdijk's respective concepts of emergence and explication; the graphic visualization angle of Morton's notion of the hyperobject; and Gilles Deleuze and Félix Guattari's concept of the smooth and striated space.[9] Shaviro explains through emergence how environmental emergencies come to the foreground of thought while Sloterdijk's explication does the same in the case of environmental terrorism; Morton provides a concept that deals with the impossibility of apprehending the climate crises, in this case, applied to the ocean; and Deleuze and Guattari's theory of the smooth and striated is adapted to express the quantification of vast spaces such as the ocean. The works of these theorists will allow us to contemplate the interlacing of data and aesthetics needed to represent hyperobjects too vast to be effectively captured by the imagination. What is the purpose of theory at a time global warming? To set parameters, to understand the visually elusive, which in turn is easily denied. To show how things are unseen and yet the mechanism of the intangible is real. Miller's strategy to bear witness is, as he himself admits, a very human problem. He writes: "'Get ready. The end of the world is coming.' It is, perhaps, distinctively human to bear witness, to use language to testify that catastrophic climate change is happening and is going to happen".[10]

Emergence and Explication: background and foreground of thought

In 2017, Steven Desch, professor at the Arizona State University, proposed a plan to stem the Arctic ice melt-off through a flotilla of pumps and fans that would bring cold water from the depths of the ocean and sprinkle it on top of the existing ice therefore thickening the ice sheet.[11] The plan would require an immense number of floating pumps and a price tag of 500 billion dollars.[12] This plan is revelatory in the sense that it brings out, in verifiable fashion, the severity of the problem of global warming and its effects upon Arctic ice. The machine's potential use makes the problem of global warming visible. In this vein, Shaviro writes about the idea of making abstract notions visible through incongruence: "The sheer existence of a thing only becomes truly apparent to us when that thing emerges from the background, and stands out on its own account."[13] This intermingling between Desch's machine and the biome it purports to support, brings into view the complex network of the Anthropocene: "Today, in the era of globalization, and of what has come to be called the Anthropocene, our lives are increasingly intertwined with, and dependent upon, complex, widely distributed technical systems and networks".[14] Both the networks of information and "mega-entities," in this case the ocean, global warming and the melting of ice sheets, are coming into view. Shaviro engages with Morton's notion of the hyperobject to discuss the emergence of a thing paradoxically too large to see: "things are altogether real; but they are so "massively distributed in time and space" that we cannot ever see them as wholes or grasp them all at once".[15] Global warming is, on the conceptual and material level, hard to process aesthetically. It is in the same league as nuclear radiation, information-based conventional systems such as the internet and the stock market—things of which we can only have fleeting glimpses. These "things" are too large to comprehend—because they are too big to encompass by our senses, like aesthetic examples of the Kantian Sublime, they constitute invisible, yet real, and constantly evolving, backgrounds.

How does Desch's technological solution to melting ice caps fit into this? Shaviro explains that technological hyperobjects shape human existence: "If we engineer them, in various ways, they "engineer" us as well, nudging us to adapt to their demands. Automobiles, computers, and kidney dialysis machines were made to serve particular human needs; but in turn, they also induce human habits and behaviors to change".[16] But what if the planet had to be put on life support with the help of device such as Desch's machine?[17] Whether the Desch's pump system functions or not, or can be implemented, the idea of it, because of its absurd size, is already bringing attention to the background, the invisible hyperobject. The need for the pumps indicates a problem with the biome and brings attention to its function like Heidegger's broken hammer, or McLuhan's fish: we notice things "when they have stopped doing what we expect and need them to do. Thus, Heidegger says that we never really see a hammer until it is broken; and Marshall McLuhan says that a fish could never have discovered water".[18] But Desch's machine does more than simply draw attention to a broken biome; it also shows a basic condition for life, taken for granted, is compromised. This bringing of attention to the background, in real terms through abstraction, is what Sloterdijk theorizes with his notion of terrorism and the environment.

The modern era, according to Sloterdijk, came about following three conditions: the "practice of terrorism," "product design," and "environmental thinking".[19] Sloterdijk pinpoints the origins of the modern era as April 22, 1915, when French Canadian troupes were struck by a chlorine gas attack instigated by the Germans. War traditions, such as marksmanship, targeting, and individual responsibility, were abandoned in favor of an approximate destruction of life.[20] Sloterdijk writes, "The 20th century will be remembered as the age whose essential thought consisted in targeting no longer the body, but the enemy's environment. This is the basic idea of terrorism in the more explicit sense." [21] What the 1915 Ypres attack made clear was that the terrorist element is directly linked to a consideration of the environment, since, as Sloterdijk writes, modern terror is defined as "suppressing the basic prerequisites for life"— in this case of Ypres, air.[22] The gas taints the air, making the transparent apparent and making apparent in the term *explication*, in which explication reveals by making the background of operations visible. How does this making visible come into play with the link between terrorism and air condition? Sloterdijk argues that a terror victim's existence is made unsustainable through the "direct immersion in an unlivable milieu for a sufficiently long period of time".[23] In fact, this milieu is the intended target. Sloterdijk explains that terrorism "comprises a form of violence against the very human-ambient 'things' without which people cannot remain people".[24] An outcome of this strike against the ambient milieu of life has led to what he calls a "black meteorology," which looks at the functioning of "toxic clouds, or theory of unbreathable spaces."[25] With the noxious advent of modernism, the breathable air, the "atmospheric envelope[,] is transformed into something whose intactness or non-intactness is henceforth in question."[26] What was once mere invisible background is now thick with bristling affect. A chasm opens between the source of the theory— the gas attacks leading to gas chambers and the nomenclature of terrorism— and the art that this apparatus is meant to investigate. It could be seen as heavy-handed, profane, or purposefully inflammatory. But Sloterdijk is positing the conditions for our culture that come out of a tragic and inhuman past event that continues to this day to organize our thoughts and lives. And one stratum that this type of environmental tainting has affected is the art world. The slow-burning environmental "terrorist" event, in Sloterdijk's definition, in this case, the rising oceans, can be considered from the perspective of "explication":

making the element of danger be seen. But, the ocean, just like air, as a hyperobject, is just too massive to conceptualize, to perceive the lurking suppression of the conditions of life.

We have a certain intimacy with hyperobjects as conditions of life. For example, it seems to be almost statistical to say that the water content in the atmosphere has increased by five percent since 1960—not much, Morton says, but enough to make the weather alarming. But an alarming posture is taken towards a hyperobject when it emerges as the "condition" of life, as Sloterdijk explains, because, of course, "global warming is an object we're in."[27] Underneath an invisible dome, we are separated from the instant danger of space which instantly nullifies earthly forms of life. And yet, the set-up is tenuous - the atmosphere, the protective dome, the "glass screen" threatens our conditions of life. Morton explains this partly as an aesthetic problem: "as if the glass in front of a painting began to attack us with radiation, shooting ultraviolet beams onto our sensitive flesh".[28] Something that melts away in our vision all of a sudden emerges and makes it self-known in an alarming way: "Our experience becomes one of disgust and pain - a default position of an aesthetic that art normally displaces."[29] This is the way the aesthetics of the hyperobject call for a different kind of aesthetic, one that calls for a visualization not simply vision. Its "intactness or non-intactness is henceforth in question," as Sloterdijk states. The atmospheric terror, the assault on the conditions of life, were taken up by artists: art provides a form to the invisible.

Global Warming Hyperobject

In *Ecology without Nature* (2000), Morton sees ambient, or atmospheric, art as being close to science because it emulates one of the things that distinguishes science from art: that is, its relationship to knowledge. Art always has a footing in the familiar, the known: "Ambient art wants to make the unknown known, like science. But it also wishes to retain the flavor of the unknown, a certain mystifying opacity—otherwise ambient art would in fact be science."[30] Morton then questions the difference between art and science, between data collection in the case of science and the artistic manipulation of this data. In the latter case, "Ambient art predicts, or sets up the parameters for, certain kinds of unknown."[31] This relationship between the unknown and data collection can be seen in a work by Andrea Polli's *N.* (2005). Polli is an American environmental artist whose art engages with science and technology. A research-based artist, she presents her findings in the guise of public artworks, media installations, performances, and the curation of public events.[32] *N.* strives to grasp and present to a remote public the "last imaginary place on earth," the North Pole[33] which is "a real-time online sonification and visualization of the Arctic,"[34] since the Arctic is an indicator of global warming. In this work, data on meteorological fluctuation was gathered daily and then transformed through a method of sounding—or sound-based data interpretation—which was then broadcast in conjunction with a projection on a round screen of images of Arctic landscapes taken with what seems to be a utilitarian camera.[35] In fact, the network of collaborations set up by Polli to make this project viable seems to come from scientific research rather than art: "N. presents a sonification of Arctic weather data modeled specifically for this project by Patrick Market, meteorologist and snow and ice specialist at the University of Missouri, and imagery from the National Oceanic and Atmospheric Administration (NOAA) Arctic research program in a sound and visual representation of the climate and conditions at the North Pole from 2003-2006". [36] Moreover, most revealing is the provenance of the sound for the sonification: "A portion of the sound used in N. comes from live atmospherics and global electromagnetic transmissions of lightning from the INSPIRE VLF receiver at NASA's Marshall Space Flight Center. Audio engineered at Harvestworks, New York City by Ken Babb. Supported, in part, by a PSC-CUNY Research Foundation Grant".[37] This work is exemplary in the way information is shaped by data used by the artist to provide a glimpse at a hyperobject through information art. The work involves a circular screen showing the horizon the icy landscape and environmental information broadcast as sonification. Polli compares sonification to an eyewitness who can provide crucial but imperfect information about an event.[38] Visually, the dominant line on a quasi-monochromatic landscape is the feint horizon line dividing the circular frame in half. This line seems to hint at the Deleuzo-guattarian dictum stating there is no line between earth and sky. It can also be seen as a feint flatline in the landscape.

The Smooth and Striated as Measurements of the Ungraspable

How do we take care of mapping abstraction, charting hyperobjects or even sketching an approach to intangible actual object, like the ocean, on the plane of art? Vast spaces, such as deserts, steppes, sea ice, and oceans are "local spaces of pure connection,"[39] according to Deleuze and Guattari. The philosophers theorize immersive spaces through a duality of the smooth and striated as a mutually mutating measuring device. These spaces of pure connection are an immersive experience requiring many data points in order to process the orientation of an ever-changing geographical landscape: "Orientations are not constant but change according to temporary vegetation, occupations, and precipitation."[40] The visualization of such space is difficult because the space is shifting and must be inhabited to be processed: "There is no visual model for points of reference that would make them interchangeable and unite them in an inertial class assignable to an immobile outside observer".[41] The issues, again, seem to be grounded in local versus global perspective. Smooth spaces, like the sea, the desert or the Arctic are hard to capture in one point of view in constantly varying conditions. But a multiplicity of points of view can also be hard to process because the observer of the smooth space complicates the assemblage of the data into a unified whole, since they are also interpreting their own relationships through haptic means.

This is where the apprehension of smooth space gets more complex from a representational point of view when considering how these objects are captured through art. The Deleuzean conceptual persona of the nomad makes its appearance as an avatar shuttling between these abstract dimensions. In this case, we can fit the nomad persona onto the figure of the artist who reveals the invisible hyperobjects. As Tom Conley explains, the nomads also function on a smooth and striated duality therefore creating a fractal plane in the very explanation of the process of the relationship between the smooth and the striated:

> The nomad, the philosopher, and the scientist and artist alike are capable of creating spaces through the trajectories of their passages that move from one territory to another and from given striations on the surface of the world to smooth and intensive areas, areas that are tantamount to the folds and creases of events that vibrate in the body, itself a place that can be affectively spatialized in infinite ways.[42]

Deleuze and Guattari invite us to experience the hyperobject in one instance. As the philosophers clarify, the relationship between the nomads, in this case, the smooth space observers, cannot be bracketed in an abstract dimension from which to assess smooth space: "The interlinkages do not imply an ambient space in which the multiplicity would be immersed and which would make distances invariant; rather, they are constituted according to ordered differences that give rise to intrinsic variations in the division of a single distance".[43] Smooth space is apprehended through orientation (too close), distance (variable) and interlinkage (complicated) and demonstrates the aesthetic complexity of a smooth object, like say, the ocean, and the way that it cannot be made into a single, simple, static conceptual object. On the other hand, this trifecta of orientation, distance and interlinkage seems to have more determined functions when striation occurs: "Striated space, on the contrary, is defined by the requirements of *long-distance vision* constancy of orientation, *invariance* of distance through an interchange of inertial points of reference, interlinkage by *immersion* in an ambient milieu, constitution of a central perspective".[44] Thus, the local spaces of pure connection are constructed through striations. We can see how a striation of a space, like the ocean, can be appropriated, edited, redacted, and politicized, which, in turn, is a negative co-option of smooth space. But there is no line between the earth and the sky, as Deleuze and Guattari write, and so the relationship between smooth and striated is not simply one of the contraries. It is about gaining insight into boundless objects by considering objects and their relations not as differing categories but as a continuously variable condition of observation.

The relationship between the smooth and the striated, where the smooth gives rise to striated space,[45] is not clear-cut with the smooth being liberating and the striated being a bureaucratic grid imposed on the former.[46] In fact, they are ineradicably comingled—the smooth element grounds its surroundings. The ocean grounds the earth and makes striation possible: "The desert, sky, or sea, the Ocean, the Unlimited, first plays the role of an encompassing element, and tends to become a horizon: the earth is thus surrounded, globalized, "grounded" by this element, which holds it in immobile equilibrium and makes Form possible".[47] According to Deleuze and Guattari, the smooth, or what could stand in as Morton's hyperobject, is the limitless element giving rise to form through its relationship with striation. But perhaps closer to a romantic view of the sublime quality of the hyperobject as ungraspable, the smooth can be foreboding. Having given rise to the striated, now the striated casts the smooth as the "loathsome deep" where smooth means non-measured and menacing.[48]

What controls the limitless smooth space are striation of all dimensions: measurements, statistics, and organization. Even though smooth space is boundless and oceanic, it nevertheless needs "to be thought of in conjunction with its 'striated' counterpart, a space drawn and riddled with lines of divide and demarcation that name, measure, appropriate and distribute space according to inherited political designs, history or economic conflict".[49] Artists transform data into information transmitted in the form of lines as a way to show the boundlessness of the oceanic but also the loathsome depth. More precisely, the data artists use is based on quantifiable calculations and measurements. Like other self-propelling dualities in Deleuze and Guattari's philosophy (for example, the creative map and the redundant tracing that nevertheless need each other despite being each other's conceptual opposites), the smooth and striated continuously seek equilibrium in terms of representation. Therefore, we can apply Morton's "solve" for the ungraspable hyperobject which needs striations: it needs to be captured through visualization.

But with all its characteristics, how do we capture the hyperobject of the ocean, or more precisely, the ocean's rise. The way to do this, according to Morton, is by capturing the effects of a hyperobject and not the thing itself. Morton suggests the link between the function of philosophy and the function of the visual diagram: "Process philosophy helps us to visualize how high-dimensional entities execute. Thus, a slightly upgraded way of seeing hyperobjects would be the *plot* or *graph*".[50] We are reminded that Polli, to show the Arctic, resorts to visualizing the northern smooth space which is out of reach to so many through distance and imagination. She uses visualizing, or sonorizing strategies to make global warming and the Arctic circle visible. The artist brings about the notion of visualization as showing, making the hyperobject visible through data-driven representation. Similarly, Morton explains how Phase Space—in dynamical system theory, a space where all possible states of a system are represented, often through complex and dynamic diagrams—requires plots and maps of algorithms to map climate: "The arithmetical calculations, called floating-point operations ("flops") that climate mapping requires are measured in petaflops, namely one million billion per second (1015)".[51] We are here dealing with numbers so large that a necessary mediation of the data operates at post-human levels of function; we are far from any possibility of accessing this information based on feeling. The transformation of the data into visualization is also part of the inaccessible function: "The graphics that draws attractors is not for providing an incidental visual aid but is instead the scientific work as such".[52] The visualization, in this case, is part of the process of the determination of information and not an ancillary function of transmission of the data as information for functional or interpretative outcomes. Time and space have to be considered not as an "aesthetic container" but rather are part of phase space: "Time is now radically inside objects, rippling through them .... And space is inside objects, differentiating their parts from one another."[53] But the dynamic phase space, the multi-dimensional possibilities generating attractor, is not perceived aesthetically, rather it must be plotted through mediation: "The trouble is that we cannot help but fail to see such high-dimensional entities when they are plotted in this way. Software "sees" them for us, then we see data or slices of that phase space, rendered in some way to make it usable."[54] For Morton, then, hyperobjects are multi-dimensional objects that cannot be perceived directly. They need a great level of mediation, but not because they are abstract to begin with, rather because a level of abstraction is necessary to comprehend their reality. And so, global warming, as a hyperobject, is real, without being visually apprehended: "Global warming is not simply a mathematical abstraction that doesn't really pertain to this world. Hyperobjects don't inhabit some conceptual beyond in our heads or out there. They are real objects that affect other objects".[55] This is why a reconfiguration between philosophy and science, and even between materiality and transcendence, is necessary within philosophy: "Indeed the philosophical view behind thinking that objects are one thing and relations ... are another positively inhibits our transition to an ecological age...."[56] Morton invites us to think about discreet things and abstract things as hyperobjects. Both objects and relations between objects are part of the same process. This dynamic relationship is at the heart of Deleuze and Guattari's smooth/striated concept. And this is why for Deleuze and Guattari smooth and striated space is more than just a way of considering a static landscape or an abstract calculation of aesthetic space, but rather constant, dynamic negotiations between the haecceity of things: "It is true that the number is the correlate of the metric: magnitudes can striate space only by reference to numbers, and conversely, numbers are used to express increasingly complex relations between magnitudes, thus giving rise to ideal spaces reinforcing the striation and making it coextensive with all of matter".[57] The object and its relations are considered at the same time. The smooth and striated are a way of capturing imperceptible objects through their abstract relations.[58] The relations generated by the smooth and striated can be perceived by the nomad, the artist. And informational aesthetic, or ambient art, as defined by Morton, which requires research, data, and the manipulation of information, contribute to the emergence and explication of the hyperobject.

Mapping Abstract Lines

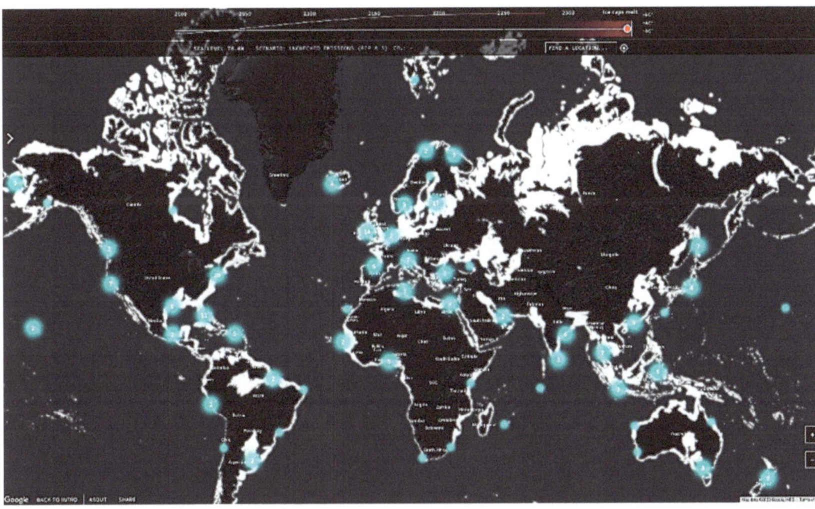

Figure 7.1: *Coastline Paradox* 2020, experimental artwork by Timo Aho and Pekka Niittyvirta in collaboration with Google Arts & Culture using data from Climate Central and the IPCC. Image courtesy of the artists.

When it comes to art, the transmission of data into an aesthetically comprehensible information skips the line drawn between a transcendental understanding of a modernist unrepresentable and the postmodernist self-reflexive unrepresentability. In this case, we go one step further, when the artist is aware of the unrepresentability of post-human proportions of multidimensional and dynamic datasets through aesthetic categories primed for representation of visual information. Timo Aho and Pekka Niittyvirta are two Finnish artists. Aho is a multidisciplinary artist who works with installation, sculpture, and intervention. His work investigates the environment through societal structures by shuttling between reality and fiction.[59] Niittyvirta's photographic and video works often touch on the human impact on the environment by engaging with society, technology, and finance.[60] They consider their work *Coastline Paradox* as an "interactive online art experiment."[61] It allows the viewer to survey the global map and enter street views of hot spots to visualize the sea level rise in the next 300 years. Click "enter map" and you are presented with a dark map resembling a command center. The entire map is in night view, with illuminated lights indicating centers of human activity (Figure 7.1). Blue glowing dots can be clicked on the screen the street view of which areas may contain a neon-colored line indicating the height at which the water will rise. If the image does not contain a white light (you may be on a bridge), the message is nevertheless devastating as it reads that "Temperatures are incompatible with human civilization, the planet is largely rendered uninhabitable." The white neon line, precisely tracing the level to which the water will rise in a city, is elegant in its minimalist aesthetic (Figure 7.2). But its elegance reveals a cold ultimatum: whatever is below the line, will be submerged with water. Particularly telling, then, is our quick consideration of what is below the line. The sophisticated city architecture is no match for temperature incompatible with human civilization.

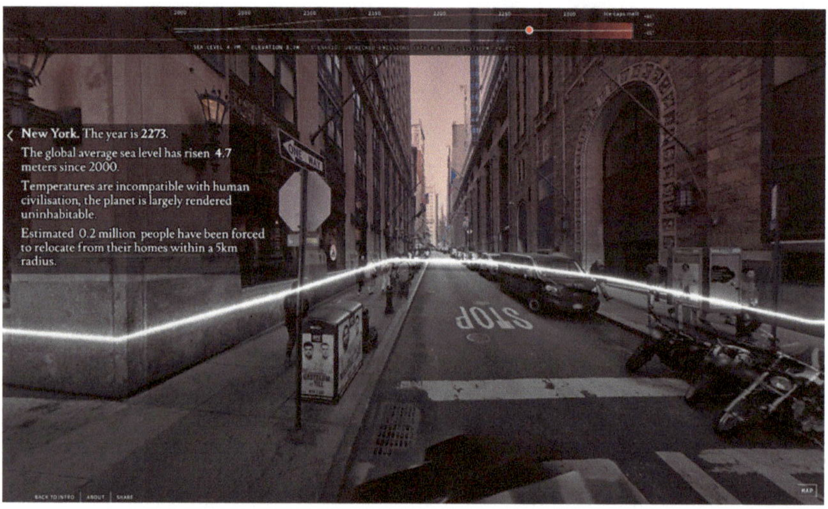

Figure 7. 2: *Coastline Paradox* 2020, experimental artwork by Timo Aho and Pekka Niittyvirta in collaboration with Google Arts & Culture using data from Climate Central and the IPCC. Image courtesy of the artists.

The interactive map of the *Coastline Paradox* was created after one of the duo's previous work *Lines (57°59'N, 7°16'W)* (2018–2019) which is an installation created in a remote Scottish coastal town which has already experienced the impact of global warming. The work involves a luminous line projected onto the landscape which shows the level to which the sea will rise in the future. With the help of this visualization, we can imagine how the rise of the sea level will impact the coastal area with its inhabitants and their use of the land.[62] The work's impact comes from the aesthetically economical eco-visualization light installation in the shape of a line: "light emitting diode neon-rope lights stretch horizontally across segments of the seaside community's landscape".[63] The light installation responds to an input of data: "Synchronized to tide data, the lights activate at high tide to indicate the potential tide level in the not-so-distant future".[64] The aesthetic quality of the visualization is important since it serves to communicate intangible data in a tangible way: "The line acts as a glowing warning—an elegant, visual marker of the impending impact of climate change. As climate projections are made visible within communities, once abstract, climatological data can become comprehensible for inhabitants".[65] In fact, the aesthetic of visualization, by transforming data into information produces a material effect on the viewer: "Through these sorts of tangible reminders, the public might be able to grasp the imminent realities of climate change and the need for drastic and swift social, environmental, and political action".[66] This relationship of art and data and its transformation into comprehensible information is at the heart of Aho and Niittyvirta's work: "We were hoping to pinpoint an important issue by the means of art: Art carries the potential to convey complex ideas, concepts and scientific data in a powerful way that other mediums, like texts or graphs may fall short of".[67] This sentiment conveys how the multifaceted way of conceptualizing smooth and striated space and how art features as a bonding element: "The creative process had a lot to do with a connection and co-existence between the contemporary society, development and oceans. We started the project within the context of physical positions of seaside communities and their futures".[68] In fact, the artists go as far as to say that it is art that can augment the tangibility of abstract visualization: "Art has the potential to convey scientific data...through this work, people can better visualize and relate to [the] reality".[69] Which is a testament to the communicative aspect of the line which allows for a clear understanding in such a minimalist form. The line not only carries quantifiable information, but it also carries an aesthetic history.

The simple line, aesthetically elegant, carries a lot of weight both as a mark of measurement in visualization in art installation but also from an art historical point of view. Here, Deleuze and Guattari, also can provide an aesthetic assessment close the minimal element of the line. They create mini-Hegelian aesthetic theory with three types of lines controlling the originary smooth space: a rectilinear line (Egyptian); organic line (Assyrian or Greek); and a supraphenomenal line (Chinese): these lines, that Deleuze and Guattari call imperial lines, make abstraction concrete: they "convert the abstract line, rend it from its smooth space, and accord it concrete values".[70] The line, which will become an aesthetic measure and manifestation of the smooth and the striated in artistic terms, demonstrates this battle of the forces of deterritorialization and reterritorialization with the progression of the history of art:

> Still, it can be argued that these imperial lines are contemporaneous with the abstract line; the abstract line is no less at the "beginning," inasmuch as it is a pole always presupposed by any line capable of constituting another pole. The abstract line is at the beginning as much because of its historical abstraction as its prehistoric dating. It is therefore a part of the originality or irreducibility of nomad art, even when there is reciprocal interaction, influence, and confrontation with the imperial lines of sedentary art.[71]

This line, or lines, which provide form to the boundless, are not simply a controlling grid that prevents a natural, unspoiled, utopian space to spread.

This relationship between art and the communicability of complex information, especially regarding sea-level rise, has been also worked out by Paul Maher, who works in Nova Scotia at the intersection of arts, visual communication, and planning at the junction of human culture and land use. The translation of data into visualization in the form of a line takes on particular significance in his *Visualizing Coastal Erosion and Sea-Level Rise* project. Maher's project features, much like Aho and Niittyvirta's experiments, a line delineating the level to which the sea will rise in a not-too-distant future. Whereas Aho and Niittyvirta's work is interactive by letting the viewer input data and browse a map on their computer screen, Maher's line depends on a more direct community involvement in which a group of volunteers place especially designed sandbags around a physical space to show to which level the sea will eventually rise. If Aho and Niittyvirta's line is minimal and virtual, Maher's line is physical and haptic. In Maher's case, the line is manipulated and materially interacts within actual space.

For Maher, the challenge was to effectively communicate the data regarding the projections of sea-level rises on a Nova Scotia coastal community. The aesthetics of visualization was a primary concern: "A number of key features are present in effective communication. Visualization material has long been known to convert the complexity of scientific jargon into readily understood information."[72] Maher was able to imagine and implement a strategy using another type of line from Aho and Niittyvirta, this time not a light projection, but a line traced in the community with sandbags:

> This visualization is a participatory art event, which takes an abstract mapping convention into a real-world context. Lines, which indicate the anticipated effects of climate change, such as coastal erosion or flooding, are taken off the map and enacted in real space. To mark out this line a series of sandbags are placed along a piece of ground in the location of an established scenario. These sandbags have been letterpress printed with words associated with adaptation planning.[73]

The issue with this line tracing was the communication of complex and often unpredictable sets of information: "Conveying the dynamic interplay between erosion, sea-level rise, storm surges and other effects is complex in nature and difficult to predict".[74] Maher created a participatory and interactive art project that provided a pedagogical aspect of the use of visualization of art in a targeted community: "project also identified that interactive visualization forms, like a floodable model or an interactive map, were more likely to be popular with audiences. These findings reinforced other research that found that scientific learning is enhanced through participatory activity."[75] The observer, at the center of the smooth space, as we saw in Deleuze and Guattari's smooth and striated model, interprets their position in the variable conditions of the milieu through a haptic, participatory processes. By creating a haptic line, a material line, the observer takes control of the shifting orientation in an increasingly changing geographical landscape: "In addition…art can communicate in ways that accommodate complexity. When at its best art can inform in nuanced ways that allow for multiple perspectives providing opportunities for debate and discussion to occur."[76] Just like Polli and Aho and Niittyvirta, Maher's project deals with the transmissibility of complex sets of data by turning them into aesthetic lines through artistic research and interpretation. The outcome of this work then, is to convey imperceptible information to an audience through aesthetic means.

In addition to Maher's painstakingly haptic line, informational art can manifest the image of an ocean through the line in different forms. The faint horizon line in Polli's work functions like a beacon to visualize Arctic ice, and Aho and Niittyvirta's line is neon white but communicates the loathsome depth of unchecked potentiality. The line has to do with display, participation, and activism. Through the data interpretation, visualization and aesthetic use of the line, these artists trace a path towards capturing the hyperobject.

What is the use of adding spilled ink to continuously raising waters, asks Miller: "All the ink we have spilt will only add to the flood, but it is better, I claim, more human-inhuman, to know what is happening than to be naïvely surprised by the rising waters".[77] He wonders what the purpose of theory is when confronted with auto-immune diseases, financial systems catastrophes brought about by post-human algorithmic technologies, or glacial ice collapsing into the ocean without global warming being reversed by carbon tax swaps. Understanding our species *modus operandi* is at stake. The smooth and the striated may conjure the rise of the ocean before our eyes, and the incomprehensibility of the hyperobject remains, the emergence and explication of atmospheric and all-encompassing systems can only occur when the said systems glitch. But trying to make sense of the distances, dimensions, and volumes of the environmental crises through lines drawn according to computed statistical data and speculative projections, does more than simply engage with a problem: the line point towards the exit.

Notes

[1] J. Hillis Miller, "Reading Paul de Man While Falling into Cyberspace", in Eds. Tom Cohen, Claire Colebrook, and J. Hillis Miller, *Twilight of the Anthropocene Idols,* (London: Open Humanities Press, 2016) 126-78; 192.
[2] Miller, *Twilight,* 128.
[3] Miller, *Twilight,* 128.
[4] Alex Migdal, *More than a billion seashore animals may have cooked to death in B.C. heat wave, says UBC researcher,* CBC.ca, July 5, 2021. https://www.cbc.ca/news/canada/british-columbia/intertidal-animals-ubc-research-1.6090774.
[5] "Another (counter-intuitive) example is the recent extremely cold and snowy winters in the United States, the worst on record in many places all the way down to the Gulf Coast, where snow and ice-storms of an intensity such as have occurred are exceedingly unusual. These winters have been accompanied by so-called "polar vortexes," a beautiful figure of speech". Miller, *Twilight,* 129.
[6] Maria Cramer, "Leaky Gas Pipeline Sparks an Inferno in the Gulf of Mexico", *New York Times,* July 3, 2021. https://www.nytimes.com/2021/07/03/world/americas/eye-fire-gulf-mexico.html?searchResultPosition=2.
[7] Henry Fountain, "Climate Change Contributed to Europe's Deadly Floods, Scientists Find", *New York Times,* August 23, 2021, https://www.nytimes.com/2021/08/23/climate/germany-floods-climate-change.html?searchResultPosition=1.
[8] Timothy Morton, "Poisoned Ground", *Symplokē* 21, no. 1–2 (2013): 37.
[9] Gilles Deleuze, and Félix Guattari. "1440: The Smooth and the Striated," *A Thousand Plateaus: Capitalism and Schizophrenia II.* Trans. Brian Massumi. (Minneapolis: University of Minnesota Press, 2005), 474-500.
[10] Miller, *Twilight,* 193.
[11] S. J. Desch et al., "Arctic Ice Management", *Earth's Future, 5,* 2017: 107–127, doi:10.1002/2016EF000410.
[12] This project was reported on in a Canadian Broadcasting Corporation radio program by Anna Maria Tremonte, "Can a $500 billion geoengineering project save the Arctic from melting?" cbc.ca, 20 February 2017, at http://www.cbc.ca/radio/thecurrent/the-current-for-february-20-2017-1.3988710/can-a-500-billion-geoengineering-project-save-the-arctic-from-melting-1.3990917.
[13] Steven Shaviro, "Thinking Blind", *Journal of the Fantastic in the Arts* 25, no. 2/3 (91) (2014): 314–31. http://www.jstor.org/stable/2435303, 314. https://doi.org/10.5250/symploke.21.1-2.0037.
[14] Shaviro, "*Thinking*", 14.
[15] Shaviro, "*Thinking*", 315 quoting Morton 207.
[16] Shaviro, "*Thinking*", 315.
[17] Peter Sloterdijk. "Spheres Volume 3: Foams: Plural Spherology", Translated by Wieland Hoban, South Pasadena: *Semiotext(e),* 2016, 295. "Whoever wishes to understand the island must build prosthetic islands that reproduce all essential characteristics of the nature island point for point in the technical replica."
[18] Shaviro, "*Thinking*", 31.
[19] Peter Sloterdijk, *Terror from the Air,* Trans. A. Patton and S. Corcoran (Los Angeles: Semiotext(e), 2009) 9.
[20] Sloterdijk, *Terror,* 13.

[21] Ibid., 14.
[22] Ibid., 15.
[23] Ibid., 16.
[24] Ibid., 25.
[25] Ibid., 23, 19.
[26] Ibid., 25.
[27] Morton, *Poisoned*, 40.
[28] Ibid., 40.
[29] Ibid., 40.
[30] Timothy Morton, *Ecology Without Nature: Rethinking Environmental Aesthetics* (Cambridge, Mass: Harvard University Press, 2009) 96.
[31] Morton, *Ecology*, 96.
[32] https://sites.google.com/andreapolli.com/main/bio
[33] https://digitalartarchive.siggraph.org/artwork/andrea-polli-joe-gilmore-n/
[34] "Data sonification means representing data as non-speech sound. The basic principles are similar to visualization, but where visualizations use elements such as lines, shapes, and colours, sonification relies on sound properties such as volume, pitch, and rhythm" (Jamieson) So that grooves and peaks on a chart read as low and high pitches, and the space the chart occupies, say, from left to right, could be read as a musical partition that unfolds over time.
[35] Andrea Polli, "Sonification of Global Environmental Data" *Environmental Sound Artists: In Their Own Words*. Ed. Frederick Bianchi and V.J. Manzo, (Oxford: Oxford UP, 2016): 5.
[36] https://digitalartarchive.siggraph.org/artwork/andrea-polli-joe-gilmore-n/
[37] Ibid.
[38] Polli, *Sonification*, 7.
[39] Deleuze and Guattari. *A Thousand Plateaus*, 493.
[40] Ibid.
[41] Ibid.
[42] Tom Conley, "Space" in Adrian Parr, (Ed.) "S." *The Deleuze Dictionary* Revised Edition, NED - New edition, 2 ed. (Edinburgh, University Press, Edinburgh, 2010), 262.
[43] Deleuze and Guattari, *A Thousand Plateaus*, 493.
[44] Ibid., 494.
[45] Ibid.
[46] In fact, Jon Protevi warns us against jumping too quickly to this conclusion: "Before we go any further, we should note that the production of smooth spaces by the armed forces and surveillance technologies of con- temporary States and quasi-State corporations, as well as the demand for identity cards and fixed addresses by asylum seekers, economic migrants, and other displaced persons, prevents any naive 'postmodernist' privileging of the smooth as somehow progressive or always beneficial and the striated as always retrograde and repressive. After all, the main text of *A Thousand Plateaus* ends with the line: 'Never believe that a smooth space will suffice to save us.' (Deleuze and Guattari, 1987, 500)," 92.
[47] Deleuze and Guattari, *A Thousand Plateaus*, 495.
[48] "However, what Deleuze identifies as the problem that will emerge in the spatiotemporal diagram of control society – a diagram, however, that was only the 'just coming into view' – is the existence of an 'outside' that is composed of 'Reimanian patches' of unstriated or unstratified forces. These forces, however, are determined neither by enclosure nor analogy,

thus creating the possibility of new un-encoded elements and a greater degree of movement between spatiotemporal relations that appear outside their former enclosures.
Gregg Lambert, 'Notes from an Investigation of 'Control Society' *Control Culture: Foucault and Deleuze after Discipline* Ed. Frida Beckman (Edinburgh: Edinburgh University Press, 2018), 23.
[49] Conley, *Space*, 261-62.
[50] Morton, *Hyperobject*, 73.
[51] Ibid.
[52] Ibid.
[53] Ibid.
[54] Ibid.
[55] Ibid.
[56] Ibid.
[57] Deleuze and Guattari, *A Thousand Plateaus*, 484.
[58] This is not exactly next-level thinking, but it is something that the world discovers again and again, especially now, in the midst of a pandemic when supply chains, which have been an afterthought for most of the population really hit home. Or the lack of understanding that closing discreet boarders won't block plane trajectories.
[59] Timo Aho, http://www.timoaho.org/about/, accessed July 21st 2021.
[60] Pekka Niittyvirta, https://niittyvirta.com/cv/ , accessed July 21st 2021.
[61] Ibid.
[62] K. Urban Lee, "Public Space as a Didactic Platform: Raising Awareness of Climate Change through Experiencing Arts," *Sustainability*, 2021: 13(5), 2915. 2, https://doi.org/10.3390/su13052915.
[63] Kayla P. Dean, and Joy G. Bertling, "Eco-Visualizations: Facilitating Ecological Relationships and Raising Environmental Awareness," *Art Education* 73 (3), (2020): 54–61, 58. doi:10.1080/00043125.2020.1717823.
[64] Dean and Bertling, *Eco-Visualizations*, 58.
[65] Ibid.
[66] Ibid.
[67] Amy Brady, An Interview with Artists Timo Aho & Pekka Niittyvirta, 2019, https://artistsandclimatechange.com/2019/05/06/an-interview-with-artists-timo-aho-pekka-niittyvirta/
[68] Gunseli Yalcinkaya, "Lines Light Installation Demonstrates the "Catastrophic Impact" of Rising Sea-Levels". *Dezeen*, 2019, np., https://www.dezeen.com/2019/03/18/lines-pekka-niittyvirta-timo-aha-light-installation/
[69] Ibid.
[70] Deleuze and Guattari, *A Thousand Plateaus*, 497.
[71] Ibid.
[72] Paul Maher. "Visualising Coastal Erosion & Sea-level Rise: Integrating Art and Design within a Community Engagement Process," https://climatechange.novascotia.ca/sites/default/files/uploads/2013-2014_EAC.pdf, 4.
[73] Maher, *Visualising Coastal Erosion*, 13.
[74] Ibid., 7.
[75] Ibid., 6.
[76] Ibid.
[77] Miller, J. Hillis, "Paul de Man at Work: In These Bad Days, What Good is an Archive?", Eds, Tom Cohen, Claire Colebrook, and J. Hillis Miller, *Theory and the Disappearing Future: On de Man, on Benjamin* (London: Routledge, 2012), 88.

VIII.
The Ocean Behind Glass

Ian Buchanan

University of Wollongong

Abstract

As Susan Davis puts it in her book *Spectacular Nature*, aquariums are in the 'feelings' business: they have to generate feelings of excitement and interest and they have to avoid "boredom, uneasiness, anxiety, disgust, and pity."[1] Nature isn't appealing – in the sense of compelling people to part with their money – all by itself, it needs to be framed in a particular way. In the early years of aquarium history, it was enough for them to render visible what had hitherto been invisible for them to generate enough astonishment and wonder to attract a paying audience. But that only lasted a few decades and aquariums soon found themselves searching for new ways to entice people through the turnstiles. In our own hyper-visual age, when scarcely anything has escaped the gimlet-eye of the camera, wonder in the face of the hitherto unseen is no longer sufficient, indeed it is barely adequate to compete with the many other visual delights constantly being generated by the culture industry. To generate the flow-through of customers, it needs to satisfy its commercial imperative aquariums were seemingly compelled to become more and more like the cinemas and theme parks their owners also have in their portfolios. No one has documented this aspect of aquariums more astutely than Davis who aptly describes public aquariums as "a mall with fish."[2] In order to find their point of difference from cinemas and theme parks, though, aquariums dressed their product in the noble robes of education, or what Davis terms 'edutainment'. But its message tends to be that the environment needs to be 'managed', and it instils the view that all of nature is somehow a resource for humans. Moreover, it frames this management in terms of one-to-one relations between individual humans and individual animals as though nature was somehow a vast assemblage of pets just waiting for their human owners to care for them.[3]

Keywords: Aquariums, fish, dead zones, assemblage theory, spectacle

***

> If Anna could not stay by the sea, she would have to bring the sea to the city. [4]
>
> – Rebecca Stott,
> *Theatres of Glass, The Woman Who Brought the Sea to the City,* 2003

As a child, I did not live near a beach or lake or river, at least not close enough for so-called 'wild water' to be part of my daily experience. But my grandmother had a small beach house on the southern coast of Western Australia, and I used to spend my summers there, swimming, surfing, and snorkeling. In those lazy days between the end and the beginning of school years, I would spend hours immersed in the ocean -- the sun scorching my back -- peering through the tiny screen of my goggles at the marine life below. The fish were not particularly abundant in the shallow coastal waters near my grandmother's house, so it took patience and diligence to find them in amongst the rocks and sea grass. Further from shore one could find plenty of fish, as well as sharks (including human eating varieties like white pointers) and even giant blue whales, but I was too young for such adventures. Whenever I did happen upon fish, I would hover above them trying not to disturb them, watching them as one might gaze upon a streetscape through a looking glass from a great height. The fish were mostly fast-moving and silvery, such as bream, whiting, and skipjack, but I'd also see pufferfish and other more sedate varieties too. I was fascinated by their comings and goings, there to-ings and fro-ings, and all their zigs and zags, as they went about the daily business of living and surviving. It was enchanting and I seemed never to tire of it as my horrendously blistered and sunburnt back could attest. I'm not sure why I enjoyed snorkeling so much, but I do recall being conscious of the fact that I was an alien in the ocean environment and desperately wanted not to be. In my idle moments, I wished I was Aquaman and could see and breathe underwater.[5] Dependent as I was on my goggles and snorkel, I was acutely aware of my estrangement from all that I surveyed. My mask was a window into another world, but it was a window I couldn't open.

For my 12th birthday, I was given an aquarium, or fish tank as I always called it, which was yet another variety of window that couldn't be opened. I'm not exactly sure why I wanted a fish tank, probably because it seemed like a logical extension of my love of snorkeling. My parents found a freshwater tank for sale in the classifieds section of the Sunday paper and bought it for me. I would have preferred a saltwater tank, so I could literally bring the ocean into my home, but the technology was in its infancy then and it was too expensive (for my family) to set up at home. The tank I ended up with was sizeable (i.e., it was more substantial than a goldfish bowl) and it came with a full complement of tropical fish, including the standard clutch of colorful Tetras, Guppies and Gouramis and a couple of tiny sharks. If I knew then what I know now about the dreadful way tropical fish were collected for sale I would not have been so keen on owning an aquarium. In the 1980s and 1990s cyanide was widely used to capture live fish for the aquarium market. This practice devastated the aquatic environments where it was used and posed a severe health risk to the fishers themselves, many of whom died of accidental poisonings.[6] So devastating is the live fish trade – the scale of which is mind-boggling, more than 20 million fish are caught each year, along with 12 million live corals – at least one critic has asked whether any responsible person can consider owning or visiting an aquarium.[7]

We set the tank up in the lounge room in the wall space that would typically be reserved for the TV in most houses – we had a TV, but it was in my parent's bedroom and my brother and I were very rarely permitted to watch it – and almost immediately it became a stand-in for the TV. However, it was my parents, rather than me, who got the most out of this gift. I quickly found the whole thing rather artificial and off-putting, not to mention tedious to keep clean and maintain, and happily ceded my sovereignty over it, and moved onto other interests (truth be told, I would have preferred an actual TV anyway). My parents, by contrast, would often spend their evenings sitting together on the couch sharing a bottle of homemade wine as they gazed at the tank, which functioned as a living screen, every bit as captivating to them as a digital screen. Now, instead of the movement of pixels their eyes were entranced by the movement of neon-lit fish and the gentle bubbling and swirling of the water. As eccentric as I thought my parents were for doing this, it turns out they were far from alone in treating their tank as a TV. In recent years there has even emerged a global 'fad' for old style TVs (i.e., not the sleek flat screens of today but the boxy old clunkers of yesteryear) converted into fish tanks, thus realizing in a more literal way what was already apparent in any case, namely that we approach the glass of the fish tank in identical fashion to the way we approach the screen of our TV.[8] However, as Jameson insists, we need to (always) historicize our perspective here and remind ourselves that the invention of the aquarium in fact precedes both the arrival of film and television.[9] I want to suggest that if the aquarium appears to imitate film and TV today, as I would claim it does, then it is because it belongs to the same technological phylum (as Deleuze and Guattari would put it), which can trace its origins back a few hundred years to the appearance of Wunderkammer, and not because it is a simulacra.[10]

As Brunner shows, without arguing it in this way, the aquarium brings together two trajectories of desire that were either current or reaching their apogee in European and North American society in the 19th and 20th centuries: the desire to collect and the desire to display. Although they are obviously related, these two desires are not identical because one does need to collect to want to display (as conspicuous consumption makes apparent), nor does one need to want to display to collect (as hoarding makes apparent). Aquariums made visible what had hitherto been invisible and in doing so, created a new world of opportunities for collecting which the Victorian world keenly accepted. The depths of the ocean were unknown and largely unknowable until the middle of the 19th century because the requisite technology needed to breathe and see underwater was lacking. These two desires (collecting and displaying) began to manifest themselves in a variety of ways from the late Renaissance onwards when cabinets of curiosities became fashionable, in step with European exploration and conquest of the non-European parts of the world, when sea-going vessels would bring back all manner of natural wonders. Some, like Australia's platypus and echidna, were so incredible they were assumed to be hoaxes, which were common. Over the years, these catch-all cabinets of curiosities gave way to more specialist and specialized passions and interests. In the 1700s, beachcombing and shell-collecting became fashionable, as did the keeping of exotic birds and ornamental poultry.[11] From there, it was a small step to collecting and displaying live marine creatures and plants.

Fish have been collected and kept in ponds and glass-sided tanks in Europe since Roman times and in China since at least the 10th century, but it wasn't until the late 1700s that people began to deal seriously and effectively with the technical problems of keeping fish alive in tanks in the home; and it took until the mid-1800s before those problems (aeration and nutrition were the most pressing) were sufficiently attenuated (not to say resolved) for aquariums to become vogue amongst the middle and upper classes of Europe and North America.[12] This coincided, happily enough, with the burgeoning of popular and essentially amateur interest in science – Charles Darwin is the most renowned example – which ennobled collecting as something other than the whimsical acquisition of nature's marvels.[13] Ironically, it was one of Darwin's most vocal opponents, Philip Henry Gosse, who popularized amateur marine science, and the corresponding desire to collect and display marine creatures. He is also credited with endowing the Latin word 'aquarium' with its current meaning.[14] He was so successful in conveying his enthusiasm for aquariums that in later life he came to lament the devastation of England's coastal areas caused by avid collectors following in his footsteps and strip-mining the shoreline for specimens to stock their tanks.[15] So popular was this passion for collecting and displaying marine life, Jules Verne's 1870 novel *20 000 Leagues Under the Sea* is thought to have been inspired, at least in part, by his visits to public aquariums, rather than an actual encounter with the deep.[16] Not unrelatedly, the first film version of Verne's novel, which was made in 1915 but wasn't released in Europe until after the First World War, inspired the surrealists with its otherworldly imagery. Breton's *L'Amour Fou* (*Mad Love*) includes an underwater still of a coral reef in the Bahamas, which he mistakenly labels as a section of Australia's Great Barrier Reef.[17] These connections reaffirm the aquarium's lineage with film and television on what Deleuze and Guattari call the expressive plane (which works in tandem with the technological phylum) because it was the aquarium's most overtly cinematic qualities that attracted the attention of the surrealists: color, movement and new shapes and forms.

I

When I began to visit large public aquariums, initially with my children when they were very young, but then on my own out of personal fascination, I became interested in and wanted to understand how they function to – presumably – mediate the way people encounter aquatic life. In particular, I wanted to know whether it enabled people to relate to aquatic life in a deep-feeling way, by which I mean in a way that would make them willing to act in a more environmentally conscious and responsible way. This question is more important and more interesting than initially meets the eye because it is my impression that most people do not have a strong affective relationship to aquatic life. This is not a proposition I wish to defend, necessarily, but I do want to be provocative in saying it. My reasoning, which I can't easily quantify, is this: I suspect most people only ever encounter marine creatures on ice at their local fishmongers or in batter on their plates and therefore tend to think of them as food, which they then classify according to their taste and disposition toward seafood. As such, I disagree with Elspeth Probyn's thesis that it is only by eating fish that humans can be induced to care for fish.[18] I also suspect that most people only ever encounter actual living marine creatures via a screen of some sort, whether that's at an aquarium or on TV. So, although the technology now exists to enable us to see underwater, life beyond the breakers and beneath the waves remains as unseen and unknown as it was in the 19th century and before. The aquarium, in this sense, takes us to places that we largely do not go, not just because they are far away or difficult to get to but more fundamentally because water is not our element (as Steve Mentz says, the ocean is deathly to humans). Moreover, precisely because water is not our element, we have no easy way to relate to fish, except perhaps as food or as exoticisms. We cannot communicate or interact with marine life beyond stimulating a flight or fight response (whales and dolphins are perhaps an exception to this rule); indeed, we seem not to even be able to empathize with marine life – it wasn't until 2002 that we finally accepted that fish do indeed feel pain, thanks in large part to the research efforts of British bio veterinarian Lynne Sneddon, though our approach to them continues to *not* reflect this knowledge (as fishing, fish farming and aquarium practices can all attest).[19]

Although I want to treat film and TV screens and aquariums as belonging to the same technological phylum, I do not mean to suggest that there are no differences between them. Indeed, it is the differences that are intriguing because what interests me most is whether the presence of actual marine life, albeit behind glass, affects us differently from the purely virtual form one sees on TV and film. I want to suggest that those differences, particularly where large public aquariums are concerned, are now seen as design faults by their proprietors which need to be overcome or somehow obscured by adding what I will call 'spectacle' elements (in Debord's sense of the word) to their displays. Aquariums are caught in a bind which they cannot easily escape, and it shapes their development in a very particular fashion. They are businesses first and foremost, so they depend on numbers through the door for their existence, and in this respect, they are in exactly the same business as film and TV, namely the so-called 'attention economy', but their commodity is 'nature' and its appeal on its own is uncertain and inconstant.[20] We humans may be fascinated by nature, but generally speaking, we do not hesitate to put our own interests ahead of the other-than-human plants and animals with which we share this planet. Evidence of this is not hard to find, though in the case of the ocean, it typically remains unseen. "In most places, the oceans have lost upwards of 75 percent of their megafauna – large animals such as whales, dolphins, sharks, rays and turtles – as fishing and hunting has spread in waves across the face of the planet." [21] For some species numbers are down by as much as 99 percent and there are dozens more that have literally disappeared.[22] And that doesn't even begin to cover the full extent of the destruction. One must also mention algal and jellyfish blooms, acidification, coral bleaching, the spread of deoxygenated 'dead zones', rising water temperatures and the incredible volume of biological and non-biological pollutants and rubbish that has been pumped into the ocean without a second thought. Environmental devastation is a measure not only of environmental neglect, but also of environmental indifference, and it is precisely that indifference which aquariums must try to counter by pretending they are something other than what they are.

By 'spectacle' I simply mean those design elements of the modern aquarium which demonstrably owe their origin to theme parks or film and television (I'll discuss the specificity of this in more detail in what follows). The question this raises for me, though, is whether the addition of 'spectacle' elements contributes to the development of deep feeling between humans and our other than human aquatic neighbors or erodes it? Over the past two decades, I have visited many aquariums all over the world with a view to answering this question for myself and I'm sorry to say I tend to think they are less effective in generating empathy towards aquatic life than we might hope.[23] I have visited the 'fish house' at the London Zoo, which was the world's first public aquarium (built in 1853 to educate the citizens of the world's then most powerful nation about the reaches of its empire), and the equally antique aquarium at Amsterdam's Artis Zoo, as well as large modern aquariums in all inhabited continents – Monterey (California), New Orleans, Toronto, Melbourne, Sydney, Auckland, Singapore, Hong Kong, Manila, Taiwan, Durban, Cape Town, Rio and Sao Paulo – and I'm yet to encounter one that contradicts this conclusion. As different as each of these aquariums are from each other, they also share several key characteristics, particularly in the way they curate their exhibits. Here it is perhaps useful to speak in terms of trends, not just in the sense of passing fashions, but in the more ideal sense of emerging archetypes. The history of public aquarium architecture has followed five main trajectories – firstly, the aquarium tanks have gotten larger, thus enabling them to accommodate a greater variety of species, including large varieties of fish such as the misnamed Whale Sharks, large sharks such as White Pointers and Hammerheads, and even small varieties of marine mammals such as Beluga Whales and Sea Lions; secondly, the tanks have been shaped so as to foster the impression that one is actually inside the tank, or at least more fully immersed in the viewing experience than one can be when confronted by a flat screen; thirdly, tanks have been created that specifically enable spectators – especially children – to touch certain non-dangerous creatures such as sponges and starfish; fourthly, thematic framing has been added, such that the newer aquariums resemble theme parks; and lastly, perhaps fulfilling Debord's prophecy that the image will eventually replace the thing, aquarium tanks are being replaced by flat screens displaying digital animations of aquatic life.

The spectacle is not only found at the level of form, though, it is also to be found in the content. Aquariums do not merely resemble cinemas in their formal arrangement, the choice of species in their display too is heavily influenced by cinema. There is probably no aquarium in the world that does not have at least one clownfish and one yellow-tailed blue tang, aka Nemo and Dory, somewhere in the display.[24] In many cases, the clownfish, particularly, are displayed on their own, giving them both a prominence and conspicuousness that is not keeping with how things are in their natural setting. To be sure, this is a general feature of all aquariums, which as Elias argues, want their displays to be visible to their paying customers, rather than camouflaged as the creatures themselves would typically want to be, but in the case of 'famous' species singled out for special treatment it makes it appear they are the only species worthy of attention.[25] This manner of foregrounding select species is reminiscent of shopwindows and the way they present merchandise in an eye-catching fashion.[26] In this way, the screen of the aquarium functions much as the TV screen does, it is simply a mechanism for driving sales. This is a double-edged sword because *Finding Nemo* (2003) and its long-awaited sequel *Finding Dory* (2016) are probably the two most widely known films about life underwater and for many children it is the only representation of aquatic life that they are familiar with, so the popularity of the films is the reason the children are at the aquarium in the first place, but it is perhaps also the reason the children leave without thinking about the actual fish. As John Berger said of zoos, at least one of the reasons adults take their children to aquariums is "to show them the originals of their 'reproductions'", but this does not necessarily convert into a deep-feeling for the oceanic originals.[27] One gets the impression watching children encounter clownfish and blue tangs in aquariums, seeing them shout excitedly in recognition that they've seen Nemo and Dory, and quickly take pictures of them, that it is as though they've entered the virtual realm of the films themselves, rather than caught a glimpse of life beneath the waves. Certainly, if the gift shops can be taken as symptomatic, then the over-representation of these two species on their shelves is a powerful indicator of the importance of the connection between visual culture more generally and aquariums.[28]

II

The first public aquarium, the Fish House at the London zoo, consists of several banks of the kind of fish tanks one might find in the home of a genuine aquarium enthusiast, each measuring approximately two or three meters across, with larger 'habitats' built around the edges. For decades this was the benchmark for what a public aquarium should look like, and it was widely emulated around the globe. Enlarging the exhibition was accomplished arithmetically by increasing the number of tanks. Now, though, in modern aquariums, enlarging the exhibition is accomplished geometrically by increasing the size of the tanks, which today are built on the scale of arenas. The largest aquarium in the world, the Georgia Aquarium in Atlanta, built with a $250 million donation from Home Depot co-founder Bernie Marcus, features as its showpiece a 24-million-liter tank.[29] The Dubai Mall in U.A.E. is the next biggest with a tank of some 10 million liters. Turkuazoo aquarium in Istanbul, also located in a shopping mall, has a 5-million-liter tank viewed by means of an 80-metre tunnel. Monterey Bay Aquarium on Cannery Row in Monterey, which was initially funded by David Packard, co-founder of Hewlett-Packard, boasts two enormous tanks, one of 1 million liters and another of 4.5 million liters. These vast tanks reconstruct ocean habitats on a cinematic scale and indeed that appears to be their intention. Often these huge tanks, which can measure more than 30 meters across and 10 meters high, are surrounded by theatre-style seating so spectators can tarry awhile. Typically, aquarium spectators move through the displays at a comparable speed to art gallery visitors, which is to say rapidly and almost without pause except briefly to snap a quick selfie or two, so these spaces offer a change of pace and an opportunity for a very different spectator experience.

In "The Age of the World Picture" Heidegger writes, "everywhere and in the most varied disguises the gigantic is making its appearance. In so doing, it evidences itself simultaneously in the tendency toward the increasingly small." He explains this paradoxical claim as follows. "The gigantic presses forward in a form that actually seems to make it disappear – in the annihilation of great distances by the airplane, in the setting before us of foreign and remote worlds in their everydayness, which is produced at random through radio by a flick of a hand."[30] Both of these trajectories – the becoming gigantic that is also a becoming microscopic – can be observed in the history of the development of public aquariums. The larger the tanks have become, and as I've just indicated some are indeed gigantic, the smaller they make the oceanic space they are endeavoring to present to their audiences seem. The microcosm does not merely stand in the place of the macrocosm, it annihilates it. This is not, however, a matter of a triumph of the simulacrum over the real thing (as Baudrillard might frame it). As Susan Davis argues in her pioneering book *Spectacular Nature*, nature simulations are as old as history itself, as such, they are not troubling in and of themselves; "it is the uses to which nature simulations are put that we should worry about, the stories about environmental crisis that are left untold and the limits on our ability to imagine solutions."[31] In dialectical fashion, she argues that it is what is invisible in aquariums that should concern us because what we do not immediately see "are the selective ways nature is shaped into something that can be looked at."[32] This selectivity, in turn, erases the long human history of the exploitation and despoliation of aquatic environments. Aquariums are pristine, apparently paradisiacal spaces, in which 'nature' has been both contained and managed, thus offering an uplifting vision for the future that – completely falsely and unrealistically – suggests we can 'fix' the messes we have created by the application of technology and 'know-how'. In other words, it encourages the view that the microcosm of the aquarium is in fact the 'truth' of the macrocosm – it is in this sense that gigantic displays make the ocean disappear.[33]

No matter how large the tanks become, however, they can never escape their apparent two dimensionality so long as they retain their flat screen design. This "produces a sense of emotional distance and remoteness that even the transparent medium of glass cannot rectify."[34] If we take literally Rebecca Stott's description of aquariums as 'theatres of glass' then we can perhaps make a parallel between the viewing situation of theatre patrons and aquarium visitors.[35] Both are confronted with an impenetrable 'fourth wall' separating them from what they are viewing, a situation that serves to remind them that what they are viewing is just 'make believe' and not something they have to take seriously or engage with. While this may be fine for certain types of theatre, for the aquarium viewer it undermines the idea that what they are witnessing in the tanks is 'real', that it is actual 'nature' and not just a theatre of glass. Consequently, at the heart of the development of aquariums for the past fifty years has been this basic situation of viewer and viewed and the need to make that feel as real as possible. In theatrical terms, aquariums needed to find a way of breaking down the proverbial fourth wall and immersing the viewer in the display and not the tank itself. The late Kelly Tarlton, a marine archaeologist, diver, and entrepreneur, was the first to experiment with a tunnel design in his Underwater World Aquarium in Auckland (now part of the global Sea Life franchise) to allow spectators to pass underneath and through aquariums, rather than move around them. He also pioneered the use of a travelator or conveyer belt to move spectators through the space, which solved two separate problems, the logistical problem of throughput, and the ambulatory problem of walking or moving without looking where one is going (this latter problem has become especially acute in the age of the smartphone!). Tarlton's idea has now been emulated all over the world. Each new iteration is bolder in both scale and ambition, again following a geometric rather than arithmetic progression. The Shanghai Ocean Aquarium has a stunning 155 metre tunnel, which is almost double the length of the Turkuazoo aquarium's similarly impressive 80 metre tunnel, and it completely dwarfs the 35-metre tunnel at Spain's L'Oceanogràfic, which is the largest in Europe.

The experience of walking through these tunnels is like watching a film in an Imax-style cinema – there is a gigantism of the literally moving image, which is both overwhelming and reality-distorting. The tank above looms so large it is impossible not to think this is what it must be like to walk on the floor of the ocean and yet one is dry. This is one of the key paradoxes of the aquarium, the closer it brings one to aquatic life, the more insistent is the separation: the screen does not disappear just because it changes shape, though for a moment or two as a shark swims overhead one can easily imagine that it has vanished. In this respect aquarium tunnels can usefully be compared to theatres because as in the theatre, no matter how hard one tries to break down the so-called fourth wall and remove the line of separation between actor and spectator it always reasserts itself in some way. This is true even of the 'touch tanks and other varieties of 'immersive experience' (such as cage diving with the sharks or walking with the penguins) which do their best to remove the barriers between seer and seen by allowing the spectator to physically enter the tanks because as I said above, we can never escape the simple fact that 'we' humans cannot live beneath the water. Our intrusions there can only ever be mediated visits supported by technology – therefore, as Mentz suggests, thoughts of drowning and death always accompany our visits to the deep.

In more recent times, aquariums have attempted to negate the fourth wall by framing their tanks with design elements adopted from theme parks. A favorite strategy, used in several aquariums I have visited (but none more prominently than Durban's UShaka Marine World), is to style the interior as though it was a sunken ship. The aquarium tanks are seen through the portals or holes in the ship's hull, thus creating the illusion that spectator and spectated upon share the same fluid space. Another favorite is to create a 'jungle scene', particularly for freshwater species from South America, replete with all the Indiana Jones-style signifiers one would expect. The tanks are then positioned in such a way that one views them from above, as though one had stumbled upon a river or lake in the furthest recesses of the Amazon. But one cannot help but think that contextualizing the displays in this way can only reinforce the view that the displays are simply that, something to be looked at for the sake of a moment's wonder, and not as representatives of a rapidly disappearing 'wild' world. But this is far from the most disturbing development. In recent times, the tanks themselves have begun to disappear, to be replaced by video screens and animation displays. The most extreme example of this, I've seen, is the Taiwan National Aquarium which has an entire building devoted to digital displays – or, to put it another way, it has an entire building which is completely absent of all forms of aquatic life. One finds it hard to believe that animation can ever build the same potential for affective relations that actual animals do, but then again, from the perspective of the ethics of keeping animals for the sole purpose of their display, this is perhaps a trend to be welcomed. This is not the place to decide that debate, but it does return us to the question of whether aquariums work to create environmental awareness and sensitivity.

III

As Susan Davis puts it in her book *Spectacular Nature*, aquariums are in the 'feelings' business: they have to generate feelings of excitement and interest and they have to avoid "boredom, uneasiness, anxiety, disgust, and pity."[36] Nature isn't appealing – in the sense of compelling people to part with their money – all by itself, it needs to be framed in a particular way. In the early years of aquarium history, it was enough for them to render visible what had hitherto been invisible for them to generate enough astonishment and wonder to attract a paying audience. But that only lasted a few decades and aquariums soon found themselves searching for new ways to entice people through the turnstiles. In our own hypervisual age, when scarcely anything has escaped the gimlet-eye of the camera, wonder in the face of the hitherto unseen is no longer sufficient, indeed it is barely adequate to compete with the many other visual delights constantly being generated by the culture industry. To generate the flow-through of customers, it needs to satisfy its commercial imperative aquariums were seemingly compelled to become more and more like the cinemas and theme parks their owners also have in their portfolios. No one has documented this aspect of aquariums more astutely than Davis who aptly describes public aquariums as "a mall with fish."[37] In order to find their point of difference from cinemas and theme parks, though, aquariums dressed their product in the noble robes of education, or what Davis terms 'edutainment'. But its message tends to be that the environment needs to be 'managed', and it instils the view that all of nature is somehow a resource for humans. Moreover, it frames this management in terms of one-to-one relations between individual humans and individual animals as though nature was somehow a vast assemblage of pets just waiting for their human owners to care for them.[38]

Notes

[1] Susan Davis, *Spectacular Nature: Corporate Culture and the Sea World Experience* (Berkeley: University of California Press, 1997), 161.

[2] Davis, *Spectacular Nature,* 2.

[3] Ibid., 146.

[4] Rebecca Stott, *Theatres of Glass: The Woman who brought the sea to the City* (London: Short Books, 2003).

[5] I am not alone in having this fantasy, see Steve Mentz's *At the Bottom of Shakespeare's Ocean* (London: Continuum, 2009), 44.

[6] Carl Safina, *Song for the Blue Ocean* (NY: Henry Holt, 1998), 343-345.

[7] Bernd Brunner, *The Ocean at Home: An Illustrated History of the Aquarium* (London: Reaktion Books, 2005), 142-145.

[8] See for example https://www.pinterest.com.au/vmterroba/television-fish-tanks/, accessed October 19th, 2019.

[9] Fredric Jameson, *The Political Unconscious: Narrative as a Socially Symbolic Act* (London: Routledge, 1981), 9.

[10] Gilles Deleuze and Félix Guattari, *A Thousand Plateaus: Capitalism and Schizophrenia,* trans B. Massumi, (Minneapolis: University of Minnesota Press, 1987), 406-410.

[11] Brunner, *The Ocean at Home,* 21.

[12] Ibid., 31-33.

[13] I must note here that I use the word 'nature' in a variety of ways throughout this piece without offering a single clear-cut definition. In part this is because it is a highly contested term and I don't think any one definition would suffice; relatedly, the literature surrounding the term is too large to engage with meaningfully here. My use, though, owes a great deal to Raymond Williams' well-considered ambivalence toward the two extremes of the debate, i.e., either everything is nature or only the non-human is. Both positions are useful and problematic, he argues, suggesting that there is no real advantage in resolving this debate. See Raymond Williams, *Culture and Materialism,* (London: Verso, 1980), 67-85.

[14] Brunner, *The Ocean at Home,* 39. Shortly before *On the Origin of the Species* was published, Gosse published a book in which he argued that fossils were placed in rocks by God to create the impression that the earth had a longer history than it really had. Apparently, this was a step too far for most people and despite his renown Gosse became something of a laughingstock and his career languished.

[15] Brunner, *The Ocean at Home,* 139-140.

[16] Ann Elias, *Coral Empire: Underwater Oceans, Colonial Tropics, Visual Modernity* (Durham, NC: Duke University Press, 2019), 33.

[17] Elias, *Coral Empire,* 32.

[18] Ian Buchanan, "Must we Eat Fish?", *Symplokē,* 27: 1-2 (2019): 79-90.

[19] Carl Safina, "Are we wrong to assume fish can't feel pain?", *The Guardian,* October 20th, 2018, https://www.theguardian.com/news/2018/oct/30/are-we-wrong-to-assume-fish-cant-feel-pain.

[20] For example, *The Sea Life* franchise which manages 53 aquariums (as of 2020) all over the world is a subsidiary of the Merlin Entertainment Group which also owns Madame Tussauds, Alton Towers and Legoland among other properties.
[21] Callum Roberts, *Ocean of Life: How our Seas are Changing* (London: Allen Lane, 2012), 3.
[22] Roberts, *Ocean of Life*, 3.
[23] Here, as an aside, I would note that we should not assume that more entertaining means more affecting; on the contrary, sometimes the exact opposite is true – it is boredom that affects us most deeply, as Heidegger argued many years ago, because when we are bored, we are compelled to use our imagination to overcome our boredom. Buchanan, I. 2017 "Disappearance of Boredom", *Lo sguardo – revista di filosofia*, 23, P 277-284.
[24] Even home tanks have been influenced by these films as this website selling tanks and related equipment amply attests https://www.reefsaltwateraquarium.com/what-types-of-fish-are-in-finding-nemo/
[25] Elias, *Coral Empire*, 143.
[26] Ibid., 156.
[27] John Berger, *About Looking* (London: Bloomsbury, 1980), 23.
[28] Sometimes this is taken to absurd lengths, as it is at Sydney's Sea Life Aquarium which uses the children's TV character Peppa Pig as its mascot, ostensibly because it has a dugong named Pig on display.
[29] The statistics relating to the size and scale of public aquariums are drawn from this helpful site https://www.touropia.com/largest-aquariums-in-the-world/
[30] Martin Heidegger, *The Question Concerning Technology and Other Essays*, trans W. Lovitt, (NY: Harper Torchbooks, 1977), 135.
[31] Davis, *Spectacular Nature*, 238.
[32] Ibid.
[33] Elias makes a similar point, though her argument is historical rather than conceptual. She writes: "By 1921, Western perceptions of the underwater were shaped by aquariums, which were understood as optical devices for visual entertainment that brought pleasure and wonder by miniaturizing the sea on land." Elias, *Coral Empire*, 126.
[34] Elias, *Coral Empire*, 52.
[35] Rebecca Stott, R. *Theatres of Glass: The Woman Who Brought the Sea to the City* (London: Short Books. 2003), 31.
[36] Davis, *Spectacular Nature*, 161.
[37] Ibid., 2.
[38] Ibid., 146.

Contributors

Catherine Bonier is an Assistant Professor at the Azrieli School of Architecture & Urbanism at Carleton University in Ottawa. Her research draws on the history of cities to imagine urban futures, using water and infrastructure as central threads to situate an ethical, critical perspective. Her past positions in construction management, mental health counseling, and video game design contribute to her focus on the conflicting effects of technologies on the creation and protection of just, healthy cities and environments. Catherine is co-director and co-founder of the Carleton Urban Research Lab (https://c-url.ca/) with Professor Ozayr Saloojee. C-url engages in collaborative interdisciplinary research, teaching, and design centered on three themes — water, cities, and equity.

Ian Buchanan is an Australian cultural theorist, currently serving as Director of the Institute for Social Transformation Research based at the University of Wollongong. He has published works on Michel de Certeau, Gilles Deleuze and Fredric Jameson. Buchanan is the founding editor of the *Deleuze Studies Journal*, as well as several important book series dedicated to the work of Gilles Deleuze.

Diana Heise's practice engages filmmaking, photography, writing, performance, and social practice. Her work has been exhibited in galleries and festivals internationally, including the Brooklyn Museum, the Film Anthology Archives, Oriel Myrddin Gallery, Cantor Art Center, Institut Français de Maurice, and the Des Moines Art Center, among others. She is a recipient of a Fulbright Fellowship in the Creative and Performing Arts, a Performance Art Fund Grant from the Franklin Furnace Inc. as well as a Presidential Fellowship at the American University in Cairo. She has participated in residencies at the Vermont Studio Center, the Visual Art Center of New Jersey, Open Wabi and the Wassaic Project. She has spoken about her work at venues such as the Parsons School of Art and Design, Stanford University, and the Kemper Museum of Contemporary Art. She holds an MFA in Photography, Video and Related Media from the School of Visual Arts in New York, NYC, and a BA in Art History from Vassar College. She is Professor and Chair of the Photography and Filmmaking Department at the Kansas City Art Institute.

Celina Jeffery is an Associate Professor of Art History at the University of Ottawa, Canada. Recent publications include *Ephemeral Coast* (2015), *The Artist as Curator* (2015), the 'Junk Ocean' issue of *Drain: A Journal of Contemporary Art and Culture* (January 2016) and the 'Towards a Blue Humanity' issue of *Symploke* (2019) co-edited with Ian Buchanan. She is the founder of *Ephemeral Coast* www.ephemeralcoast.com, a SSHRC (Social Sciences and Humanities Research Council) funded, curatorial research project (2015–2019). She has curated exhibitions internationally which explore the visual cultures of climate change.

Andrea Hurst is a Professor in Philosophy at Nelson Mandela University, Gqeberha, South Africa. She holds a PhD in Philosophy from Villanova University, Philadelphia, USA, 2006. This research was focused on bringing complexity-thinking in continental philosophy into contact with psychoanalytic theory, leading to the publication of a book entitled Derrida vis-á-vis Lacan: Interweaving Deconstruction and Psychoanalysis (New York: Fordham University Press, 2008). She has also published numerous journal articles and book chapters examining the interfaces between complexity-thinking, psychoanalytic theory (particularly a Lacanian model of subjectivity), and philosophy as a way of life in its many dimensions. She currently holds a South African Research Chair Initiative (SARChI) Chair in Identities and Social Cohesion in Africa and is engaged in a research programme that fuses philosophical inquiry with practice-based knowing in the various arts.

Anna (Ania) Paluch is a Polish Canadian PhD student in Cultural Mediations at Carleton University, situated on unceded Algonquin territory in Ottawa, Canada. Her research focus is on Indigenous North American and Eastern European Futurism, spaces of cultural hybridity, and post-memory in the diaspora. She is a curator, mixed-media artist, cultural educator through the Young Polish Canadian Professional Association (YPCPA), and a board member of various Polish-community organizations based in Ottawa, Montreal, Toronto, Winnipeg, and Vancouver.

Belinda du Plooy has worked in higher education for close to 25 years in various capacities, both academic and managerial. She holds qualifications in Public Relations Management and Communication Studies (NDip: PRM) and in English Studies (BA, BA Hons (cum laude), MA (cum laude)). Her highest qualification is a DLitt et Phil degree. Her Master's dissertation was on the topic of pain and healing in the work of Nobel Laureate Toni Morrison. Her doctoral thesis was on the topic of compassion as metanarrative in postmodern discourses. She lives in Port Elizabeth, South Africa, and works at Nelson Mandela University as Academic Engagement Manager. She also acts as a postgraduate supervisor across a variety of Social Science and Humanities departments and disciplines. Her areas of academic specialisation, publication and supervision include Literature, Philosophy, Popular Culture, Film Studies, Women's and Gender Studies, Communication, Media Studies, Academic Engagement and Higher Education practice.

Sherena Razek is a PhD candidate and SSHRC doctoral fellow in the Department of Modern Culture and Media at Brown University. She researches visual cultures of resistance and refusal from Palestine to Turtle Island, amplifying practices of transnational Indigenous solidarities from the perspective of critical racial and decolonial theory. Sherena has curated and co-organized exhibitions that address the politics and aesthetics of surveillance, oceanic degradation, and the militarization and materialization of nation-state borders between the Global North and the Global South. She holds an M.A. in Art History, Visual Art, and Theory from the University of British Columbia (2018) and a B.A. in the History and Theory of Art from the University of Ottawa (2016).

Jakub Zdebik is an Associate Professor of Art History and Theory and Chair of the Visual Arts Department at the University of Ottawa, Canada. He is the author of *Deleuze and the Diagram: Aesthetic Threads in Visual Organization* (Continuum, 2012) and *Deleuze and the Map-Image: Aesthetics, Information, Code and Digital Art* (Bloomsbury, 2019). He published in *Screen Bodies*, *RACAR*, *The Semiotic Review*, *ESC: English Studies in Canada*, *The Brock Review*, and *Esse*. He has curated exhibitions at the Kennedy Museum of Art, Ohio, Galerie R3, and Gallery Karsh-Masson, Ottawa, Canada.

Index

E

F

G

H

I

J

K

L

M

N

O

P

R

S

T

U

V

W

Y

Z

CPSIA information can be obtained
at www.ICGtesting.com
Printed in the USA
LVHW071338100422
715714LV00046B/854/J